PENGUIN BOOKS

LIVING ON THIN AIR

Charles Leadbeater is an independent writer, Demos research associate and consultant to leading companies. He was Industrial Editor and Tokyo Bureau Chief at the *Financial Times* before moving to the *Independent*, where he devised *Bridget Jones's Diary* with Helen Fielding. He can be contacted at: charlie@malvernrd.demon.co.uk

LIVING ON THIN AIR

THE NEW ECONOMY

Charles Leadbeater

PENGUIN BOOKS

PENGUIN BOOKS

Published by the Penguin Group
Penguin Books Ltd, 27 Wrights Lane, London W8 5TZ, England
Penguin Putnam Inc., 375 Hudson Street, New York, New York 10014, USA
Penguin Books Australia Ltd, Ringwood, Victoria, Australia
Penguin Books Canada Ltd, 10 Alcorn Avenue, Toronto, Ontario, Canada M4V 3B2
Penguin Books (NZ) Ltd, Private Bag 102902, NSMC, Auckland, New Zealand

Penguin Books Ltd, Registered Offices: Harmondsworth, Middlesex, England

First published by Viking 1999
Published, with the addition of Chapter 18, in Penguin Books 2000
10 9 8 7 6 5 4 3 2 1

Set in Sabon
Typeset by Rowland Phototypesetting Ltd
Bury St Edmunds, Suffolk
Printed in England by Clays Ltd, St Ives plc

For G

CONTENTS

Preface   ix
Acknowledgements   xiii
1 We're Going on a Bear Hunt   1
2 Dianomics   18
3 Delia Smith not Adam Smith   28
4 Knowing is Competing   37
5 Collapse   53
6 Creating Knowledge   65
7 If Organizations were like Brains   87
8 The Rise of the Knowledge Entrepreneur   93
9 Building the Knowledge Society   108
10 Is Knowledge Always Good?   121
11 The Networked Economy   124
12 Silicon Valley: The Intelligent Region   139
13 Trust: The Ethics of the New Economy   149
14 Who Should Own Knowledge?   169
15 Financing Social Capital   183
16 Creating Social Capital   202
17 The Power of Fantasy   219
18 A Manifesto for the New Economy   232
Select Bibliography   251
Index   257

It is very hard to keep a sense of balance these days. The turbulent economy in which we all have to make our livings, constantly throws things out of kilter.

At times we seemed blessed. We are living in an era of unprecedented productivity and creativity, in which science and innovation are bestowing upon us families of new products with exciting possibilities: genetic treatments for disease, powerful computers the size of a television remote control, robots smaller than the size of a coin. The generation, application and exploitation of knowledge is driving modern economic growth. Most of us make our money from thin air: we produce nothing that can be weighed, touched or easily measured. Our output is not stockpiled at harbours, stored in warehouses or shipped in railway cars. Most of us earn our livings providing service, judgement, information and analysis, whether in a telephone call centre, a lawyer's office, a government department or a scientific laboratory. We are all in the thin-air business. That should allow our economies, in principle at least, to become more humane; they should be organized around people and the knowledge capital they produce. Our children will not have to toil in dark factories, descend into pits or suffocate in mills, to hew raw materials and turn them into manufactured products. They will make their livings through their creativity, ingenuity and imagination.

Despite the cornucopia of the emerging knowledge economy, most of us feel more uncertain, stressed, insecure and less in control of our lives. Our society seems ludicrously confident in some areas – for example, the capacity of our scientists to uncover our genetic make-up – and yet beset by doubt closer to home – for example, over the welfare state's capacity to deliver decent pensions. We have devised ways to make complex tasks easy – moving billions of dollars around global financial markets – while relatively simple tasks – improving living conditions on poor housing estates – seem beyond us. Many people feel their lives are in the grip of forces beyond their comprehension: global companies and markets, which bring with them the modern plagues of downsizing, re-engineering and restructuring. Jobs, careers and occupations come and go. While a global super-class grows fat on markets in which the winners take the lion's share of the rewards, many others find their life chances closed down. Inequality has become an acute, chronic and endemic feature of modern societies.

Our powerlessness is not a personal failing, but an institutional one. Most of the institutions we rely upon to protect and guide us through this tumult – governments, trade unions, companies – seem paralysed. Our traditional institutions, many of which were designed for an era of railways, steelworks, factories and dockyards, are enfeebled. We are on the verge of the global twenty-first-century knowledge economy, yet we rely on national institutions inherited from the nineteenth-century industrial economy. The contrast is instructive. The nineteenth century was revolutionary because the Victorians matched their scientific and technological innovations with radical institutional innovations: the extension of democracy, the creation of local government, the birth of modern savings and insurance schemes, the development of a professional civil service, the rise of trade unions and the emergence of the research-based university. We are timid and cautious where the Victorians were confident and innovative. We live within the shell of institutions the nineteenth century handed down to us. Our highly uneven capacity for innovation is the fundamental source of our unease. We are scientific and technological revolutionaries, but political and institutional conservatives.

This book is about how we can create the organizations, both public and private, economic and social, to unleash and spread the benefits of the knowledge economy. We must not retreat from modernization, but instead embark on a wave of radical innovation in many of our most basic political, social and economic institutions: companies, markets, banks, schools, universities, public services and government departments.

Living on Thin Air is optimistic. It has little time for the Jeremiahs who want to retreat from globalization. Globalization is good. Through global trade in products and services people learn and exchange the ideas that in turn drive economic growth. If we turn our backs on the global economy, we turn our backs on the most vital force in modern societies: the accelerating spread of knowledge and ideas. A thriving knowledge society must be cosmopolitan and open; it must reward talent and creativity; it must invest in people and education. The radical innovation and knowledge creation that underpins modern economic growth thrives in cultures that are democratic and dissenting; that are open to new ideas from unusual sources; in which authority and élites are constantly questioned and challenged. That vision underlies the institutional revolution this book recommends.

We must not retreat into the illusory comfort of a closed, nostalgic communitarian society. That dead end would kill off innovation. Nor must we fall prey to the naïve over-optimism that infects so many starry-eyed advocates of the new economy, who believe that technology will solve all our problems. Above all, we must not be timid. Indeed, for modernization to succeed, it must become more confident and radical. Modernizers must be prepared to take on larger questions which have been put to one side, questions about: how a knowledge-based economy should be owned; the scope for social ownership of basic knowledge, for example in genetics; whether the market should be the dominant determinant of value; the essential role of collaboration and co-operation, alongside competition, in promoting economic efficiency. The rise of the knowledge economy challenges many of our most cherished assumptions about how the economy works; that is why modernization will inevitably raise such fundamental questions about how we organize ourselves. Modernizers – in business and politics – who want to be more than good managers, must be confident enough to pick up these questions. Only then will they be counted as visionaries and radicals.

The Blair government's project of modernization has faced criticism from many quarters. I will add to that criticism, but from a distinct vantage point: I think the government's problem, in the long run, will be that it is not modernizing enough; it needs to go much, much further, and more confidently, for modernization to succeed. *Living on Thin Air* is the blueprint for what a radical modernizing project will entail in the years to come.

ACKNOWLEDGEMENTS

This book was conceived during the long boom of the 1990s, researched when the boom was at a peak and written when it seemed to be on the verge of collapse amid the financial turmoil of late 1998. In the course of the writing many of my ideas developed, changed and evaporated, largely thanks to conversations with interesting people more insightful than myself.

Were it not for David Godwin, my entrepreneurial agent, I might not have written a book at all. Juliet Annan at Penguin Viking was extremely patient as I sailed past one deadline after another.

Many of the ideas for this book were gathered during research projects organized with Demos, the think-tank, which has been an important source for my ideas. So thanks to Tom Bentley, Ben Jupp, Perri 6, Lindsay Nash, Debbie Porter, Ian Christie et al. and especially Geoff Mulgan, who has been an invaluable collaborator for several years. My work as an adviser to BP-Amoco's chief executive John Browne has been challenging and creative and I am grateful to him and Nick Butler, his policy adviser.

In the course of researching the book I made several trips to California, and Silicon Valley in particular. Two conferences at Berkeley University, organized by Ikujiro Nonaka, helped me clarify my thoughts, and I owe particular thanks to David J. Teece, from whom I learned, and borrowed, a lot. A variety of people helped me, including Paul Romer at Stanford, John Freeman at Berkeley, a host of Silicon Valley companies, Steven Levy at the Center for the Continuing Study of the Californian Economy, and Doug Henton and his partners at Collaborative Economics. I am grateful to the Gatsby Foundation for a generous grant to research knowledge entrepreneurs in the UK.

In the second half of 1998 I was asked by Peter Mandelson, then

Secretary of State at the Department of Trade and Industry, to develop a White Paper, published in December that year, entitled *Building the Knowledge Driven Economy*. Developing that policy document with Dan Corry, Stephen Haddrill, Ed Harley, Ken Warwick and others helped me a great deal.

Over the years a variety of other people have helped me to develop the ideas in this book, among them: David Abraham, Douglas Hague, Charles Handy, Ian Hargreaves, Anthony Hopwood, Will Hutton, Andy Law, Baruch Lev, David Miliband, Jane Taylor and Martin Taylor. I have benefited from reading work by Brian Arthur, Ulrich Beck, Max Boisot, John Cassidy, Diane Coyle, Daniel Dennett, Anthony Giddens, Kevin Kelly, Rosabeth Moss-Kanter, Dorothy Leonard, Hamish McRae, Annalee Saxenian, Adam Seligman, Thomas Stewart, Karl Erik Sveiby, Hirotaka Takeuchi and many others.

I could not have written this book, nor done anything else for that matter, without the support of my parents, my wife Geraldine Bedell, and the kids, Henrietta, Freddie and Harry, who make it all worth while.

CHAPTER ONE WE'RE GOING ON A BEAR HUNT

Allow me, briefly, to describe where I am coming from. I do not work for a company or a university. I am neither a business consultant nor a civil servant. I have no job title nor job description, no office or expense account and I do not belong to a clearly defined occupational group. When people ask me, 'What do you do?', I find it hard to come up with a clear, concise answer. I work from home, writing mainly, sometimes books, sometimes reports, often for a think-tank, sometimes for the government or a company. The kids are perplexed by my lifestyle. They like my being around, but part of them would quite like it if I had a proper, dependable job to go to, in an office, like other people's dads. Yet my life is far more comfortable than my father's was at a similar age. As a young man he had to fight in a world war and he did not have the chance to go to university. My family goes on foreign holidays, has several computers, cable television, a microwave, two mobile phones, uses the Internet daily and drives around in a vast 'people carrier'. There are two much more significant differences: the kind of jobs we do. My wife has a job; my mother toiled for her family but not for an employer. My father had a steady, predictable, dependable career, which carried him through to a well earned, properly funded and enjoyable retirement. In contrast, although I am not yet forty, I have already had several mini-careers. For three or four years after university I worked in television. Then I had an eleven-year career as a newspaper journalist, which I brought to an end after I became exhausted by corporate upheaval and disillusioned by working sixty-five hours a week as an executive. Now I am self-employed, independent, working from home. I am one of Charles Handy's portfolio workers, armed with a laptop, a modem and some contacts. Peter Drucker anointed people like me 'knowledge workers'. Put it another way: I live on my wits.

As I sit at my desk at home I sometimes marvel at the risk I am taking. I have commitments to my family, which mean I will need to work for another thirty years, to pay for the education of our offspring, our weakness for holidays and a retirement pension. In the last ten years I have managed, by the skin of my teeth, to keep pace with the technological changes sweeping the 'media' industries. But how will I manage to keep up in fifteen or twenty years' time, when my reflexes will be even slower and presumably I will be on my fifth or sixth career? Occasionally, usually when the cash dispenser has done something unpleasant, it seems too daunting and implausible that I should be able to make my way in such a competitive world on my own, without protection from some larger organization. At times like that I fondly imagine joining a newspaper perhaps or a television production company or an investment bank even: something solid, dependable, with a recognized brand name.

That fantasy of acquiring safety in numbers never lasts more than a minute. Most large organizations seem pretty soulless, increasingly focused, driven, lean machines, designed to deliver shareholder value. The lights never go out these days in modern companies; no sooner have you found a cosy corner of the organization to settle down in than some ambitious manager points the spotlight at you, questioning your contribution to profitability. Life within such organizations is forever clouded by the threat of downsizing, reorganization or merger. Such a life seems to me to be no more secure and certainly less interesting than the slightly perilous independence I have plumped for. I have decided I will organize my work around myself and my family, and earn my living by finding people who will pay me to do things I am interested in. It's skating on thin ice, but the ice is getting thinner wherever you go these days.

Of course I am lucky. I have a good degree. Through my career as a journalist I made a lot of contacts, in business and politics. I live in London. I have marketable skills. Yet the dilemma I face – how best to provide myself with a degree of security in a more competitive, unsentimental, relentless world – faces most people. To go it alone is risky, demanding and stressful. Yet to rely upon larger organizations and institutions, companies and trade unions, isn't much of an improvement, because they seem either too cumbersome or too callous. Where can we turn to find greater security in an environment as hostile as the modern global economy?

The unlikely starting point for an answer is *We're Going on a Bear Hunt*, one of our family's favourite children's books, in which a family sets out to find a bear, only to meet a series of daunting obstacles: deep mud, a cold river, a dark forest, a violent storm. At each of these the family chants: 'We can't go under it. We can't go over it. We'll have to go *through* it.' That is the challenge most of us face in the precarious economy on which our livings now depend. We have to steel ourselves to press on, not really sure what lies ahead, but knowing that retreat is no alternative.

We have to go forward because if we retreat we end up with gridlock. Our societies and governments often seem paralysed, or at best enfeebled, in the face of economic and technological change that outstrips their capacity to respond. We are weighed down by institutions, laws and cultures largely inherited from the industrial nineteenth century; yet we confront a global economy driven by an accelerating flow of new ideas and technologies which are creating the industries and products of the twenty-first century. We have welfare systems which are impervious to reform, parliamentary systems which are recognizably Victorian and schools which still resemble their nineteenth-century forebears. Imagine fighting a modern war using cavalry: that is the position we are in.

Yet as soon as our institutions become unblocked, everything threatens to spiral out of control. As soon as outmoded old institutions are shunted out of the way, nothing stable replaces them. Nowhere is this more evident than in the world's highly strung financial markets. The Bretton Woods system of fixed exchange rates has long had its day. We cannot go back to that system. But we seem to have unleashed in its place a monster that no one can control, even that small minority which profits from it. Few people feel their lives, particularly their work lives, are more secure and under control. Instead, most people feel ensnared by the impersonal forces sweeping the global economy. It is difficult to be convinced that this is progress.

This book's first aim is to explain the swirling forces which are shaping our economic lives. These forces are partly malign but potentially very beneficial. The second is to explain why we need to reconstitute many of our institutions – social, political and economic – to enable them to withstand the gale around them and exploit the benefits on offer to the full. People feel less in control of their lives not because they suffer a lack of confidence. We will not overcome our anxiety by going into collective therapy, willing ourselves to become more entrepreneurial and flexible. Nor will we get very far by reining in the dynamic and creative forces which are driving the global economy, in particular the creation and spread of new ideas and technologies which are the well-springs of higher productivity and improved well-being. Our problem is that the institutions to which we turn to protect us from volatility and to shape our world – large companies, trade unions, welfare states, national governments – seem incapable or uninterested. Public, collective institutions seem enfeebled and overrun. Private-sector institutions seem too self-interested to be fully trusted. Piecemeal reform of old institutions will not be enough. We need to embark on a wave of radical institutional innovation and invention; to create new kinds of companies, banks, welfare organizations, governments, schools, universities which can gather our resources more effectively and so put people more in control of their lives.

Although technology has moved on in leaps and bounds in this century, we are largely living with an institutional inheritance from the Victorians. Most of our modern institutions can trace their roots to the nineteenth century. In the UK, the joint-stock company reached legal maturity with the 1862 Companies Act and became the dominant form of capitalist organization in the 1880s. Consumer co-operatives and burial associations became the basis for the modern building societies, given legal form in the friendly society and building societies law of 1874. The local authority emerged from the consolidation of the poor laws of 1834, the public-health legislation of 1848, the highways act of 1862 and the education act of 1870. Trade unions gave voice to organized labour. Institutions of higher education, incorporating scientific research, were created as the century progressed. The nineteenth century was so revolutionary because technological innovation went hand in hand with institutional innovation, itself the product of political and social change. By contrast with the Victorians we are scientific radicals but institutional conservatives. The Victorians had a grand political and social imagination to match their achievements in science and industry. Our era, thus far, has failed that test of imagination.

To understand the scale of the renewal we need, we must first understand the three forces driving change in the economies of modern societies: finance capitalism, knowledge capitalism and social capitalism.

Finance Capitalism

The most obvious and maligned force, which sends a shiver down most people's spines, is the disruptive power of deregulated, interconnected global financial markets, which swill around the world in pursuit of shareholder value. Imagine a boat that combined the scale and mass of a super-tanker with the speed and instability of a speedboat. That is the world's financial system; the force that sanctifies downsizing, restructuring and re-engineering.

There is no better case for greater regulation of world financial markets than the turmoil that began in July 1997, when Thailand was forced to devalue the baht. By the end of the year, Thailand, the Philippines, Indonesia, Malaysia and South Korea had watched their currencies and stock markets collapse, bringing down banks and large businesses around them. The joy of living in such a tightly interconnected world turned sour in 1998 when Japan finally admitted the true scale of a decade's mismanagement in its banks and plunged into its deepest post-war recession. Russia essentially went bankrupt in the summer of that year and the world's stock markets waited with bated breath to see if Mexico, Venezuela and Brazil would follow suit. By the start of 1999 the world economy was largely being kept going by the spending and borrowing of US consumers. Their confidence was almost entirely due to the buoyancy of the US stock market, which many outsiders thought to be over-valued. Put it another way: the world economy was hanging by a thread – the capacity of US investors for collective self-delusion.

This rolling crisis had a simple cause. The world's financial system is able to switch vast resources around the globe in an instant. A dealer in London can buy stocks in the Lebanon, government bonds in Thailand, futures in Brazil, and take a punt on the Indonesian currency, while sipping a *café latte*. Combine these powerful and volatile financial flows with attractive but fragile emerging economies, equipped with feeble, sometimes corrupt and poorly regulated financial systems, and you have a recipe for disaster. The flood of capital into emerging economies in the early 1990s was like a seriously overweight adult trying to sleep in a baby's cot. The costs are still being counted.

In Indonesia and Thailand alone 25 million were expected to fall back into poverty in 1998. The World Bank expected thirty-six countries, accounting for 40 per cent of world output, to experience a fall in per capita income in 1998. Korea's unpayable external debt was estimated at $30 billion (thousand million), Indonesia's at $22 billion and Thailand's $13 billion. Bad loans made by Korean and Thai banks were thought to be worth 40 per cent of those countries' GDP. The effects of this financial twister were soon felt even in more robust economies. As Asian demand slumped, the oil price dropped to a twelve-year low of less than $10 for a gallon of benchmark North Sea crude. As a result of the oil-price fall the Saudi Arabian government's budget deficit rose in a year from $4.8 billion to $15 billion, forcing the once mighty Saudis to scurry to near neighbours for emergency loans. A year and half after the crisis began, Exxon and Mobil, the oil companies, announced the fall in the oil price had forced them into the largest industrial merger in history to create a company with revenues larger than the gross domestic product of Belgium. Commodity prices around the world fell off the cliff made for them by the financial system. The World Trade Organisation reported in late 1998 that coffee prices were 33 per cent down on the year before, agricultural raw materials 23 per cent down and cereals 17 per cent down. Farmers around the world were left a lot poorer. A precipitate fall in semi-conductor prices led to the closure of a string of factories, including several in the UK. At the low point for world equity markets, in October 1998, about £1,400 billion in world financial assets had been wiped out. All that wealth simply disappeared into the thin air from which it had come.

The rolling financial collapse of 1998 was waiting to happen. Banks and brokerages can hire the brightest people money can buy and equip them with the most sophisticated computers. Yet, as global financial markets have liberalized since the 1970s, this system has become prone to ever larger accidents, from the obscure Latin American debt crisis in the 1980s, through the property bubble in the US, the UK and Japan of the early 1990s, to the Asian financial crisis of 1997–98. Since the collapse in 1973 of the Bretton Woods system, which was set up after the Second World War to regulate world financial markets, there have been banking crises in sixty-nine countries. These have been combined with recessions, massive tax-funded bail-outs for bankrupt banks and currency crises, of which there have been eighty-seven since 1975, according to the World Bank. As Martin Wolf, the chief economic commentator at the *Financial Times* put it: 'Financial systems are not so much an accident waiting to happen, as one that is constantly happening.'

It might be worth putting up with such wasteful volatility if it delivered impressively higher growth. But it does not. Between 1945 and 1973, the heyday of the Bretton Woods system, the developed world enjoyed annual growth rates of about 4 per cent, tripling its total output. In 1973, a speculative attack on an over-stretched dollar forced the Nixon Administration to float the US currency, bringing the Bretton Woods system – inspired by economist John Maynard Keynes – to an end. In the decades since, average growth rates have halved across much of the world, unemployment has become a more intractable problem and economic crises have become more commonplace.

Despite all that, the argument of this book is that globalization is good. A retreat into defensive, inward-looking, nationalistic economic policies, would not be progress. One of the few good things to come out of the crisis of 1998 may be a *more* integrated global financial system, strengthened by the creation of steering mechanisms to prevent it careering out of control: stricter and more transparent regulation of banks and stock markets in emerging economies; a world financial authority; an International Monetary Fund, with the resources to prevent crises snowballing; the creation of stronger regional currency blocs such as the European Single Currency, to provide greater stability; and, possibly, punitive taxes to deter short-term speculative capital movements in and out of vulnerable countries. No one put the case for such a steering mechanism better than Keynes himself, writing in 1942 on proposed international finance controls to follow the war:

The advocacy of a control of capital movements must not be taken to mean that the era of international investment should be brought to an end. On the contrary, the system contemplated should greatly facilitate the restoration of international credit. The object, and it is a vital object, is to have a means of distinguishing a) between movements of floating funds and genuine new investment for developing the world's resources; and b) between movements which will help maintain equilibrium between surplus and deficit countries, and speculative movements.

That is still our goal today.

This would be a turn away from the pure market, but not from the global economy. On the contrary, these measures would be designed to make global financial markets more effective by making them more transparent. The task is to maintain beneficial long-term global investment flows to emerging markets and innovative economies while taming hot money and speculative excess. The creation of a globally integrated and interconnected economy, for finance and trade, is a huge achievement. Flows of trade and investment carry ideas and people which bring with them innovation and creativity, the well-springs of economic growth and productivity. Trade encourages creativity and breeds relationships which cross borders and cultures. Global trade and investment, in the long run, will make the world stronger and more peaceful than nationalism and protectionism.

Global finance is just one force driving the modern economy. The second force, with which this book is mainly concerned, is just as pervasive and powerful as financial capitalism but less well recognized. This is 'knowledge capitalism': the drive to generate new ideas and turn them into commercial products and services which consumers want. This process of creating, disseminating and exploiting new knowledge is the dynamo behind rising living standards and economic growth. It reaches deep into our lives and implicates all of us as consumers and workers. If we were to turn our backs on the global economy, we would also leave behind the huge creative power of the knowledge economy.

Knowledge Capitalism

The modern economy's most impressive feature is its ability to create streams of new products and services. The spectacular growth of organized science, the consequent acceleration of technological change and the speed at which new ideas are translated into commercial products distinguish our era from previous ones. To list the changes in this century, particularly in its second half, in travel, communications, medicine, pharmaceuticals, robotics, information-processing and genetic engineering – to take just a few examples – is to chronicle a revolution in what we make and consume, largely enabled by the commercial application of human intelligence.

Across a wide range of products, intelligence embedded in software and technology has become more important than materials. Radios got smaller as transistors replaced vacuum tubes. Thin-fibre optic cable has replaced tonnes of copper wire. New architectural, engineering and materials technologies have allowed us to construct buildings enclosing the same space but with far less physical material than required fifty or 100 years ago. When Henry Ford began mass-manufacturing cars, the miracle was that all those materials – iron, steel, rubber, glass – could be brought together in the same place. The steel in the latest luxury cars in the US costs $1,000, the electronics cost $3,000. The laptop I am using to write this book weighs a little less than the old laptop I bought five years ago. Both machines have broadly the same ingredients – plastic, copper, gold, silicon and a variety of other metals. Yet the new machine is ten times more powerful, far faster and more adaptable than the old machine. None of this extra power is due to new materials, but to human intelligence that has allowed its makers to reorganize the available materials in minutely different ways. The key to economic advance are the recipes we use to combine physical ingredients in more intelligent and creative ways. Better recipes drive economic growth.

We are developing new recipes more quickly than ever before. More scientists are at work today than in the rest of human history. Scientific research is far more productive than in the past and its results are being translated into commercial products more quickly. As a result, we are in the early stages of the development of families of entirely new products and industries: materials that mimic biology; genetic treatments for major diseases; drugs that can target specific parts of the brain that produce emotions; and miniature robots that could work inside the human body. Take just one example. Scientists at the Imperial College of Science and Technology in London have developed a breathalyser which can tell a doctor what is wrong with a patient by analysing the smell of his breath. The market for this product is estimated to be worth £13 billion.

The knowledge-driven economy is not made up by a set of knowledge-intensive industries fed by science. This new economy is driven by new factors of production and sources of competitive advantage – innovation, design, branding, know-how – which are at work in all industries from retailing and agriculture to banking and software.

There are downsides to this relentless flow of new ideas. Innovation threatens familiar routines, institutions and occupations. Technology, particularly information technology, is full of false promise. New knowledge – for instance the power to manipulate our genes – creates dilemmas over its acceptable use. Yet despite these drawbacks, knowledge capitalism is the most powerful creative force we have yet developed to make people better off – something it does by generating and spreading intelligence in the usable form of products and services. Modern consumers can call on the intelligence of thousands of people embedded in the intelligent tools that they use every day: computers, cars, telephones, microwaves. Modern economies are a system for distributing intelligence. The potential of the knowledge economy will not be unlocked by defensive measures to regulate financial capitalism. Instead, we need to redesign our economies to release their potential for creating and spreading knowledge throughout our populations.

Social Capitalism

Collaboration is the driving force behind creativity. That is why social capital, to promote collaboration, is the third motive force of the new economy. At root the idea of social capital is very simple. Making your living in a market economy involves risk. When you buy a product in a shop you run the risk that it may not work.

When you invest in a company you take a risk that it may go belly-up. When you agree to partner someone in a venture, you run the risk that they may let you down. Unless you are prepared to take risks, you cannot get much done, as a consumer, investor or producer. The more you can depend on people you can trust, the less risk you take. So it's easier to take risks when you have relationships with a range of people you can depend upon or if you can rely upon rules, institutions and procedures to provide you with guarantees. The more an economy promotes this capacity for sharing risks, information and rewards, the more able it will be to bring people together to back investment in new products or enter new markets. Successful economies are underpinned by social relationships which help people to collaborate, whether those are the dense web of relationships between banks and business in Japan and Germany, the co-operative relationships among craft producers in northern Italy or the social networks which thread through Silicon Valley in California. Networks of social relationships create social capital, which is absolutely critical in this new economy. An ethic of trust and collaboration is as important in the new economy as individualism and self-interest.

We rely on institutions of welfare, insurance, education and mutual self-help to withstand the turbulence of the global economy. The welfare state was designed for a world of male full-employment and stable nuclear families which has gone for good. That is why we need to reinvigorate and revive organizations capable of creating social solidarity. This is critical for an economy that seeks to trade on its know-how and ideas. Any society that writes off 30 per cent of its people through poor schooling, family breakdown, poverty and unemployment is throwing away precious assets: brainpower, intelligence and creativity. Our tolerance of this social failure is akin to the Victorians choosing to dump millions of tonnes of coal at sea, or Henry Ford leaving tonnes of machinery out in the rain to rust. An innovative economy must be socially inclusive to realize its full potential.

That goal – an innovative and inclusive society – is particularly important because the forces promoting inequality are so powerful. Inequalities have grown as knowledge has become more important in economic growth. As David Landes puts it in *The Wealth and*

Poverty of Nations: 'The difference in income per head between the richest industrial nation, say Switzerland, and the poorest non-industrial country, Mozambique, is about 400 to 1. Two hundred and fifty years ago, this gap between richest and poorest was perhaps 5 to 1.' Knowledge-rich nations, regions and classes have pulled away from the knowledge-poor that are producing commodity products.

The knowledge economy threatens to amplify existing sources of inequality while also creating distinctive divisions. Imagine we lived in a world where, due to genetic mutation, income translated directly into height. The richer you were, the taller you would be. Then imagine that the entire population of the UK were to march past you, in an hour, ranked in order of their income. After three minutes the walkers would be 2 ft tall. After a quarter of an hour the marchers would still be dwarfs of about 3 ft and they would only reach 4 ft after 24 minutes. You would have to wait until 37 minutes before a person of average height, about 5 ft 8 ins, walked by. In the final quarter of an hour, abnormally large people, more than 7 ft tall would start to appear. With three minutes left, people twice average height, 12 ft 3 ins, would pass by. It would only be in the final minute that the real giants appeared, people 30 yards high. Yet that would still not be the top. In the final seconds single men earning more than £1 million a year – top barristers, superstar city analysts, some chief executives – would lope by: they would be 235 yards tall.

These giants are the winners in a society that is increasingly organized so that the winners take all, or if not all, then a dispro-portionately high share of the rewards. The same dynamics are at work in television, entertainment, films, pop music and book-writing. John Grisham and Danielle Steel get multi-million dollar advances for their books, while authors whose writing is better write for nothing (an inversion of the economic law that the more you pay the better the product you get). Confined to these celebrity markets, extreme inequalities might be overlooked. Yet the cult of celebrity is spreading. In virtually every profession, an élite is pulling away from the middle and leaving the bottom trailing. Markets for many goods, whether they are computer games, books, films or legal services, are becoming more international. Larger markets mean larger rewards for the people that win. Being the winner in a local market – a school sports day – might bring you a small cup; winning in a global market – the Olympics – brings you vast rewards. As more markets internationalize, there will be a few very big winners. Success will breed success, celebrity will beget celebrity.

A trend towards inequality is deeply ingrained in modern society. Poorer people are less able than rich people to cope with the risks inherent in the global economy. To reverse this trend we need to invest in new institutions of social solidarity. That is the defensive case for social capital. There is a creative case as well. An ethic of collaboration is central to knowledge-creating societies. To create we must collaborate.

Ideas for new products usually emerge from teams of people drawing together different expertise. Few companies have the resources to make global products that combine several different technologies. That is why joint-ventures, partnerships and alliances are proliferating. Cities such as London and Los Angeles will be at the heart of the knowledge economy because these are places where ideas and people circulate at great velocity. Collaboration is driving progress in science. In the 1890s Sir J. J. Thomson, a professor of physics at the Cavendish Laboratory in Cambridge, and a handful of co-workers discovered the electron, using simple equipment. In the early years of the twentieth century Lee de Forest and Irving Langmuir, two US scientists, developed the vacuum valve, working in small, isolated groups. Thereafter developments in this basic technology, which is at the heart of electronics, involved progressively larger teams working with the support of large organizations and wide networks of research contacts. The development of the transistor at AT&T's Bell Telephone Laboratories, by a group led by John Bardeen, Walter Brattain and William Shockley, stemmed from a project to replace the vacuum valve. The result emerged from the co-ordination of many scientists, not an isolated stroke of inventive genius. The development of the microprocessor and computer chip, the modern equivalent to the vacuum valve, took the combined work of hundreds of researchers. Biotechnology is even more collaborative: a recent research paper on yeast had 135 authors from eighty-five institutions.

Sir Alec Broers, the vice-chancellor of Cambridge University, studied twenty innovations in information and communication technologies to find out where the new ideas came from. He concluded:

> We are in an era where the ideas of a single person alone seldom lead to fruition. All ideas originate with individuals, but their ideas must fit into a matrix of innovation before progress is made. The innovation matrix extends across groups of researchers and, in many cases, across nations and the world. If a researcher is not a part of the world technology network, he is unlikely to succeed. This is perhaps the area of greatest change [in scientific research] over the last 100 years.

Collaborative networks, not companies, are fast becoming the basic units of innovation and production in the new economy.

Welcome to the Knowledge Society

Three forces are driving modern economies – finance, knowledge and social capital. It is no coincidence that all are intangible: they cannot be weighed or touched, they do not travel in railway wagons and cannot be stockpiled in ports. The critical factors of production of this new economy are not oil, raw materials, armies of cheap labour or physical plant and equipment. These traditional assets still matter, but they are a source of competitive advantage only when they are vehicles for ideas and intelligence which give them value.

When the three forces of modern economic growth work together the economy hums, and society seems strong and creative. When they are at odds, as they have seemed to be for much of the last twenty years, society seems in danger of fragmenting and becoming more volatile. The task is to combine finance, knowledge and social capital in a virtuous circle of innovation, growth and social progress. There are three ways this could be done: by organizing society around the leadership of the market, the community or knowledge and creativity.

Those who believe that self-interest and the search for profit are the main motive force for economic growth argue that the market and private companies should primarily organize the economy. That was the argument of the new right for much of the 1980s and 1990s: that society should be rationalized, restructured and ultimately revitalized by unleashing self-interest and extending the market. The more people looked after their income, housing welfare, education, health, the better-off we would all be. This free-market argument is still influential but has run its course. A free-market society would put us at the mercy of the impersonal and capricious forces of the financial markets, widen inequalities and under-invest in the long term and the public goods on which we all rely. The rise of the knowledge economy will force us to revise many of the claims of the new right which have passed into conventional wisdom, for example that something's value can be read from its price, as set by an open market.

In the 1990s, most critics of free markets have chosen to prioritize social capital, often with the ambiguous but superficially appealing rallying cry that we should strengthen our sense of 'community'. The argument that society should be organized to maximize a sense of community comes in many guises. Stakeholder economists, such as Will Hutton, argue that we need to regulate market capitalism by enforcing upon companies obligations to communities and employees as well as shareholders. Communitarians, such as John Gray and Amitai Etzioni, argue that individuals can only realize themselves within a strong, supportive community. They share the belief that global capitalism is the enemy of community and that we need to make our societies more caring and compassionate. The communitarian critique of market capitalism is superficially appealing but eventually disappointing. Strong communities can be pockets of intolerance and prejudice. Settled, stable communities are the enemies of innovation, talent, creativity, diversity and experimentation. They are often hostile to outsiders, dissenters, young upstarts and immigrants. Community can too quickly become a rallying cry for nostalgia; that kind of community is the enemy of knowledge creation, which is the well-spring of economic growth.

This battle between market and community has been central to the politics of the 1990s. The clash between market and community encouraged a string of attempts, none entirely convincing, to reconcile them: Tony Blair's and Bill Clinton's Third Way, Gerhard Schroeder's radical centre in Germany, Lionel Jospin's hope to create a market economy but not a market society in France, George Bush Jnr's compassionate conservatism, were all attempts to marry the market and community, efficiency and social justice. Governments of the right and the left have continued with broadly pro-market policies, while also strengthening social institutions. This middle way is better than the market extremism which went before. But too often this course, tacking between the demands of market and community, is reduced to a balancing act. Politics with a compromise built into its core unsurprisingly leads to piecemeal, cautious reform: one step forward, half a step back. It does not produce a new vision of how society should be organized, nor a radically new kind of politics, with a new uplifting, inspirational goal and new means to achieve it.

The emergence of the Third Way and its continental variants marked the end of free-market dominance. But the way ahead is not to navigate a middle course between the old left and the new right, the community and the market. The way ahead is to adopt a different destination altogether. The goal of politics in the twenty-first century should be to create societies which maximize knowledge, the well-spring of economic growth and democratic self-governance. Markets and communities, companies and social institutions should be devoted to that larger goal. Finance and social capital should be harnessed to the goal of advancing and spreading knowledge. That will make us better off, put us more in charge of our lives and make us better able to look after ourselves. The free-market agenda has run out of steam. Communitarianism is fraught with difficulty: when it is not vague it sounds authoritarian. The goal of becoming a knowledge-driven society, however, is radical and emancipatory. It has far-reaching implications for how companies are owned, organized and managed; the ways in which rewards are distributed to match talent, creativity and contribution; how education, learning and research is organized; the constitution of the welfare state and the political system. Knowledge is our most precious resource: we should organize society to maximize its creation and use. Our aim should not be a Third Way to balance the demands of the market against those of the community. Our aim should be to harness the power of markets and community to the more fundamental goal of creating and spreading knowledge. How we do that, is what this book is about.

CHAPTER TWO DIANOMICS

We are all in the thin-air business these days. It is slightly frightening to work out just how little supports most of our livelihoods. In the past, people made their living by extracting ore, mining coal, making steel, manufacturing cars, bringing cattle to market. They mined, they made, they forged. Work was hard physical labour. As Bertrand Russell, the philosopher, put it in *In Praise of Idleness*: 'Work is moving things around at or near to the earth's surface.' The output of this labour could be weighed on scales, shipped in railway cars, measured with rules, stockpiled. These days most people in most advanced economies produce nothing that can be weighed: communications, software, advertising, financial services. They trade, write, design, talk, spin and create; rarely do they make anything. The assets they work with are as ephemeral as their output. Of course many of us work in large buildings, offices and factories and we work with machinery and equipment, computers and robots. Yet the real assets of the modern economy come out of our heads not out of the ground: ideas, knowledge, skills, talent and creativity. Indeed, the richer and more powerful the person, the more likely it is that they make their money by manipulating ephemera and intangibles rather than from labour in any recognizable sense.

There is no better example of this than one of the most successful thin-air businesses ever created, the British Royal Family, and one of the world's leading practitioners of thin-air economics, the late Diana, Princess of Wales.

The British Royal Family has no output other than symbolism, a vague sense of well-being it occasionally induces in its citizenry and a lot of gossip. Of course, the Royal Family is very rich. It owns a lot of prime real estate. But that is not the source of its power or standing. People do not come to see Buckingham Palace because it is a beautiful or striking building. They come because the Queen lives there. The Royal Family's value is as a national symbol: it's a brand. Its power and influence stem entirely from the ephemeral world of gestures and symbols. Its most precious assets are not physical but intangible: public popularity, loyalty, affection and the dwindling stock of human capital that are its members. Princess Diana proved particularly adept at thriving in this thin-air business.

While the Royal Family remained rooted in the past, imprisoned by the assets and protocol which were once its strength, Princess Diana exploited one of the first laws of thin-air economics: those with the best image and ideas are more agile, quicker to adapt and better able to communicate directly with people than those weighed down by tradition, trapped by protocol or encumbered by physical assets which have outlived their usefulness. The Royal Family was trapped by its past, like a lazy, complacent incumbent in an industry it had long dominated: the very lucrative monarchy franchise for the United Kingdom. Diana was the upstart challenger, an entrepreneur who used new technology to outmanoeuvre the established but tired incumbent. For the Royal Family, read IBM; for Diana, read Microsoft and the new challengers in the computer industry which have emerged in the last decade. For the Royal Family read Barclays and NatWest; for Diana, read First Direct and the telephone and electronic banks which are the new competitors.

Britain was not just shocked by Princess Diana's death, it was surprised by its own reaction. Almost everyone felt touched by her and yet the scale of the mourning seemed out of proportion, because it was so difficult to pin down Diana's claim upon our affections. Diana was stunningly beautiful, but not uniquely so and certainly no more so than Princess Grace of Monaco, who also died tragically in a car crash. John Lennon like Diana died a peculiarly modern death, in which fame played a part. Lennon, shot by a fan, was a gifted musician who spoke for a new generation. Yet vacuous Diana was mourned more. Winston Churchill was mourned by the nation, but then he was a great wartime leader. What explains her peculiar hold on our emotions?

Diana's celebrity was a product of modern economics. She was a celebrity on a global scale because we live in an era of global media, which allows a kind of global gossip. Celebrities have risen in tandem with the communications technology that makes them possible: it started with telegraph and wireless, now it is satellites and the Internet. When Charles and Diana got married in 1981 there were 11.7 television sets per 100 people in the world; now there are 23 per 100 people and broadcasting has been transformed by a digital revolution which is spawning hundreds of channels. It took 38 years for radio to reach 50 million users in the US. It took 16 years before the same number of Americans used personal computers. The Internet reached 50 million Americans within four years of being available to ordinary consumers. Global communications allow instant distribution of news and images at little cost to tens of millions of people. Pictures travel better than words. Words have to be translated; Diana's face was universal. Lennon and Churchill came up with memorable phrases; Diana came up with memorable looks. Gestures and symbols are the currency of global communications. Diana became a celebrity in the era in which Coke, McDonald's, Nike and Calvin Klein all became truly global brands, with symbols that could be recognized instantly from rural Turkey to Tokyo. So did Diana's smile. Images cross geographic and social borders far more easily than words. Diana was a largely silent star in a cacophonous age. Her life was meant to be seen, not heard. When she opened her mouth she destroyed her classless appeal and we remembered that she was just another Sloane. Princess Diana was a creature of the modern communications revolution. The current Royal Family, like so many of our other outmoded institutions, is rooted to its Victorian origins.

But visual images alone do not sell; brands need personality. We seem increasingly attached to celebrities, through whom we live vicariously. Although Diana was rich, jetted about for endless holidays and lived behind high railings, she managed to conjure a reputation for being popular and accessible. She broke through protocol and convention to talk in public about bulimia and adultery. Celebrities of old were meant to be flawless heroes who were held up as moral exemplars: intrepid explorers, ingenious discoverers, inspired performers, visionary leaders. Diana, on the contrary, was compelling because she was flawed and seemed to acknowledge it. We knew more about Diana than most of us know about our neighbours. Diana was an intimate celebrity. Intimate celebrities – the famous people that ordinary punters feel close to and can trust – are among the most valuable commodities in the modern economy. They sell global products.

Consumer-goods companies increasingly use celebrities to promote their brands: they want that mixture of excellence, ubiquity and intimacy that celebrities offer. Nike is the prime example of a company which built its brand around its association with idolized sporting celebrities: Michael Jordan and Tiger Woods. There is a good economic reason for this. It's a response to competition. As markets become more crowded and competitive, it becomes ever more important for products to stand out by being distinctive. One way to achieve that is to associate the product with a celebrity the consumers admire, by investing his or her character in the product. Consumer-goods manufacturers have a vested interest in celebrities who can front their products to help them stand out from the crowd. The rewards for celebrities are rising. Even Sarah Ferguson managed to make close to $5 million in a few months by endorsing a range of products in the US, including Cranberry Juice and Weight Watchers.

It should be no surprise that after Diana's death the biggest controversies were about her after-life as a brand, in particular who should control the rights to use her name and image to promote products and make money. Our emotional response to Diana's death was fleeting. The anniversary of her death drew a muted response. Her commercial value will be more enduring. Fame is the basis for some of our most important industries: entertainment, music and sport. As Diana's career in the Royal Family was unfolding, so was this structural shift in the character of the British economy. Britain earns more from exports of rock music than it does from steel. She started her royal career as a blast from the past: a gawky adolescent, seemingly bred for a life of duty, wellies, gun dogs, children and forbearance. She metamorphosed into the embodiment of global chic, style and independence. She went from the old Britain of landed aristocratic wealth to a new Britain in which wealth comes from the media, fashion, styling, branding. Diana was just one product of this celebrity economy.

Diana's reach exemplified another aspect of modern economics:

the power of directness. Diana went direct to the people by using the media. She bypassed formal channels. The Royal Family found that the protocol designed to entrench its power left it marooned, out of touch, unable to learn about the world around it. Diana, by contrast, seemed spontaneous, youthful, unstuffy. As Diana's brother, Earl Spencer, put it in his funeral oration, she was very British yet she had a global following (a combination British Airways still yearns for). The Royal Family was a national industry, trapped by its dependence upon a safe local market. The Windsors were cut off, locked in the past, introverted, trapped by their own past success: not a bad description of many established companies, for example the high-street clearing banks. In financial services, as much as the royalty business, the rewards will go to those who go direct to the consumer.

British financial services are being shaken up by a new breed of competitors. It all started with First Direct, the telephone bank set up by Midland, the bank, and Direct Line, the telephone-based insurance company. Now supermarkets are entering the fray to challenge the staid, old-fashioned banks. In late 1998, the Prudential launched a new bank, called Egg, targeted at young people. Egg will have no premises; it will deal with its customers over the telephone, through the Internet and by using digital television. These new electronic competitors have three advantages over the traditional high-street banks. First, they go direct to the customer. A customer can call up a telephone bank anytime they like, bypassing the old branch network. In the new economy, intangible assets such as communications and software (or in Diana's case a gift for a good picture) are more valuable than physical assets: lots of high-street branches (or large chilly palaces). Second, this gives the new banks cost advantages. Rather than employing lots of people, in buildings which need heating and other services, the new banks operate with large centralized databases and telephone systems. They save on real estate but have to spend a lot on advertising to build brand recognition. Third, high-street banks have an image problem: they all look very much alike. Supermarkets and retailers are more adept at managing brands and customer relationships. That is why the new banks are being fronted by the likes of Tesco and Virgin.

High-street banks have been caught out. Vast branch networks used to be the only way to distribute banking services to customers. Until a decade ago these were a great asset. Banks used to measure their market share by the total length of their counters. The more miles of counters a bank had, the more customers it could serve. The branch network used to be a great obstacle to new competitors: entering the banking business was very expensive because setting up a branch network on high streets up and down the land cost a lot of money. The branch networks were a commercial Maginot Line. The new banks are bypassing the branch network and going direct to the customers, using new technologies. The branch network has become a liability, a millstone around the banks' necks. Traditional high-street banks are set up to deal with money as a flow of physical things – cheques, coins, notes, paying-in slips. The new banks deal with money as a flow of information.

This transformation of banking mirrors that of the monarchy. Diana was Royalty Direct. She turned her lack of assets – she had few staff, no great houses and at the end no HRH title – into a strength. Her lack of traditional assets allowed her to be quicker than the Royal Family to respond to public opinion. In the old economy, of objects and buildings, a company could see a competitor coming from a long way off: a new bank had to build a presence on the high street; a new manufacturer had to build a factory; a competitor for the throne had to launch an invasion. In the weightless economy where intangible assets are critical, new competitors can spring from unexpected sources. Supermarkets can challenge banks, television companies can challenge telephone operators, Internet service providers can challenge building societies, biotech companies can challenge giant pharmaceuticals groups and divorced single mothers can launch a challenge to the Crown.

This is one reason why life has become so hard for established institutions and those who work for them: the ground can disappear so rapidly from beneath their feet. Competition and radical innovation can suddenly emerge to threaten the identity and purpose of established institutions. Telephone companies, which were once publicly owned, have to become fashionable Internet service providers. Public-service broadcasters have to compete in the world of digital television. The Royal Family has to think of itself as a brand in the communications business. Intense competition, especially from unexpected sources, means that institutions have to learn rapidly and reinvent themselves repeatedly, something the Royal Family continues to find difficult.

The volatility and uncertainty of life in the intangible economy also helps to explain why we found it so hard to get Diana in proportion. In the late summer of 1997, she was mourned as if she were the prized daughter of a vast extended family. A year later many people were scratching their heads to work out what it was all about and why such a powerful sense of distress could dissipate so rapidly. This lack of perspective is a condition of life in the modern economy. In the old economy, it was easy to get things in proportion: you weighed them, counted them go by, measured their size, calculated how much material had gone into making them. In the intangible economy, judging the value of something is much more difficult, because value is so much a product of fashion and perception. Sudden surges in popularity and value are a feature of the modern economy, where gossip and rumour spread like wildfire and the true worth of a company or a product is difficult to pin down. An oil company can be valued on the basis of its known reserves, the published price of oil, and the efficiency with which the company pumps the oil out of the ground. In contrast the share prices of most biotechnology companies are highly volatile because few of them have any products. They have ideas and ideas are difficult to value. The stock-market valuation of biotech companies swings up and down depending on what the company says about its research to test its ideas. Internet stocks follow the same pattern. Before the Netscape Navigator went public, Netscape was almost impossible to value; it had no product, no track record and no market. A few weeks later, Netscape was worth billions of dollars. Several months later Netscape's value collapsed. We live in a world where the value of a company increasingly depends on perception, branding and fashion. We should not be surprised that we found it so difficult to judge what was appropriate in our response to Diana's death: speculative bubbles which inflate and then implode are a feature of our times.

Putting an enduring, accurate value on a product, service or celebrity has become all the more difficult because the nature of consumption is changing. We are increasingly implicated in producing what we consume, as the line between production and consumption blurs. In the past two decades, many companies have made themselves more productive by abolishing demarcation lines – within factories and offices, between skilled and unskilled, white-collar and blue-collar workers – to create more flexible workforces. The largest productivity gains of the next decade will come from companies that demolish the demarcation line between consumption and production. Consumption is becoming more interactive and often the last stage of the production process. Most software programmes, for example, are developed by companies in conjunction with their users. As more products become digitalized and downloaded via the Internet, we – the consumers – will play a larger role in tailoring them to our needs. Soon we will be able to mix our own CDs, for example. Our homes are like mini-factories, stuffed with high-tech machinery that will produce the digitalized services we will consume. Federal Express, the overnight mail company, allows consumers in the US to fill in their own despatch dockets by logging in over the Internet. The consumer fills out a form that used to be filled out by a Federal Express employee. This shift of work, into the hands of consumers, has saved Federal Express perhaps one million computer key strokes a day and $500 million a year in clerical salaries. That work is being done by consumers. Yet Federal Express's consumer satisfaction ratings have gone up because consumers feel more in charge. Consumers are being enlisted as workers, designers and joint-producers.

This fuzzy line between production and consumption helps to explain why we found it so difficult to keep Diana's value in perspective: we were consuming an image we were partners in creating. The Royal Family has an old-fashioned relationship with its consumers. We get what they choose to give us, as and when they choose to give it to us. Diana was created in part by her consumers. She was jointly owned by the people who consumed her image, the readers of *Hello!* magazine, the media and Diana herself. This shared ownership was evident in Kensington Gardens in the days after her death. The park was awash with flowers and messages, ostensibly addressed to Diana and her sons. Yet actually these messages were from the mourners to one another. The nation communicated with itself through bunches of flowers. People placed their messages in great piles, round trees, along walls, to be read by thousands of other people passing by. It was like posting a message on a bulletin board on the Internet. A personal message became more valuable because it was surrounded by so many other messages of grief and condolence. The point of putting flowers in Kensington Gardens was not diminished as more flowers arrived; the incentive to join in rose the more that other people joined in. The emotional significance of a single bunch of flowers – a few scrawny carnations in some Cellophane – was dramatically enhanced by there being so many other, similar bunches dotted around it.

Precisely the same principle applies to many of the products of the new economy. The point of owning a piece of Windows software is not to be the only person with Windows. That would be virtually worthless. The value of my Windows software derives in part from the fact that so many other people have Windows software as well. That commonality means we can communicate more easily and share tips. My laying flowers at Kensington Gardens made more sense because so many other people were doing it. Diana stopped belonging to herself and became shared property, to be consumed jointly.

There are many downsides to this world. One is the risk of monopoly and conformity. With a lot of modern products, such as personal computer software, it pays to use what everyone else is using. That is one reason why Microsoft has such a stranglehold on the personal-computer industry. Becoming a dissident, using an Apple Mac, becomes more difficult. Every teenager in a generation of individualists seems to want to wear Nike, Air Walk and Calvin Klein. In the week after Diana died, it paid to be doing what everyone else was doing: to be mourning and laying flowers. To be a dissenting doubter was to be an outcast. In the days after her death, Diana enjoyed what economists call increasing returns: the more grieving there was, the more of an incentive there was for other people to join the grieving, the more valuable the process seemed to become and the more that other people took part. Traditional economics and common sense tells you the opposite should happen: the more people use a park the less attractive it becomes for other people. Yet, as we shall see, many of the products of the new economy enjoy a measure of increasing returns, when, for a time at least, success begets success and the normal laws of old economics get turned on their head.

And, of course, there is another problem. Diana shook up the Royal Family but she did not displace it, nor could she have done. There was no revolution along the Mall and had she lived it's far from clear that her challenge to the Windsors could have been sustained. The extraordinary public emotion which followed her death disappeared almost as quickly and mysteriously as it surfaced. The story of Diana's challenge to the Royal Family exemplifies the vulnerability of complacent incumbents in established industries but also their stamina. Reform to the large, established institutions which play such a central role in our lives is far more difficult than creating short-lived, freelance competitors which blaze through the sky and then fall to earth. Diana exposed the Royal Family's frailties, but she could not replace it or even show in much detail how to reform or modernize it. Flair and creativity count for a lot, but to be effective they have to be combined with other assets – buildings, machinery, staff. Diana had flair without the assets or the machinery of state; the Royal Family had the assets without the flair and creativity. This has left the Royal Family stuck in no man's land: its vulnerability has been exposed but it has been unable to reform. It will not go away but nor is it capable of radical renewal. Many of our traditional institutions are mired in this no man's land.

Princess Diana was modern: she crossed social boundaries, she talked in public about experiences normally kept private, she challenged convention. Yet almost unrecognized she was one bearer of the new economy in which more and more of us make our livings. Diana, Princess of Wales is one icon of the modern, weightless economy. A figure who explains much of what the knowledge economy is about is Delia Smith, Britain's most popular cookery writer.

CHAPTER THREE DELIA SMITH NOT ADAM SMITH

Each year at Christmas, millions of people around the world give millions of other people cookery books, in the hope that those who receive the books will become better cooks in the following year. This exchange of gifts is an annual, global knowledge transfer on a vast scale. A few thousand cookery writers around the world distil their knowledge and deliver it to tens of millions of cooks. It is a world-wide upgrade of the software which runs our kitchens. The size and scale of this transfer of know-how is one mark of how much economic activity revolves around the production and distribution of knowledge. There is no better metaphor for the products of the knowledge economy than the recipe.

Our annual download of kitchen software exemplifies the value of different kinds of knowledge. A distinction that will recur in this book is between two kinds of knowledge: tacit and explicit. Tacit knowledge is not written down and is hard to articulate. It is often learned by osmosis, over long periods, in very particular contexts, by an apprentice learning at a craftsman's elbow, for example. Tacit knowledge is robust and often intuitive, habitual and reflexive. Most of us know how to ride a bike but could not write down in detail how to do it. It is knowledge best acquired by doing, and best communicated by example. Explicit knowledge is codified. It is articulated in writing and numbers, in books and reports. As a result, explicit knowledge can be taken from one context and transferred to another more easily than tacit knowledge. A manual that explains how a computer works can be used around the world. Explicit knowledge is more transferable than tacit knowledge, but less rich. Often tacit knowledge becomes valuable only when it can be communicated to a large audience. To make that possible it has to be conveyed in explicit, transferable form: an insight has to become an explanation, a rule of thumb a procedure. In the translation from tacit to explicit knowledge, many of the critical nuances may get left out. When people receive knowledge conveyed in explicit form, the process goes into reverse. Explicit knowledge, conveyed as information, has to be internalized to be brought back to life as personal knowledge. This internalization often makes knowledge tacit once more. A recipe is just information; to bring it to life, the cook has to interpret and internalize it by making his own judgements.

Knowledge is not just spread through this process; it is created. As an idea is transferred from setting to setting, person to person, kitchen to kitchen, it grows and develops. The original idea is modified and adapted; it is in perpetual motion. In traditional industries, dominated by craft skills, this motion is slow, constrained by tradition. In innovative, radical fields, ideas circulate at high velocity. Knowledge sharing and creation is at the heart of innovation in all fields – science, art and business – and innovation is the driving force for wealth creation. This is not an abstract process. It requires human initiative. Information can be transferred in great torrents, without any understanding or knowledge being generated. Knowledge cannot be transferred; it can only be enacted, through a process of understanding, through which people interpret information and make judgements on the basis of it. That is why so much of the hype about the information age leaves us cold. Great tides of information wash over us every day. We do not need more information; we need more understanding. Creating knowledge is a human process, not a technological one.

There is no better way of conveying the economic value of knowledge transformation than to think about the home economics of food. Think of the world as divided up into chocolate cakes and chocolate-cake recipes. A chocolate cake is what economists call a rival good: if I eat it, you cannot. A chocolate cake is like most products of the industrial economy: cars, houses, computers, personal stereos. A chocolate-cake recipe, by contrast, is what economists call a non-rival good. We can all use the same chocolate-cake recipe, at the same time, without anyone being worse off. It is quite unlike a piece of cake. The chocolate-cake recipe is like many of the products of the knowledge economy. Software, digital codes and genetic information are all like powerful recipes which control how hardware – computers and bodies – work. We are moving into an economy where the greatest value is in the recipes, rather than the cakes.

There are two different ways of distributing a recipe and the knowledge embedded within it. One is to spread tacit knowledge. This is how my mother learned how to cook beautiful chocolate cake: by watching her own mother. It's a time-consuming business, but it can produce lasting knowledge and very good results. The other distribution method is to put the know-how into an explicit form, by writing a cookery book, for example, or putting a recipe on the Internet. This kind of knowledge may be less nuanced than tacit knowledge, but it travels a lot further to a lot more people. Delia Smith, Britain's most successful cookery writer and a multi-millionaire, is really a knowledge entrepreneur. She makes money by selling her know-how. According to the *Sunday Times*, Delia is worth at least £24 million, all of it made from thin air, by understanding how to package recipes in an accessible, attractive form. Delia Smith and the stream of cooks who have followed in her wake, Rick Stein, Gary Rhodes, Nigel Slater and so on, have created a new market in cookery knowledge. In the process they have exemplified why transferring know-how that way is more socially and economically efficient.

Transferring knowledge through tacit means is inefficient. Tacit knowledge is limited by the context it is learned in. My mother's cookery knowledge was largely learned in Lancashire. My mother is a great cook but she could not teach me how to cook curry, pizza or sweet and sour pork. As our tastes have become more cosmopolitan so people have wanted to cook a much wider range of food. At bookshops we can buy in cookery know-how from Thailand, Korea, Tuscany and Australia. All the know-how which was locked into localized markets can be sold around the world. Tacit knowledge confines our range of recipes to those we learned from traditional, localized sources. The global market in cookery know-how provides us with a much wider range of expertise to draw upon. Globalization is good for our palates.

Learning how to cook at someone's elbow is inefficient. My mother studied in kitchens as a daughter and wife when she could have been studying for a degree or starting a business. The lengthy learning process that lies behind my mother's roast beef with crispy roast potatoes and Yorkshire pudding was made possible only by a social division of labour in which men went out to work and women stayed at home to rear children and cook the meals. That social division of labour was sustained by a relatively primitive knowledge economy: cooking based on transfers of tacit knowledge between women. The old knowledge economy has given way to a new economy in which knowledge is imparted through several different channels to men and women. The student cook has more choice about the speed at which they learn. I cannot sit in a kitchen watching Delia Smith to learn at first hand what makes her chicken in sherry wine vinegar quite so tasty. Instead I can read her recipe, over and over, and try it out, once (disastrously) and a second time more successfully. Learning becomes more efficient, less wasteful.

Knowledge about how to cook food, once a craft skill, has become a commodity. Instead of acquiring our own knowledge, we economize on learning by buying in the knowledge we need in standardized form from any number of fast-food restaurants or through cook chilled meals from Tesco and Marks & Spencer. I like Thai noodles but I do not know how to cook them. Learning the skill would require a lengthy investment of time replete with repeated failures and doubtful results. That is why I prefer to buy in the knowledge, when I need it, by going to a Thai restaurant.

Yet there is a crucial difference in the economics of recipes and the economics of food. Go back to the comparison between chocolate cakes and chocolate-cake recipes. Imagine for a moment that you had invented the perfect chocolate-cake recipe. You have two options to exploit this invention. One is to make chocolate cakes using the recipe and to sell the cakes. You would need to buy extra ingredients for each cake you made. You would need to install ovens and refrigerators. There would be a limit to the number of cakes that could be made and distributed efficiently. The second way to exploit the value of your creation is to turn it into a recipe. The fixed cost of developing a new recipe can be large: it takes repeated attempts and many failures to find just the right combination of ingredients, in the right proportions, cooked in the right way. Yet once the recipe is perfected and written up in an accessible, easy-to-understand form, with glossy pictures, it costs very little to reproduce it. The cost of producing another 100 or 10,000 versions of the same recipe is not that different from producing just one. That is why recipes are like software. It costs Bill Gates many hundreds of millions of dollars to develop a new generation of his Microsoft Windows software for personal computers. But once the software is perfected it costs him virtually nothing to reproduce it endlessly for a mass market.

The similarities between recipes and software do not end there. As with computer software, consumers are intimately involved in producing and reproducing the product. Cooks at home have to interpret the recipes to understand them. The transfer of knowledge is even more time-consuming than downloading a piece of software. A recipe has to be interrogated to be understood. This changes the character of consumption in a knowledge economy. We have been brought up with a physical, sensual notion of consumption inherited from agriculture and manufacturing. We are used to thinking that when we consume something it becomes ours, we take it into ourselves, we eat it up, like a piece of chocolate cake. Consumption is the pleasure of possessing something. Yet when we consume knowledge – a recipe for example – we do not possess it. The recipe remains Delia Smith's; indeed that is why we use it. By buying her book we have bought a right to use the recipes within it. Ownership of the recipe is in effect shared between Delia and the millions of users. Consumption of the recipe is a joint activity. This is not consumption so much as reproduction or replication. The knowledge in the recipe is not extinguished when it is used; it is spread. The more knowledge-intensive products become, the more consumers will have to be involved in completing their production, to tailor the product to their needs. Consumption of knowledge-intensive products is not just joint and shared but additive as well: the consumers can add to the product's qualities. This is one of the most important ways that software producers learn about whether their products work: they give them to consumers to try them out and to develop them further. In a knowledge-driven economy, consuming will become more a relationship than an act; trade will be more like replication than exchange; consumption will often involve reproduction, with the consumer as the last worker on the production line; exchange will involve money, but knowledge and information will flow both ways as well. Successful companies will engage the intelligence of their consumers to improve their products.

As Britain's food economy has become more knowledge-intensive so it has become more efficient, choice has expanded and resources are being used more efficiently and creatively. Resources, mainly women's time, have been freed from the old, time-consuming way of learning. Women's opportunities for employment have expanded. An old, inefficient social division of labour which enshrined this tacit, traditional way of learning is being eroded. In cooking, as in so many other fields, we have made social and economic progress by replacing a relatively narrow, inefficient method of knowledge transmission with a far more effective range of mechanisms to spread know-how more widely, which is both more efficient and more fun.

An economy which becomes more knowledge-intensive has the potential to become more inclusive and meritocratic. Everyone with an education can have a go. That is what makes people like Delia Smith so intriguing. We all know people who are good cooks, and who might be able to come up with great recipes. Perhaps one day they could become famous for their cooking. In an economy which trades know-how and ideas, everyone seems to have a chance to make it, working from a garage, their kitchen or their bedroom. Twenty-five-year-old drop-outs can create best-selling computer games; a nerd fresh out of college can create the Internet's best browser; a boy with no formal education can become Europe's most precocious fashion designer. Knowledge empowers people to take charge of their lives. That is because knowledge can make a lasting impact on well-being: a recipe stays with you long after the cake has been eaten. The more an economy promotes the production and spread of knowledge, rather than just the exchange of goods and services, the better-off we become.

The rub, however, is that know-how on its own is never enough to make money. What stands out about Delia Smith is not just the quality of her recipes but how well she packages and communicates them. Delia Smith's skill is to combine her know-how with the complementary assets and skills – marketing, branding and publishing – which she needs to make money from her ideas. We do not buy Delia Smith's recipes; we buy her books. The tangible product – the book – is the way she makes money from the intangible content – the recipe – which is the true source of its value. It is because the recipes are packaged so attractively, in books which are marketed so skilfully, that we pay so much for them. Recipes may be used simultaneously by lots of people, but books cannot be. To make money from know-how, it is not enough to have good ideas; one has to be able to appropriate the value in them.

Recipes are the engines of economic growth: Paul Romer, Professor of Economics at Stanford University, in California, has formulated an economic theory based on the principle of the recipe. Romer argues that every economy is made up from three components: people; physical things, like raw materials and machines; and rules. Rules are recipes: different ways to combine people and things. As Romer put it in an article in *Worth* magazine:

> We used to use iron oxide to make cave paintings, and now we put it on floppy disks. The point is that the raw material we have to work with has been the same for all of human history. So when you think about economic growth, the only place it can come from is finding better recipes for rearranging the fixed amount of stuff we have around us.

The great advances in modern economies have come from the application of new recipes. A new recipe, invented by chance, created the modern chemical industry. Will Henry Perkin, a British inventor working in the mid-nineteenth century, came up with the first synthetic dye as a chance by-product of a failed attempt to make quinine. Working in a laboratory at home, Perkin obtained a precipitate from naphtha, called aniline black, from which he derived aniline blue. Perkin built a plant to manufacture the dye, which quickly led to an explosion of artificial colours: fuchsia, magenta, purples, pinks and oranges. Perkin's coal-tar industry eventually produced many other chemicals used in photography, medicine, fertilizers and plastics. Thanks to Perkin, Britain led the early chemical industry. Yet within a generation of Perkin's discovery most of the modern chemical industry had migrated to

Germany. By 1881, Germany was making about half the world's artificial dyestuffs, and in 1900 between 80 and 90 per cent. British uniforms in the First World War were dyed with German dye. Germany left the rest of the world so far behind that when its major patents (recipes) were confiscated after that war, the best firms in the US could not make them work and had to hire German chemists to provide the tacit knowledge they needed.

The way Germany deposed Britain as the leader of the modern chemical industry marked a turning point in the role of knowledge in economic development. Before Perkin, technology had led science. Steam engines were invented and a few years later scientists explained how they worked. Inventions came from bright sparks on the shop-floor and heroic, amateur inventors in household laboratories. Inventions were the products of learning by doing. After the rise of the German chemical industry, swiftly followed by the electrical industry concentrated around Berlin, the roles of science and technology, explicit and tacit knowledge, were reversed. Science became the most important source of new technologies and products. Formal knowledge took precedence over hands-on experience. Institutions, such as universities and research laboratories, which produced and exploited formal knowledge, became more and more important to economic growth. Germany won leadership in the chemical industry because it had well-developed formal institutions of further education – which produced well-qualified technicians and scientists – and also the first global corporations – the German chemical giants, BASF, Bayer and Hoechst – which were organized to exploit this know-how to the full. Britain fell behind thanks to its reliance on pragmatic amateurism, learning by doing.

This transition marked the start of the rise of the modern knowledge economy. The Second Industrial Revolution in the second half of the nineteenth century was unleashed by complementary technical and organizational innovations – the rise of the joint-stock company and the internal-combustion engine, the university and the telephone. The power behind the Second Industrial Revolution was explicit knowledge, generated in institutions of learning and exploited by a new breed of company. Since then, knowledge, both tacit and explicit, codified and uncodified, formal and informal, has played a growing role in how our economies generate wealth and well-being and how companies compete with one another. At the end of the century, knowledge is not just one among many resources; it is becoming *the* critical factor in how modern economies compete and how they generate wealth and well-being.

CHAPTER FOUR KNOWING IS COMPETING

Dearborn, Detroit was the birthplace of Henry Ford's revolutionary approach to mass-manufacturing that was adapted to become a model for industries throughout the world. Rubber, coal and iron ore were carried up the River Rouge to the plant that bore its name, where they were processed to make all the components for a car: steel, windshields, tyres, engines. Armies of labour were sucked in and out by the factory siren as appendages to a scientifically managed, industrial machine. From the other end of the machine, finished cars appeared. The River Rouge plant was still working in the late 1980s, after a fashion. I went there as a young reporter to interview one of Ford's most senior executives, its head of global human resources. The executive stared from his penthouse office in Ford's World Headquarters and mused: 'We used to tell people to leave their brains in the car park before they came to work, to make them more compliant. We cannot afford that any more. This is all coming to an end. The car industry will not be a major employer of unskilled and semi-skilled labour in the future.'

That was a decade ago. Ford was in the midst of its painful response to the competitive onslaught from the Japanese car makers, which had so exposed the poor quality, low productivity, lack of innovation and complacency of the European and US industry. Even the most far-sighted executives would have been hard-pressed to imagine how far the transformation of the industry would go. Production lines have been transformed by computer-controlled machines and self-managing work teams. Much of the work that used to be done in-house, at great integrated plants like River Rouge, is contracted out, to suppliers who deliver sub-assemblies, such as dashboards or drive shafts, to the production line, ready to be slotted into the car. The term 'car manufacturer' is a misnomer.

The 'car makers'' main skills are increasingly intangible. They excel at designing and assembling cars, marketing them and arranging consumer finance for car buyers. Cars too are increasingly physical platforms to carry intangibles like software and electronics.

The miracle of plants like River Rouge was that all those raw materials could be transformed so efficiently into a car. Increasingly the real value in a car lies in what weighs least. We are buying an object with intelligence embedded within it. There are more semi-conductors in the average car than there are sparkplugs. The steel in the average US luxury car costs about $1,000; the electronics cost about $3,000. Toyota estimates that by 2005 at least a third of the value of the car will be in its electronics. The advertising for the Volvo saloon launched in 1998 boasted that it carried no fewer than twelve computers. The software that controls a car engine is often more important than the mechanics. John Seely Brown, the chief scientist at Xerox Parc in Palo Alto, California, regales audiences with the story of how he increased the power of his BMW by 30 per cent by reprogramming the software. Cars will drop in weight as new materials get cheaper. As they get lighter, it will be possible to start using new fuel sources and electric engines. That should allow car makers to do away with expensive, heavy equipment such as gears and drive shafts. The wheels could be controlled by wires and computer chips rather than mechanical controls, just as the engines and wings of a modern plane are. By that stage it might have struck us just how boring driving can be. Driving is an industrial-age activity: we sit at the wheel of a machine, controlling it for hours on end. Already satellite communications and navigational devices can pinpoint our position on digitized maps. Smart roads with electronic steering controls embedded in them will soon be able to steer cars for us. Instead of wasting our time driving we could watch a film, play a computer game or do some work.

The car symbolizes the modern industrial age. This transformation in its character and how it is designed and made is within reach. Car-manufacturing is not alone. Similar changes will sweep through other traditional industries – food, drugs, banking – for example. That is because the centre of gravity of our economies is shifting. The old economy was organized around physical, material and tangible assets and products. The old economy had a large service sector but it was largely organized to service physical products: processing paper, taking orders, managing production, selling, servicing and repairing. In the new economy more of the value of manufactured products will come from the software and intelligence that they embody, and more of what we consume will be in the form of services. Across all sectors the knowledge content of products and processes is rising. Everything is getting smarter, from computers and photocopiers to cars and corn. Knowledge push and market pull have made know-how the critical source of competitive advantage in the modern economy.

Knowledge Push
We are doing more scientific research, more productively than previous generations, and translating the results more quickly into commercial products. As Michio Kaku puts it in *Visions*: 'In the past decade, more scientific knowledge has been created than in all of human history. Computer power is doubling every eighteen months. The Internet is doubling every year. The number of DNA sequences we can analyse is doubling every two years.' Scientific research has been made vastly more productive by information technology, which, for example, allows biotechnology researchers to scan scores of compounds in the time it took a researcher three decades ago to survey a handful. After the Second World War it took a decade for the fruits of electronics research to become mass-produced products. These days it takes a few months for a discovery in a biotechnology lab to be patented. One reason for this collapsing gap between scientific discovery and commercial exploitation is that more science is being done in the private sector. In the UK, for example, there are 5,000 recognized institutions of scientific research which have produced patented scientific inventions. About 1,000 of these are in universities, but 2,000 are housed in companies.

As Eric Hobsbawm, Europe's leading historian, remarks in *The Age of Extremes*, no period in history has been more penetrated by and more dependent upon the natural sciences than the twentieth century. Yet, perhaps as a consequence, not since Galileo clashed with the Catholic Church has society been more troubled by the implications of its new knowledge. Genetics is the best example of the potential and the peril of this explosion of scientific inquiry. Modern science and computing power have combined to put us on the verge of the largest explosion of biological diversity and creativity for billions of years. We are in a position to sample and experiment with millions of combinations of amino acids to create new proteins which evolution has never sampled. What should we do with this knowledge?

This explosion of scientific knowledge has been made possible by huge state investment in research, particularly through two world wars and the Cold War. That state-led investment provoked moral dilemmas about whether research should be used for military ends, and economic dilemmas about whether money was being wasted on 'blue-sky' projects. For the foreseeable future the private sector will play the leading role in funding and directing research. That provokes dilemmas of quite a different kind. Companies that turn scientific discovery into commercial products make knowledge widely available. According to one estimate, US pharmaceutical companies invested about $14 billion in research on a set of drugs in the 1970s, which in the 1980s and 1990s yielded a saving of $27 billion a year in terms of extended life expectancy. The downside is that scientific knowledge that might have been publicly owned is being privatized. Is it right that basic scientific knowledge – for instance, about the make-up of human genes – should be owned and exploited for profit by private companies? Private companies may excel at applying and exploiting scientific research, but will they reinvest in the public sharing of knowledge which underpins basic research? These questions will force us to address quite fundamental issues about how the knowledge economy should be owned and organized for the public good.

We invest far more than previous generations in education. It is easy to forget just how recent and incomplete this investment has been. In the UK a national system of secondary education was only created after the Second World War. Further and higher education, in universities, was an élite experience in the UK until the mid-1980s. The most significant policy promoting knowledge-intensive industries in the US was the post-war GI Bill, which opened further education to a majority. The foundations for the world's most dynamic regional economy, Silicon Valley, rest on public investments in California's outstanding universities made between the 1930s and the 1960s. Both the demand and the supply of education will increase rapidly in the next few years, partly through government policies but also through the spread of technologies that will make learning easier. The fastest-growing university in the US is the University of Phoenix, a so-called Drive-Thru university, which teaches entirely through distance learning and virtual classrooms. The fastest-growing form of university is the corporate university, set up by a company to provide its staff with an opportunity to study for a degree. Our ability to compete in the knowledge era will turn on how inventive public policy can be, to invest more in education and to open up the market for learning, to break down the barriers between the public and private sectors in education and to take learning beyond the classroom and the university, into living rooms and offices.

Education and science are joined by the spread of information and communication technologies as the final main push factor. The spread of cheap computing power allows us to collect, analyse, retrieve and re-use information about a widening range of activities, from scientific research to selling insurance. The growth of voice and data communications means we are increasingly able to share and spread this information at great speed, over large distances. A prime example is the way that information about the make-up of the human genome, the complete map of human DNA, is posted by researchers each night on the Internet for millions of people to see. In 1997 there were about 200 million computers in the world. Soon there will be 500 million. Far more important will be the computers and microprocessors that will become embedded in our everyday life, sitting on top of our televisions, inside our cookers, controlling our heating systems, threaded through our clothes. In 1997 there were about 6 billion semi-conductors at work around the world. Soon there will be 10 billion. In late 1997 Texas Instruments, a leading US chip maker, announced plans to introduce a chip so powerful that it would be capable of putting the equivalent of a super-computer used in scientific research into an everyday product like a microwave. In the summer of 1998 IBM announced it had found a way to power chips small enough to turn hand-held devices like mobile telephones into a mini-computer.

More information is not better information. We are deluged by useless information. Our capacity to generate information far outstrips our ability to use it effectively. About 20 million words of technical information are published every day around the world. A fast reader, reading 1,000 words in three minutes, non-stop for eight hours, would need a month of solid reading to get through a single day's output. About 1,000 books are published each day around the world. There has been more telephone traffic in the world in the last seven years than in the rest of human history. More data will soon be carried over telephone lines than conversations. These floods of information make people anxious that they are missing out, being left behind.

This explosion in our ability to communicate explicit knowledge and to share information has made us far more productive, but only if we can get the right information to the right place, at the right time. Better information should allow us to use our resources more effectively. Examples of this abound. Seven-Eleven, the hugely successful Japanese convenience store, uses a point-of-sale information system which tracks sales of every product and automatically re-orders stocks that run low. Safeway, the British supermarket chain, is using satellites to keep track of its fleet of lorries, to make sure they are used most efficiently. The satellite tracking systems cost £1.5 million to install and £300,000 a year to operate, but they should save that money in a year by improving fuel efficiency and vehicle maintenance. Safeway's truck drivers clock up 80 million kilometres a year, the distance of a return journey to Jupiter.

The most successful companies will be those that make the best use of the least information. The smartest organizations and entrepreneurs need only snippets of the right information to make a decision about how a product might develop or a market might change. Information is cheap and plentiful. What matters is not information but the capacity to make sense of it quickly, turning it into understanding, insight and judgement. Bill Gates and Rupert Murdoch are not rich and powerful because they can process more information than the rest of us. Their skill is to focus on the most important information, to see their way into emerging markets.

The world is made better-off by our ability to communicate so freely and to collect information so easily. The spread of explicit knowledge makes economies grow. But in a world awash with information, it is insight and understanding that will set apart the successful companies. To compete, companies need to call upon knowledge which is distinctive to them.

These push factors – science, education and information – are making available to our economies unprecedented amounts of valuable know-how. Yet the rise of the knowledge economy is not driven just by supply; demand is every bit as influential. A powerful set of competitive pressures are pulling companies towards know-how as a durable source of competitive advantage. The globalization and penetration of markets is intensifying competition and volatility. That pressure is driving companies to base their competitiveness on know-how and other intangible assets which competitors find hard to imitate.

Market Pull

Shortly after he took over Waterford Wedgwood, the Irish fine-goods company, Tony O'Reilly, the aspirant media magnate and former top man at Heinz, commissioned research to find out whether US consumers knew that Waterford crystal came from Ireland. If they did, then it would be important to keep production in Waterford, home of the crystal. If they did not know that their fine bowls and glasses came from Ireland, then it might be possible to outsource some production more cheaply, as long as it met Waterford's exacting standards. The research reportedly concluded that, in the minds of most American consumers, Waterford was a brand, not a location, and the brand was a mark of quality rather than confirmation of where the product had been made. There was, in theory, no reason why Waterford crystal should not be made in the Czech Republic as long as it bore the Waterford hallmark. The findings were not music to the ears of the workforce in Waterford, which believed their skills were so distinctive that their jobs were secure. O'Reilly was accused of wanting to turn Ireland into a brand rather than a place. Yet the story of Waterford crystal is common to many other companies: their distinctive assets, those that competitors cannot match, are intangible – brand names, design traditions and know-how. Something similar happened to Rolls-Royce Motors in 1998, when it was bought by Volkswagen. Fifty or a hundred years ago, a buyer would have bought Rolls-Royce to acquire its production and technical skills, as well as the brand name. The two went hand in hand. These days the old-fashioned factory in the North-west of England is probably a liability; the brand will be of far more lasting value. Volkswagen found to its dismay that the Rolls-Royce brand was owned not by the motor-car company, but by Rolls-Royce, the aero-engine company. The aero-engine company sold the right to the Rolls-Royce car brand to its long-term partner BMW for £40 million. BMW was confident it could provide all the tangible assets to make the cars: a factory, a workforce and new machinery. All of those inputs could be bought on the open market. What BMW could not provide was the intangible asset it most needed: the brand.

Intangible assets such as brands have become more important as product markets have gone global and become more competitive. The winners in global markets make a lot more money than they did in purely national markets. Yet the competition is also more intense. To be a success a product has to stand out from the jostling crowd. Brands are one feature that help products stand out.

Globalization is driving companies to base their competitive advantage on brands and other intangible assets such as know-how. Since the 1960s international trade has been liberalized, import restrictions have been removed and tariffs reduced. Partly as a result international trade has blossomed, consistently growing far faster than the world economy as a whole for the past two decades. In the past ten years the reach of the market has extended further, with the integration of most former Communist bloc economies into the global economy and the easing of restrictions on foreign trade with regulated economies such as India. As a consequence the manufacturer of a basic product – a bag, a stereo, a laptop computer – can make that product virtually anywhere and ship it to any market in the world, without facing significant tariff barriers or other restrictions. As a result, manufacturers have a strong incentive to invest in low-cost production sites, for example in the Far East. To put it crudely: China is becoming the world's factory. Low Chinese wages mean that for a wide range of basic manufactured goods it makes little economic sense to make them anywhere else.

Companies in developed economies such as the UK will find it increasingly difficult to sustain their competitiveness on cheap labour, access to raw materials, protection from imports or preferential rates for borrowing. In a world where products are getting lighter and less energy-intensive, access to raw materials is less important than it was. Instead companies in advanced economies will need to base their competitiveness on distinctive, durable, value-creating assets which their competitors will find it hard to imitate: their know-how. Strong brands, such as Waterford and Rolls-Royce, are difficult to copy because they are so value-laden and rich with history. Tacit knowledge, often held in the heads of employees, falls into this category: it is distinctive, durable and hard to copy.

David J. Teece, Professor of Business at the University of California at Berkeley, explains why intensified competition in liberalized markets has made intangible assets so valuable:

> The decreased cost of information, the increase and spread in the number and range of markets in which companies can buy production inputs, the liberalisation of product and labour markets and the deregulation of financial flows, is stripping away traditional sources of competitive differentiation and exposing a new fundamental core to wealth creation. That fundamental core is the development and astute deployment of intangible assets, of which knowledge, competence and intellectual property are the most significant. Other intangibles such as brands, reputation and customer relationships are also vital. Special access to natural resources and skilled labour, economies of scale and scope, are fading as sustainable bases for competitive advantage. In the end, wealth creation in a world of heightened competition comes down to developing, orchestrating and owning intangible assets which your competitors will find it hard to imitate but which your customers value.

Markets penetrate more deeply into industries that were once vertically organized by large integrated companies. It is increasingly common for assemblers of products, such as personal computers, to buy many of their components through sub-contractors or on open markets. Some Silicon Valley computer companies, for example, do not even touch products assembled for them by sub-contractors who put a Cisco or an Oracle badge on the final product. This spread of markets for intermediate inputs means a company will increasingly face competitors who can procure similar inputs from other sub-contractors. That makes it harder for a company to base its distinctive advantage on the quality of its inputs. Instead the company has to control and appropriate assets which cannot be bought from a supplier: the company's own capabilities.

Consumer demand, especially among more affluent consumers, in richer countries, is a further factor driving companies to come up with more intelligent products and services. Consumers want products and services which provide them with integrated solutions: printers which are faxes; washing machines which are dryers. To meet that demand, companies need to be integrate different technologies and complementary products: clothing with computing power woven into the thread; hand-held devices which are personal communicators and computers; windows covered in self-cleaning bio-mimetic materials. Consumers are demanding more knowledge-rich, intelligent products. To meet that demand, companies have to become more able to integrate different kinds of know-how and expertise. The rapid rate of knowledge creation, especially in newer industries, makes them competitive and entrepreneurial. Small companies play a critical role in industries such as software and biotechnology because they can transform an idea into a product at such speed. The leaders of these emerging industries will have to compete to generate, acquire and exploit technologies and know-how which could set global standards for their products. Competition to lead emerging markets is about backing radical new ideas which could break or make the mould.

What This Means for Companies

Most of the value of most companies comes from 'stealth assets': intangible assets such as brands, research and development, patents and other intellectual property which are not recorded on the company's balance sheet. The tangible assets recorded on most corporate balance sheets – so-called 'book assets' – are often no more than a fraction of the total worth of a company, as reflected in its stock market share price. That gap between the value of a company's tangible assets and its true worth, known as the 'market-to-book ratio' is especially large for service and high-technology companies. In May 1997, for example, the market to book ratio for General Motors was 1.6, compared with 13.4 for Microsoft. Only about 7 per cent of Microsoft's stock-market value at that time was accounted for by traditional, tangible assets – land, buildings, machinery, equipment – recorded on its formal balance sheet. The missing 93 per cent of the company's value was due to intangible assets which accountants do not measure: brands, research and development, and people. This trend is not confined to high-tech companies. In 1997 a working group organized by the Centre for European Policy Studies examined the market-to-book ratios for thousands of companies in Europe and the US between 1990 and 1995. They found that the market-to-book ratios of European companies rose from an average of 149 per cent in 1990 to 202 per cent in 1995. Over the same period, the US ratio went from 194 per cent to 296 per cent. These figures may reflect the overheating of the US stock market and they may be affected by different accounting treatments. Yet the trend is unmistakable and it is confirmed by Professor Baruch Lev, an accounting professor at New York University's Stern School of Business. Lev examined the accounts of thousands of US companies over a 20-year period, through recessions and booms. He found that, by the mid-1990s, traditional book assets explained perhaps as little of 20 per cent of the stock market value of these companies.

Know-how is increasingly important to how all companies compete, across all sectors of the economy. This phenomenon is not confined to high-tech industries or an élite of knowledge workers. The knowledge-driven economy extends beyond science-based industries such as biotechnology. The increasing supply of know-how and the growing demand for innovation affect virtually every part of the economy and all organizations within it, large and small, manufacturing and services, high-tech and low-tech, public and private. Know-how will matter for different reasons, depending on the competitive conditions that companies face, the kind of know-how they need and where it comes from. There is no 'one-size-fits-all' solution.

In traditional industries and services – for example, high-volume process industries, such as oil and chemicals, or low value-added services, such as fast food and retailing – companies need to marshal the know-how of their staff, suppliers and customers in a continuous effort to improve quality and productivity. Many large companies have begun to recognize this, partly through quality and continuous improvement programmes and more recently through knowledge-management initiatives designed to disseminate best practice or to create corporate learning programmes. These companies do not need rocket science but continuous, incremental improvements to be efficient, flexible and high-quality. Most of the know-how they need is already in the heads of their suppliers, staff and customers. Companies in these industries will need to devise far more effective ways to enlist the ideas of the shop-floor and the sales-force.

Even traditional, relatively slow-moving industries can be subject to sudden and disruptive competition brought on by new technology. The upheaval in retail banking should be a warning to all complacent, established, incumbents. This kind of competition may soon affect other industries, as traditional intermediaries who have sold products to consumers – insurance brokers, for example – find themselves competing with new entrants who go direct to the consumer, using the telephone and the interactive television. Companies in traditional industries have to be able to combine continuous improvement with a capacity to reinvent and renew themselves in the face of new competitors. Radical innovation may require companies to bring in unfamiliar people and ideas from the outside – for example, from industries such as retailing and advertising – to combine with their own resources. As we shall see, the remarkable revival of the US semi-conductor industry in the 1990s was due to its ability to acquire and digest novel ideas from outside the industry. The Japanese and Korean producers fell behind because they relied on tried and tested, internal sources which produced incremental innovations.

Knowledge plays a critical role in a range of industries – such as pharmaceuticals and aerospace – which have traditionally invested heavily in research and development. In these industries there is no alternative to heavy expenditure on research and development, either in-house or through other companies, to develop leading technologies. In these and other industries, innovation increasingly depends on the way different disciplines and technologies are brought together: the use of new composite materials to replace metal, electronic controls and navigational software in modern aeroplanes is an example. These are capital-intensive industries in which companies need scale and financial resources to generate and exploit the know-how they need.

Know-how is critically important but in a quite different way in high-value-added services, such as accountancy, business consulting, law, design, architecture and financial services, in which firms trade on the training, insight and judgement of their staff. These services account for a very large share of the exports of the British service sector. The competitiveness of companies in these industries is indistinguishable from the quality of the people working in them, which is in part a reflection of their own recruitment programmes and in part a product of professional training and education. Creative industries, such as music, entertainment and fashion, are also driven by people. But in this case they are not trained professionals but cultural entrepreneurs who make the most of other people's talent and creativity. In creative industries, large organizations provide access to the market, through retailing and distribution, but the creativity comes from a pool of independent content producers. Britain, for example, has one of the largest computer games software industries in the world, largely organized around young, self-employed producers, who sell their products to Sony and Nintendo. The knowledge base of these creative industries is far less formalized than in professions such as law or accountancy, where training is tightly controlled by the professions.

Even in knowledge-intensive high-tech industries there are marked differences in how companies acquire and apply their know-how. In electronics, for example, competition is driven by innovation to create smaller, more powerful devices. New ideas come from small entrepreneurs but also from large companies, with heavy research-and-development budgets. The most striking example of this process of dynamic learning is the resurgence of Silicon Valley in California. Its recovery in the 1990s has been driven by revitalized large companies, such as Intel and Hewlett Packard, and a plethora of younger high-growth companies such as Sun Microsystems, 3Com and Oracle. Silicon Valley companies and engineers learn from one another more than from universities. By contrast, in biotechnology and genetics, the knowledge base is less industrial and corporate, more formal and academic. Firms are being formed directly from the science base as venture capitalists back academics to create start-ups. The knowledge base for biotechnology is multi-disciplinary – it comes from several fields of biology and genetics – and multi-institutional: the know-how is in hospitals, universities and charitable foundations as well as companies.

Know-how will play a different role in different companies, depending on the competitive challenges they face, the know-how they have access to and the market opportunities they want to exploit. The kind of learning and continuous improvement which a hotel chain needs to engage in, for example, is quite different from the creativity of a designer or the inventiveness of a biotechnology entrepreneur. A few companies will be clearly in the 'old economy' of bulk processing and commodity products – McDonald's falls into this camp – where competitiveness largely depends on incremental innovation and continuous quality improvements. Other companies are clearly part of the knowledge-intensive 'new economy' – leading biotechnology companies such as Amgen and Novartis, for example – these are engaged in risky, radical innovation. But most large companies, in industries such as cars, banking, retailing and mobile telephones, will find themselves with a foot in both the 'new' and 'old' economies at the same time. This is why working and managing these companies is becoming increasingly uncomfortable. These companies, caught in the middle, often have structures, cultures and routines designed for the old economy, while they face the threat of fleet-footed, more creative, younger competitors from the new economy. In more and more industries Dianomics will be at work: an established incumbent will face younger, nimbler contenders, armed with new technologies.

Some companies excel at managing in this confusing middle ground. One such company is Nokia, the mobile telephone manufacturer. Nokia has to be an efficient, high-quality, low-cost manufacturer. It makes millions of telephones for a global market. To achieve that, Nokia needs to match the best-practice manufacturing standards of its global competitors from the US and the Far East. But manufacturing know-how will not be enough to sustain Nokia. The company needs deep reservoirs of technical know-how. The latest generations of mobile telephones combine at least five different technologies. The next generations will be more like mini-computers. That will bring Nokia into competition with a new breed of competitors, such as Microsoft. To prosper in that competitive battle, it will need its own technical expertise. That will entail investments in research and development. Yet even that will not be enough. For, in addition, Nokia needs to reproduce its brand through design and styling. Mobile telephones are high-tech fashion accessories. Nokia needs to be able to conjure the flair, creativity and independent thinking associated with fashion-driven industries, to compete. So a world-class company such as Nokia has to be a hybrid: it has to combine different kinds of know-how. Most companies are good at competing by deploying just one kind of know-how. They speak one language: science, manufacturing, marketing. The best companies are able to combine different – and often competing – kinds of knowledge, people and cultures. They must be multi-lingual.

Public-sector organizations will not be exempt. They will play a central role in the knowledge-driven economy, not least because it plays such a central role in the most basic knowledge-creating process: education. The public sector controls some of the richest assets in the information economy: the tax, insurance and health databases which the state holds. The public sector is home to some great brand names: the BBC and the NHS. Many of the public sector's most acute problems stem from its inability to learn and adapt at the speed of the society around it. The public sector suffers not just from poor productivity compared with much of the private sector, but from an innovation deficit as well. The public sector's investment in research and development is pitiful compared with the private sector. New industries, such as software and biotech-nology, are driven on by entrepreneurs exploiting new ideas; yet entrepreneurship and risk-taking are discouraged in the public sector. Many of the features which allow the private sector to learn are denied to the public sector.

Almost by chance, Britain is relatively well placed in many of the industries of the future: biotechnology, media and communications, pharmaceuticals, international business services, the creative in-dustries, some aspects of software. Britain has some world-class universities and companies, one of the more entrepreneurial, cosmopolitan cultures in Europe and it is investing more in the science base – though still not enough – and slowly getting better results from the education system. Yet Britain has long-standing weaknesses, which need to be addressed: too many children leave school without a good grounding in basic literacy and numeracy; there are too few high-growth entrepreneurial companies; our investment in training, skills and lifelong learning is still too feeble; there are too few skilled engineers and technicians; start-ups find it too hard to raise money for high-technology projects.

Competing in the knowledge era will present us with large challenges. Life will be more volatile and insecure; skills and technologies, careers and jobs will change more frequently. We will face ethical dilemmas, particularly over how new knowledge, especially from genetics, should be exploited. Learning and entrepreneurship will be of equal importance. Our national identities and cultures will be challenged. The most dynamic economies will have cultures open to new people and new ideas, which have global horizons. They will not be closed to the world but at ease with diversity and experimentation. The knowledge-driven economy will require a new raft of economic policies, covering everything from intellectual-property rights, to investment in science and innovation. Our institutions, public and private, will all have to change quite fundamentally for us to release the potential of the knowledge-driven economy.

CHAPTER FIVE **COLLAPSE**

Each evening hundreds of crabs scurry across the idyllic beach at Krabi in Thailand. They form a fractious, self-governing community which in many respects mirrors our own. They fight over territory, squabble over food and get along, with just enough co-operation to survive. What distinguishes humans from the crabs, apart from the lack of claws, is the degree of co-operation we are capable of. Crabs and sunbathers may share a beach but crabs have not built beachfront hotels, with swimming pools and restaurants, served by nearby roads and airports, to which planes are guided by sophisticated computers. By organizing collectively, people have learned how to produce more food from the same acreage of land, to extend known energy resources and to search for new ones, to invent new methods of communication and transport. Our organizations distribute our combined intelligence around us. Each day we pick up, without thinking, the intelligence of other people, which has been embedded in easy-to-use products. To write this book I relied on the intelligence of people at Compaq and Intel. When I use the telephone I rely on decades of intelligence of other people invested in telecommunications. Humans have become more intelligent than other species not because we have markedly bigger brains, but because we have learned how to store and distribute, share and re-use our intelligence, combining it to greater effect. Organizations of all sorts – schools, libraries, monasteries, universities – have played a role as creators and distributors of intelligence. In the twentieth century, companies have played the leading role, embedding and spreading knowledge in products and processes. As Dorothy Leonard Barton puts it in *Wellsprings of Knowledge*: 'Products are physical manifestations of knowledge, and their worth largely, if not entirely, depends on the value of the knowledge that they embody.'

The nineteenth century was a revolutionary period in industry and commerce because the potential implicit in the telegraph, the train, the car, the telephone, the aeroplane, the cinema and machines of all shapes and sizes was unleashed by a new generation of organizations. The power of these new institutions was borne out by the improvements to living standards they brought to the following century. In contrast, in the twentieth century, technological and scientific innovation has accelerated, but our institutional and organizational innovation has been pitiful. This imbalance between the rate of technical change and the rate of institutional innovation is one reason why we feel so uneasy. Our societies are lopsided. We have not created new institutions of co-operation and collective endeavour, to protect us against new risks, to share the rewards and to match the pace of innovation and knowledge creation.

The time for incremental institutional innovation, to modify Victorian institutions, is over, because the foundations of modern economies are shifting. Our corporate organizations are heirlooms. They were designed to make the most of the physical assets they traded upon. The corporate organizations of the next century will have to be owned and managed in a quite different way to make the most of their distinctive assets, which will be intangible. To understand why our corporate organizations need not just restructuring but revitalizing and redesigning, we have to understand why old organizations have had their day.

The Rise and Fall of the Old Order

The world might have been very different had Frederick Winslow Taylor not suffered as a teenager from severe headaches brought on by bad eyesight. Due to a physical collapse in 1874 at the age of 18, Taylor turned down a place to study at Harvard and took a job as an apprentice patternmaker at Ferrell & Jones, a Philadelphia pumpmaker. Taylor was privileged: his father was rich enough to allow his son not to work. By day Taylor, the apprentice, would work on the shop-floor; at night he would dine with his family and friends, some of whom were factory owners. This dual perspective upon work and business, combined with a fanatical attention to detail and an abhorrence of waste, encouraged Taylor to develop his theories of scientific management, which had a profound impact on organizations throughout the world in the following decades. Taylor is not well known. Millions dispute Freud's work. Marx inspired political revolutions as well as legions of academics. Darwin is back in fashion thanks to the rise of genetics. Taylor's influence upon us has been as great as that of Freud, Marx and Darwin. Lenin and Mussolini admired the principles of Taylor's scientific management, which were also taken up by capitalist manufacturers such as Ford. Yet Taylor's most famous book, *The Principles of Scientific Management*, published in 1911, four years before his death, goes largely unread.

Taylor was a prophet of one of the dominant ideologies of our times: that we should make ourselves more efficient and productive by applying scientific methods to work and organization. Taylor showed how scientific knowledge could be married to mass production to increase material well-being. His ideas helped to create the mass-manufacturing industries that produced consumer affluence in the twentieth century, spewing out washing machines and televisions, cars and refrigerators. Taylor decreed that higher productivity was possible only if managers could standardize and simplify work into a series of easily imitated steps, turning organizations into well-oiled machines, operated by brainless drones. The strengths of Taylor's de-humanized organizations – their regimentation and repetition – became their weakness: they eliminated initiative and individual responsibility.

Large organizations, with structures and hierarchies, have become so commonplace it is difficult to imagine life without them. Yet there was a time before big organizations, when people thought working for a wage was demeaning. That tradition of independent self-employment, in cottage industries, developed in the nineteenth century into a system of 'putting-out'. A merchant who owned raw material, such as wool or cotton, would 'put it out' to be worked on by independent craftsmen who owned their own machinery and set the pace of their work in their own workshops. The merchant would sell the finished product. By the mid-nineteenth century this system had developed into a system of internal contracting, in which teams worked within a factory as independent contractors, responsible for their own machinery and work methods. By the end of the nineteenth century US industry was reorganized into larger, integrated production plants, in part to eliminate cut-throat competition between smaller producers. These vast plants, with lines of heavy-duty machinery, were costly to build. They had to be run at higher capacity, to serve larger, national markets, to make the most of all the machinery and to keep the shareholders happy. That meant that managers, who were responsible to the shareholders, had to exert much greater control over production, by taking it away from the independent craftsmen.

When Taylor started work in Philadelphia, most managers knew very little about production. Skilled workers jealously guarded the knowledge of how a job could be done, how long it would take and so how much could be produced each day. Taylor believed the skilled workers' monopoly of production know-how was a bottleneck. Taylor's reforms broke the knowledge monopoly of skilled workers, broke down their know-how, into small, easy-to-imitate parcels and distributed them throughout the organization. Taylor's detailed time-and-motion studies (he died with his watch in his hand) showed that the steps in each task could be set down on a card. Knowledge held in the heads and hands of skilled workers was made explicit. That allowed these tasks to be copied and picked up by semi-skilled workers, often brought to urban centres from rural communities. As learning did not require months of apprenticeship, the workforce could be more mobile and shifting. As knowledge about production passed from skilled workers to a new breed of expert and engineer, so power also passed from workers to managers and owners.

Taylor's ideas were successful only because they were implemented to give workers more security, and unions more say, than Taylor wanted. Much of the economy remained small-scale and escaped the rigours that Taylorism brought to large organizations. Scientific management was applied quite differently in different countries, which had different systems of trade-union organization and craft training. Despite these qualifications, Taylor's influence was pervasive and powerful. His ideas are at work in every outlet of McDonald's. Taylorism has shaped our schools, with their standardized regimes and specialization. It is reflected in the departmental organization of public-sector bureaucracies. Taylor's insights keep returning in new garb as companies downsize and focus, restructure and re-engineer. Taylor was part of a larger movement in pursuit of order and organization in the name of efficiency and growth. He helped to persuade us that rational analysis could teach us the one best way to do something. Each time you think that you should do something more efficiently by planning how to do it in simple steps, unknowingly you pay homage to Taylor.

Taylor bequeathed a world of standardization and specialization. He put the stamp of science on work and taught us to treat organizations as machines to be regulated, and into which people had to be fitted. Taylor transformed how organizations created, assimilated, disseminated and applied knowledge, particularly technical knowledge about production processes. His central insight was that the control of knowledge was the key to productivity, profits and power. In the process, Taylorism created the fundamental and flawed division in work between white-collar brain-workers and operatives who have to be controlled. The large factories that Taylor helped to make possible sucked in armies of former rural workers. They were complete strangers who had been brought up to the rhythms of agricultural life; they came from different backgrounds and cultures, often had a limited formal education, yet had to be co-ordinated on complex production lines. For that to be possible, these strangers had to be brought together within a common code and set of rules, laid down in published documents. Work became routine only because it became semantic: it required workers who could read and understand instructions, add up numbers and measure output. Only a couple of generations before, these semantic skills were confined to an educated élite; mass production required mass knowledge and education.

How the Old Order Came Apart

Hierarchies first developed to run military and religious organizations many centuries ago. Hierarchies are ancient. Deep hierarchies however, with many layers, are quite recent. Most tribes, clans and agricultural societies have flat hierarchies. The Roman Catholic Church, for example, has just four formal levels. In their prime, the big corporate organizations, particularly the big US corporate organizations of the twentieth century, had perhaps fifteen or twenty levels. These organizations have been exhausted by their hierarchies. Harold Gennen, the architect of ITT, which in the 1960s became the apogee of the big corporation, said the goal of management was to 'make individuals as predictable and controllable as the capital assets for which they were responsible'. Corporations became large and complex in the post-war era, with mergers and acquisitions that created multi-divisional, international conglomerates. The specialist functions within these organizations – marketing, sales, manufacturing, engineering – had to be brought together by managers skilled at co-ordination and planning. The organization was controlled by a pyramid of managers in which everyone reported to a superior through a clear chain of accountability and control. The job of management was to allocate how the capital should be used to best effect; plan for the future; use its authority to organize work to make the most use of the machinery.

These organizations were modelled on machines; they were proud of boasting that they were cleansed of eccentricity or individuality. Each part of the organization had a clearly defined relationship with every other part and lacked any purpose of its own, other than to serve the organization as a whole and for the organization to serve the owners. Each worker was responsible for just one task. Each department was responsible for a discrete aspect of production. Juniors were responsible to superiors; managers, to shareholders. Everything was in its place. These old corporate organizations made largely standardized products, for relatively stable national markets. Their aim was consistency and control; creativity and initiative were frowned upon.

This portrait of Corporate Man is a caricature. Yet aspects of this model were reflected throughout most large US – and, to a lesser extent, European – corporations in the second half of the twentieth century. In the past two decades this old corporate model has run out of steam. It stopped delivering the gains in productivity and quality that it had delivered earlier in the century. This shortcoming in US and British industries was exposed in the 1970s by Japanese competitors that combined a hierarchical organization with an ability to mobilize the intelligence of their workforce through repeated in-company training, quality circles and product-improvement teams. The old corporate model was designed for a predictable world, delivered by Keynesian economic management, of expanding consumer demand and spreading affluence. After the oil shocks of the 1970s, growth become more volatile. With the liberalization of world trade, international competition became more intense. Consumer demand became more complex and shifting: standardized products were overtaken by products more closely tailored to specific types of consumer.

In this more fluid environment the hierarchical organization started to stumble and fall. Hierarchical firms tend to be myopic, focusing only on a limited set of objectives, customers and competitors. IBM's myopia blinded it to the emerging challenge from Microsoft, just as it took years for Detroit to wake up to the challenge from Japanese car manufacturers. Hierarchies focus people on specific tasks but reduce their scope for initiative, trapping them within rules. Deep hierarchies obscure responsibility. Worse, they can create a licence for collective irresponsibility, the ethos that seemed to rule much of British manufacturing in the 1970s. Problems which did not fit neatly into a departmental pigeon-hole were often passed up the management hierarchy, creating a log jam of indecision at the top of the organization. The old organization promoted specialization but also licensed people to refuse to take responsibility for anything beyond their narrow task: the 'not my job', 'not invented here', 'not this department' mentality that plagues large organizations, was a by-product of Taylorism. Sprawling, opaque bureaucracies create endless opportunities for the buck to be passed around. A work culture that was meant to promote focus and diligence often sanctioned apathy and carelessness, as well as sowing resentment and depression.

The initial response, in the late 1970s and early 1980s, to the growing exhaustion of the old corporate order was panic and confusion, dressed up as strategy and renewal. In many factories in the US and the UK, demarcation lines erected in the name of efficiency were brought down or blurred. Workers were encouraged to become multi-skilled. The blue-collar/white-collar divide, enshrined in pay and conditions, was almost abolished in the late 1980s in British manufacturing. Team working became increasingly common, not only on the shop-floor but also to bring different departments together – marketing, research and development, manufacturing, engineering – to speed product development. In the 1980s and 1990s a string of initiatives – Employee Involvement, Total Quality Management and Knowledge Management – were launched to mobilize the intelligence of shop-floor workers in the cause of corporate competitiveness. In some factories, workers had restored to them a power they lost more than a century earlier: the right to stop the production line to correct a quality fault.

Yet as Taylor's methods were being modified on the shop-floor, they were taking on new life in corporate strategies. 'Focus' became the mantra of corporate reorganization, as companies insisted they would concentrate only on a small range of goals, outsourcing much of the rest of their non-core work. Many large companies in the 1980s realized they could not prosper as fenced-off organizations. They needed partners, to give them access to technologies, markets and ideas. Joint-ventures, marketing agreements and product-development partnerships proliferated. Companies were pulled in different directions. Partnerships and joint-ventures cannot be managed by command and control, authority and hierarchy. They need patience, persuasion and negotiation. The old scientific methods of management don't work. Yet, in other ways, this drive to focus companies only on their core tasks made them more driven and directed, apparently more ruthless and unfeeling, as they re-engineered and downsized.

At the end of the 1990s the giant corporation has a new lease of life. As national governments have retreated from economic management, in the face of the power of global financial markets, corporations seem to have acquired more power. Only global companies, it seems, are robust enough to survive the volatility that globalization has brought, while also exploiting its opportunities for economies of scale, selling to markets across the world. A new breed of corporate giant is being created through a wave of global consolidation, with unprecedented mergers such as Daimler-Benz and Chrysler in cars or BP and Amoco, Exxon and Mobil in oil. In China, India and much of the former Communist bloc, modern large corporations are still being established. The 'organization as machine' is thriving, in modern, high-volume process industries such as fast food. The modern service economy is creating its own factories: telephone call centres. The public sector, which in the UK accounts for more than 40 per cent of the economy, is still largely a hierarchical bureaucracy.

Yet in much of the rest of the economy the old corporate regime is being stripped down and new organizations are slowly emerging. These new organizations tend to be based on networks of corporate relationships. They have very little hierarchy and encourage team working among multi-skilled staff. They reward and promote initiative. The most impressive of this new breed of company – the likes of Intel, Nokia, Ericsson – combine global scale with low-cost manufacturing, deep reservoirs of technical know-how and the flair to create fashionable branded products. The most successful companies in the new economy will be mutants and hybrids that can combine different kinds of know-how. The most fertile breeding ground for these hybrids are the industries at the leading edge of the new economy – software, communications, media, and biotechnology. Companies in these knowledge-intensive industries compete on the basis of their intangible assets, which are developed by methods of work and styles of management quite different from organizations of the old economy. Amid the slow collapse of the old corporate order, a new one is emerging, but its shape is still hard to discern.

The pressure to create new kinds of companies will not abate. Incremental innovation will not do. The old organization was good at the repetitive production of standardized products, for standard prices. The old organization does not cope well with a world in which technological change is rapid and disruptive. Old organizations plan for the future. The new organizations recognize the future is shifting and uncertain, and so it has to be shaped and strategies have to be hedged with flexibility. The old hierarchical organizations were meant to excel at controlling costs. That will remain a competitive imperative. They were less good at generating growth and creating value. Managers in the old organization were mainly focused on its inner workings: how to get the work done in the most efficient way. New organizations will have a much larger surface area: they will be much more exposed to the competitive world around them, in order to learn quickly about their changing environment. They will be less like bounded organizations and more dependent upon networks of relationships with suppliers, vendors, partners, governments. Managing the new company will be synonymous with managing this web of relationships.

Brian Arthur, an economist based at the Santa Fe Institute in New Mexico has provided one of the most trenchant explanations for why we need a new model for the company. Arthur argues that there are two worlds of business, in which different competitive pressures encourage different sorts of organizations to emerge. The old world of business, dominated by bulk processing of physical products, favoured standardized products and prices, management by command and control, organizations defined by hierarchies and rigid boundaries. The goal of these organizations was optimization: to find the one best way to complete a task. In the new world of fast-moving knowledge-intensive industries, the prize is to be the first to catch the next wave of technology. The task is not to refine what an organization does, but to invent new products and re-configure the corporation to open up new markets, as well as serving existing ones. Senior executives have to be leaders and entrepreneurs, rather than managers or administrators. They have to give an organization a sense of purpose, to take it forward into an uncertain future. Companies need to be efficient but also adaptive and innovative. Senior managers must constantly scan the horizon for opportunities and ideas rather than burying their noses in the internal machinery.

Arthur compares life in this economy to gambling in a giant casino:

> We can imagine the top figures in high-tech – the Gateses and Gerstners and Groves of their industries – as milling in a large casino. Over at this table, a game is starting called multimedia. Over at that one, a game called Web services. In the corner is electronic banking. There are many such tables. You sit at one.
>
> 'How much to play?' you ask.
>
> 'Three billion,' the croupier replies.
>
> 'Who'll be playing?'
>
> 'We won't know until they show up.'
>
> 'What are the rules?'
>
> 'Those will emerge as the game unfolds.'

'What are my odds of winning?'

'We can't say . . .'

The art of playing the tables in the Casino of Technology is primarily a psychological one. What counts to some degree – but only to some degree – is technical expertise, deep pockets, will and courage. Above all the rewards go to the players who are first to make sense of the new games looming out of the technological fog.

The old world of business will be with us for a long time. Companies are not going to give up on efficiency and cost-cutting. As a result most companies, especially large companies, will find themselves in an uncomfortable middle ground, between the new and the old worlds that Arthur describes. In many areas of the economy modernized versions of the old hierarchical organization will still be best. Yet even basic, bulk-processing and consumer industries will become knowledge-intensive; products are likely to become more brand-intensive. As these industries change, so will their organizations, as their centre of gravity is pulled away from the old capitalism to the new capitalism. Life in the organizations of new capitalism will be creative, innovative and entrepreneurial but risky, insecure and prone to repeated disappointment. Life in the surviving organizations of the old capitalism will involve working for even larger, global companies, with complex hierarchies spread across many countries. Life in the middle ground will be a process of uncomfortable transition as old routines, products, know-how and cultures are left behind and new ones take their place.

Life in the fluid organizations of the new economy will be more exciting, but only for some people, and only for some of the time. These organizations will be less hierarchical, less domineering and less intolerant of different lifestyles. They will be managed by a generation of executives brought up in the wake of the liberal 1960s. Work probably will be more creative and self-governing. There will be greater scope for entrepreneurship. Many of the new organizations will provide staff with stock options which could make them rich. Yet these new organizations will create psychic pressures as well. This new economy is not for the risk-averse. Organizations only become fluid if people can easily leave behind old routines and colleagues. Imagine working in the film business, moving from film to film, crew to crew, set to set, a success one month and flop the next, a progress in which you are only as good as your last project. Work may be like that for many more of us in the next decade: at times fun and rewarding, but itinerant and punctuated by bouts of insecurity.

On this score the currently fashionable, fluid, networked organization compares badly with the old organizations. For all their shortcomings, these old organizations brought unprecedented wealth and well-being to many millions of people. Between 1870 and 1970 US real gross domestic product per labour hour rose more than tenfold, while real GDP per capita rose more than seven times. The success of the US economy, particularly in the 25 years after the Second World War, was largely due to these giant corporations. These corporate behemoths were grey but they had a potent fantasy life: they provided a fable of security and stability, a lifetime career of steady promotion would be followed by a comfortable retirement for a large and reasonably affluent middle class. Any company that could reliably offer this prospect in the first decade of the next century would recruit very easily. The old organizations produced not just goods and services, but the post-war dream of affluence and full employment that now eludes us. The new organizations will employ fewer people in more turbulent conditions and so have no comparable fantasy to offer middle-ranking, middle-income people in middle-skill jobs. This new economy will reward celebrities and stars, gamblers and entrepreneurs, but it offers less, at the moment, for a very large swathe of people who would have had stable jobs under the old order. A central challenge for managers and policy-makers is how to create a sense of security and confidence amid the volatility and turbulence of the new economy. That is a question to which we shall return at the end of the book.

CHAPTER SIX **CREATING KNOWLEDGE**

The staff at St Luke's are in raucous mood. The office administrator reels off the shortcomings and good deeds of the staff, all sixty of whom are gathered around her, swilling beer and wine. This Man of the Month Award to the most helpful staff member is one item on the agenda of the monthly Flag Meeting of the advertising agency. This is no ordinary staff meeting: it is also a monthly meeting of all shareholders. The Flag Meeting is the heart of one of the most dynamic and imaginative company cultures to have been created in Britain in the past decade. St Luke's is an extraordinary kind of company, but one we are likely to see more of. The employees own the agency. At the Flag Meetings they review and celebrate their work over the previous month, discuss new business opportunities, make awards and have fun. The Flag Meeting has a voice on the big issues facing the company.

St Luke's is a knowledge business. Its output is intangible: ideas and images. Its most important skills are weightless: creativity and imagination. Employee ownership underpins a participatory management style and a creative approach to the organization of work. In an industry known for the scale of its expense accounts and egos, St Luke's represents a revolutionary model for all companies which compete by creating and exploiting their know-how.

St Luke's began life as the London office of the US advertising agency Chiat Day. In its time, Chiat Day, which was set up in 1968, was revolutionary itself: it pioneered open-plan offices and, in the 1990s, the 'virtual office', in which no employee had a dedicated desk. In 1992, two staff from Chiat Day's London office, Andy Law, who was then in charge of acquiring new business, and David Abraham, a young account director, joined a small group from Chiat Day's international network, which was given the task of renewing the company. Jay Chiat, the agency's founder, threw out their plan to turn Chiat Day into an ethical advertising company. Yet the attempt to reinvent Chiat Day paid dividends for Law and Abraham. Back in London they started working with clients in more co-operative, open ways; their ethical ideas started to attract new business; Law was invited to sit on the board of Chiat Day Inc., in the US; he became Jay Chiat's surrogate son. Everything went swimmingly, until 30 January 1995.

That evening, as Law was preparing for his daughter's birthday party the following day, Jay Chiat telephoned to let Law know that the entire company, including the London office, had just been sold to the media and advertising giant, Omnicom. Law's job, according to Chiat, was to merge the London office with the operations of a rival agency, TBWA. It did not take long for Law, Abraham and the creative team at the heart of the London operation to realize they did not want to be swallowed by a large conglomerate. They revolted. Law told Chiat that the London office had no assets other than its people, who had brought in the business. Law and Abraham quickly won round other employees and the agency's major clients to the idea that the London office could go it alone as a new company. Law and Abraham were summoned to Madison Avenue, New York for tense talks with their new owners. Omnicom had the financial muscle, but Law and Abraham had the leverage of the real assets: the relationships with clients and loyalty of the staff. By chance, the London arm of the business was just large enough that any ructions could upset the rest of the deal. The US parents, keen to avoid adverse publicity, agreed Law and Abraham could buy the London operation for £1, in exchange for paying Omnicom a share of their profits, worth £1.2 million, over seven years.

At that point, in March 1995, Law and Abraham could have become paper millionaires. But on the plane back over the Atlantic, they realized that without the support of the rest of the staff they did not have a company. While they had been in New York negotiating with Omnicom, the rest of the team had kept the business going. Law and Abraham realized they had the opportunity to create a new kind of company: employee-owned, co-operative, open and creative. They wanted the company's ownership to reflect everyone's contribution to the business. Realizing those ambitions was easier said than done. Over the summer of 1995 a small group tried to devise an ownership structure. The company's lawyers urged the company to adopt a traditional limited-company form. Law and Abraham toyed with the idea of calling the company a 'craft-guild'. As the talks dragged on, the company risked losing momentum. Quite by chance, the finance director stumbled upon the idea of turning St Luke's into an employee-owned company using a little-known statutory vehicle known as a Qualified Employee Share Ownership Trust or Quest. The new employee-owned company was launched in October 1995. About 30 per cent of the shares in the company were distributed to employees in equal portions, regardless of salary, rank or length of service. Each year more shares will be transferred to employees but the plan is that the trust, which represents the interests of the employee-owners, will always have a majority.

St Luke's is governed by a five-strong board, known as the Quest, which is elected by the staff. The Quest sets maternity leave (a year at full pay), sick leave, hiring-and-firing policies, and employment contracts. It meets about once every two weeks. Any member of staff can attend as an observer. The monthly Flag Meetings, which are open to all staff, review performance as well as future business prospects and strategic questions facing the company. All staff attend a Monday morning start-the-week meeting which is chaired by a different junior member of staff each week. The chair has to inform the rest of the company of major events that week, such as pitches for new business. Employees work largely free from supervision but as a result they have to take more responsibility for decisions than in a traditional company. David Abraham explained: 'People feel relieved they do not have someone looking over their shoulder the whole time, but they have to take more responsibility themselves. It cuts both ways. It is our company but that means we have to take responsibility for it.' A striking example of what this responsibility entails is the way pay is set. Every employee's performance is appraised twice a year, by peer and colleague review. One of these reviews determines the employee's pay rise. The finance director sets parameters for how much the total pay bill can rise on the basis of the company's overall financial performance. The employee is asked to judge what sort of pay increase would be justified, in the light of these guidelines. The pay decision is reached by agreement with the staff member's mentor.

The atmosphere at St Luke's is a cross between a café and a library. There are no offices. The building is organized around the clients, each of whom has a specially decorated, dedicated 'brand meeting room'. Meetings about that client's account take place in this brand room. Staff work at large, communal tables. No one is allowed to colonize a regular place. Each night at 5.30p.m. the office manager comes around with '5.30 boxes' to clear away work that staff have left at the tables. All staff carry personalized mobile phones which they pick up at reception when they come in. They can be contacted wherever they are in the building, which is networked with computers. No one has a dedicated terminal. To unwind, staff can retreat to a womb, a round room, decorated with plush red velvet, with computers connected to the Internet and other relaxants.

St Luke's employee-ownership structure, participatory management and creative work culture has won the company a string of awards, including advertising agency of the year in 1997. St Luke's has made an impressive start, but it is only a start. The open management style requires patience. In traditional organizations, managers can issue instructions; at St Luke's everything has to be negotiated. St Luke's was born on an advertising boom; its revolutionary business model is just being tested by a fully fledged downturn. The employee-owned culture put a brake on its entrepreneurial drive. If the company grows too fast it will find it more difficult to embrace the new employees in a common culture.

St Luke's represents a new breed of company which thrives because it does not have a top-heavy hierarchy. Information and responsibility is devolved to front-line employees. Employee ownership is the 'glue' that binds these networked companies together. These companies promote a high-performance culture in which employee ownership helps to provide a sense of membership, common purpose and creativity. The traditional wage packet is a thing of the past in this new breed of company in which equity pay and stock ownership form a significant share of total compensation. Fixed, detailed job descriptions are on their last legs. Clients and customers want to deal with motivated, committed employees capable of solving complex problems and coming up with new ideas. In this new breed of company, employees will not be paid a wage for a fixed amount of effort; they will be rewarded with a blend of wages and equity pay, for a blend of innovation and problem-solving. St Luke's and companies like it are using employee ownership and equity pay to create a new social contract between the employee and the company. At their most radical, companies like St Luke's are a community of interests, a set of relationships rather than a financial entity or a neatly bounded hierarchy. St Luke's is far from alone. Many of the most dynamic new companies to have emerged in the US in the 1990s, particularly from Silicon Valley, combine elements of this new business model designed for the knowledge era.

What Companies are for

We have become so familiar with an economy populated by companies that we find it hard to imagine a world without them. Yet companies, at least in their modern form, are an invention of the last 100 years. We used to find other ways of co-ordinating economic activity. Take the Victorian East End of London as an example. Nineteenth-century maps of London have on the back a directory of who lived where and what they did. In the street in which I lived, Wimbolt Street, in Bethnal Green, I could have bought furniture and had it french-polished, had my hair cut and bought a wide range of food, including cakes and chocolates. In the few streets near by were hundreds of independent producers, all selling to localized markets. It is not inevitable that companies should provide most of the goods and services we consume, especially in a world of advanced telecommunications and networking, which should allow people to work on their own, from home more easily. So why do we need companies at all?

One answer is that companies process work more efficiently than groups of independent contractors. Anyone who has had teams of builders in to do major work on their house will testify that it is time-consuming and risky to organize contracts with a group of independent suppliers to get a complex job done. But efficiency is only part of the story. Modern companies are repositories and distributors of commercially valuable know-how. This view is not new. The economist Alfred Marshall, writing in 1920, said: 'Capital consists in great part of knowledge and organisation: and of this some part is private property and the other is not. Knowledge is our most powerful engine of production; it enables us to subdue nature and force her to satisfy our wants. Organisation aids knowledge.' Edith Penrose, the mother of what academics call the resource-based view of the firm, argued that the firm's productive potential was largely determined by its distinctive stock of knowledge and experience. In the 1980s, Richard Nelson and Sidney Winter embellished Penrose's account by arguing that an organization's knowledge resides in its memory, which in turn was to be found in its routines and procedures. This explains, for example how the *Financial Times*, on which I worked for nine years after leaving university, keeps going despite frequent rotations of personnel. The editor could go missing for days and the paper would still appear, because people knew how to follow routines, which were never written down, to produce the different parts of the paper. There was an *FT* way to do things. This reliance on routines is a strength, but also a potential weakness.

Companies are confluences of several flows. First is a flow of work, which transforms inputs into outputs as efficiently as possible. Second is a financial flow. Money spent to create products and services is recouped by selling them. Third, firms are flows of ideas and know-how. Ideas are generated or acquired from innovators, designers and consumers, and knowledge flows out in the products and services a firm makes. The financial flow has to run in the company's favour for it to make a profit. To be efficient the company has to use as few inputs as possible to make its output. But, in the long run, a company's health depends on whether it has the flow of ideas it needs to renew its products. If the knowledge flow runs dry, so will a company's reservoirs of know-how, and that will be a leading indicator of its eventual decline.

A company needs to invest not just in new machinery to make production more efficient, but in the flow of know-how that will sustain the business. A company has to excel at finding or generating distinctive and potentially valuable knowledge. That knowledge has to be packaged into a form that makes it easy to replicate and to sell to a large market. Yet the company also has to prevent its know-how from being easily imitated by competitors, by branding, patents or copyrights. The company has to appropriate the value embedded within its products. Modern companies have to be good at all the elements of that process, from knowledge generation through to appropriation and exploitation. This process is fraught with difficulty. Knowledge that is visible tends to be explicit, teachable, independent, detachable, but also easy for competitors to imitate. Knowledge that is intangible, tacit, less teachable, less observable, is more complex but more difficult to detach from the person who created it or the context in which it is embedded. Knowledge carried by an individual only realizes its commercial potential when it is replicated by an organization and it becomes organizational knowledge. This process of converting personal, often tacit, knowledge into an organizational capability is far from easy. The most successful companies of the future will be designed to make this process of knowledge generation and appropriation flow as powerfully as possible. Knowledge creation within companies occurs through two quite different processes. One promotes incremental knowledge creation; the other, more radical innovations. Both have implications for how know-how companies should be organized.

Incremental Knowledge Creation

The night air was cold and Roger Boisjoly was uneasy. The following morning, 28 January 1986, the space shuttle Challenger was due to be launched from Cape Canaveral, Florida. Boisjoly, an engineer with Thoikol, one of the leading contractors on the Challenger programme, was worried something would go wrong. The shuttle was carried by a rocket which was divided into segments which were joined and sealed by very large rubber rings. These rings worried Boisjoly. On take-off the rings were eroded by hot gases escaping from the rocket. Concern about erosion had persuaded NASA to install a second ring on each joint as a back-up. The back-up had always been effective on past launches, but a shuttle had never before been launched in such low temperatures. Boisjoly and other Thoikol engineers persuaded their superiors to hold three telephone conferences on the evening of 27 January to debate whether the launch should be delayed. The engineers argued that the first ring would not seal properly in the cold. More gases would be allowed through than normal and the second, fail-safe ring would be eroded. NASA officials were unconvinced. They pressed Boisjoly to present hard, written evidence to back up his hunch. Boisjoly admitted he had no data; he just knew there was a significant risk. Thoikol managers initially supported Boisjoly but subsequently they changed their minds and the flight was approved. At 11.38a.m. on the following morning, 28 January, in an ambient temperature of 36°F, the Challenger was launched. Seconds after launch, hot propellant gases flew past the aft joint of the shuttle's right solid rocket booster, vaporizing both sealant rings, which had been too cold to seal. The mission ended 73 seconds after take off. All seven crew members were killed. Boisjoly's hunch had been correct.

There can be no more graphic explanation of the value of tacit knowledge than Roger Boisjoly's story (this account is drawn from Diane Vaughan's account of the Challenger launch decision, *Risky Technology, Culture and Deviance at NASA*). Yet the Challenger catastrophe also shows how hard it is to validate and defend knowledge that is not articulated in explicit form, especially in organizations which pride themselves on explicit, written evidence and procedures. Creativity often involves the conversion of knowledge from a tacit into an explicit form and back again. Hunches become proposals and prototypes which are tested and improved. This process is central to Ikijuro Nonaka and Hirotaka Takeuchi's study of how Japanese companies create knowledge, *The Knowledge Creating Company*.

Companies have to be good at converting the tacit knowledge held in the heads of employees, suppliers or customers into explicit knowledge, in the form of products or services. Nonaka and Takeuchi use the example of the best-selling Matsushita bread-making machine, which was designed by engineers who distilled the tacit techniques of one of Japan's top bread makers into the design for a machine. The chef's tacit knowledge was made explicit through a long process of observation, design and testing of prototypes. Nonaka and Takeuchi identify several steps in this process. Tacit knowledge is shared by socialization: apprentices watch and work alongside master craftsmen. Employees in Japanese corporations socialize a lot. Nonaka and Takeuchi argue that socialization can help people to trust one another and share their ideas. Explicit knowledge is often shared by combination: reports are edited together; data is gathered to back up an argument. Socialization and combination are important, but they are not the most potent processes of corporate knowledge creation. The most important processes meld and combine tacit and explicit knowledge. Explicit knowledge becomes tacit, held in people's heads and fingertips, when rules and procedures are internalized. It is all very well, for example, for an insurance company to have a rule that all telephones must be answered after three rings, but it is worthless unless employees internalize this rule and act upon it. Tacit knowledge becomes explicit when it is externalized, when, for instance, the bright idea of an employee becomes translated into a new procedure. All these steps – socialization, combination, externalization and internalization – are linked in what Nonaka and Takeuchi call a knowledge-creating spiral.

Through this spiral, knowledge held by an individual or a group can be converted into organizational knowledge. Good ideas come from particular people; to be valuable they have to be spread across a company. Take the example of Kathryn Kridel, a purser with American Airlines. No matter how many first-class passengers there were on her long-haul flights, the catering department always gave her a 200-gram can of caviare, costing $250. On most flights during the Gulf War, in 1991, this was opened and went to waste. Kridel suggested the purchasing department should buy two 100-gram tins. She thought no more about it. Two years later all pursers got an e-mail from the purchasing department. From January 1993 all first-class cabins were to get two 100-gram tins of caviare. The switch saved the company $567,000 a year. Kridel's idea became valuable because American Airlines, albeit slowly, translated a good idea from a person into an organizational routine. In this migration, Kridel's idea was tested, justified and tried out, before it was ampli-fied across the company. Take another example: in most companies there is huge potential to improve performance by bringing the average plants or offices close to the performance of the best. One 1986 study of forty-two almost identical food plants within the same company found that the best plants were three times more efficient than the worst. The profitability of the best plant was more than 80 per cent above the mean; the worst was 40 per cent below. The gains from effectively transferring best practices within a company can be huge. Texas Instruments generated $1.5 billion in annual semi-conductor fabrication capacity by transferring practices from its best to its worst plants. Chevron, the US oil company, estimates it has saved $650 million through the activities of a best-practice team which trawls the company looking for good ideas to spread elsewhere.

The Knowledge Creating Company highlights the strengths of Japanese approaches to knowledge creation, and the weaknesses of the dominant approach in the US. Companies in the US largely focus on collecting, distributing, re-using and measuring their existing codified knowledge and information, particularly through corporate Intranets and other networks. Sending an e-mail, writing a memo, distributing a report is the stuff of knowledge management in US companies. In Japan, knowledge creation is a more subtle, continuous, social process in which tacit knowledge plays a far more important role. Western companies tend to focus on knowledge as a stock to be located, captured, measured, manipulated and valued. Japanese manufacturing companies have a continual cycle of knowing and learning, involving a large majority of the workforce. Knowledge creation is a collective endeavour which usually involves sharing, borrowing and publicly testing ideas; it is rarely the act of an individual genius.

Yet there is a downside to how Japanese companies create know-how about which Nonaka and Takeuchi say little. Tacit knowledge can be an obstacle to innovation as well as an untapped source of new ideas. Tacit knowledge includes the mind-sets and assumptions people use to make sense of the world. These tacit assumptions are deeply held, poorly articulated and often prevent change by justifying people saying: 'We don't do things that way around here' or 'That is not our job'. Corporate knowledge is like an iceberg. What can be seen on the surface is explicit. Tacit knowledge is below the surface; huge and powerful but very difficult to budge. Tacit assumptions need to be made explicit to test them, and show why they are wrong or outdated. Tacit knowledge is often limited to a specific context in which it is learned: the particular kitchen, workshop or office. That makes it hard to transfer. The Japanese rely on tacit knowledge in part because they are taught at school and in corporations not to interrogate or question teachers or texts but to revere, respect and learn from authority. Western education encourages a sceptical, individual challenge to received wisdom and authority, based on evidence and argument; Japanese education upholds the wisdom of seniority and authority. This is borne out by the story of Captain Kohei Asoh, a pilot with Japan Air Lines, told by Peter Senge in *The Fifth Discipline*. Captain Asoh landed his DC-8 jetliner in textbook fashion, two and a half miles short of the runway at San Francisco international airport, in ten feet of water. His crew, bound by Japanese decorum that prohibits criticism of a superior, had been too timid to point out that he was making a mistake.

This respect for authority means young people often have to sit and listen as their superiors bore on endlessly. Women and foreigners are usually excluded from such discussions. Japanese companies excel at generating ideas from within; they are less proficient at absorbing radical new ideas from the outside. Nonaka and Takeuchi explain how large organizations create new products. Yet in many of the fastest-growing industries the brightest new ideas come from young knowledge entrepreneurs, running small, nimble organizations.

A great deal of managerial effort in large companies is devoted to Nonaka and Takeuchi's model of incremental innovation and knowledge creation. In large companies know-how often seems to go missing, getting lost in bureaucracy and procedures that stifle initiative or promote departmental turf wars. Most knowledge-management initiatives, and before them quality and employee-involvement programmes, were designed to enable an organization to tap into its existing stock of know-how more efficiently. Steady improvements in know-how can yield big benefits for large corporations, especially in fields where there is little radical product innovation. Yet in faster-moving areas of the economy, in fields where product innovation is more frequent and systemic, incremental innovation will not do. For a more radical approach to knowledge creation we have to turn to the West Coast of the US and the revival of the US computer industry.

Radical Knowledge Creation

In the late 1980s the US semi-conductor and computer industry seemed to have been brought to its knees by remorseless competition from the Far East. America's victory in the Gulf War seemed to mask its growing dependence upon Japanese and Korean technology. A decade later, the tables have been turned. Intel and Microsoft dominate the world personal-computer industry. The future of the Internet is being fashioned in Silicon Valley. A host of new companies have emerged – Sun Microsystems, Oracle, Sybase and Cisco Systems – which were barely a glint in an entrepreneur's eye when President Reagan was in power. Hewlett Packard is regarded as a role model round the world and even IBM is reviving. The Japanese and Korean companies have lost their way. This turn-around, one of the most dramatic industrial stories of the decade, came about because the US industry innovated a new approach to translate a stream of radical ideas into commercial products. The US industry's revival carries lessons for all companies seeking to acquire, generate, apply and appropriate knowledge for radical innovation, to open up new markets or to create new generations of products.

US dominance of the computer industry in the 1960s and 1970s was based on products which emerged from large research laboratories, the Thomas J. Watson Lab at IBM, the Xerox Palo Alto Research Center at Stanford University and Bell Labs at AT&T. By the 1980s, these research centres had become too cumbersome and slow-moving to generate new ideas at the pace needed to compete for leadership of the industry. The Japanese and Koreans delivered better products, more quickly, at higher quality and lower costs, thanks to the way they mobilized and integrated the intelligence of their workers. In the 1990s the US semi-conductor industry responded with new approaches to innovation and knowledge creation. The components of that model could apply equally well to other industries, as far afield as retailing, consumer goods and automotive products, in which companies need to engage in bouts of radical innovation.

The US computer industry developed an 'intelligence network' to spot new ideas among bright graduate students working in university laboratories. The companies realized there were many more ideas outside their walls than inside. To generate radically new products a company has to be open to ideas from unusual sources. That is why some US car companies have relocated some design and management away from Detroit to California, to get closer to fashionable, environmentally conscious consumers. To come up with radical ideas, companies have to learn from unusual and interesting sources.

The US semi-conductor companies recruited young Turks into positions of responsibility and gave them budgets to play with. In a Japanese company these youngsters would have had to wait patiently for their turn before leading a design project. In the US they were given their heads. They were absorbed directly into organizations which had cultures open enough to recognize talent rather than status or length of service. The US companies were not only better at identifying novel ideas, their capacity to absorb these ideas was far greater than their Japanese competitors'. Well intentioned failure is the most valuable knowledge-creating activity. An organization that wants to generate more knowledge has to generate better failures than it did in the past. The important thing is to fail forward, rather than backwards, as Dorothy Leonard Barton puts it in *Wellsprings of Knowledge*. Alexander Fleming discovered penicillin by chance when he spotted some mould growing on a plate that had been discarded as a failure. The ubiquitous Post-It note started life as a failed attempt to devise an adhesive for car ceiling covers. Failure is central to Karl Popper's elegant theory that scientific knowledge develops through a continual process of conjecture and refutation. There is no such thing as the truth, according to Popper, just better and better conjectures. A commercial version of this process of conjecture and refutation is Hewlett Packard's approach to product development. HP aims to obsolete its own products, in a sense refuting its own conjectures about what the market wants. What matters is not whether you fail but how. The British are terrible at failure. We fail a lot and we tend to fail backwards, sentimentally.

Creative failure involves testing new ideas to see if they stand up to scrutiny. Asking people to justify their ideas in public is a fragile and fraught process. A tendency to avoid tests and hide mistakes is entirely normal. Yet radical innovation comes from applying stringent and demanding tests. The US semi-conductor companies welcomed radical ideas but these ideas were so novel they required extensive testing to refine them. The US semi-conductor industry has a much larger capacity for experimentation and devotes far more time to testing than the Japanese and Koreans, who rely on incremental improvements to tried and tested designs. Radical knowledge creation requires a commitment to extensive experimentation and testing. The US semi-conductor companies became adept at integrating the different skills they needed to turn a prototype into a product. Products used to be developed sequentially, with each department playing its role, from research to engineering, manufacturing to sales and marketing. In the 1990s product development was handled by integrated teams which combined these skills. The companies had to retain deep reservoirs of specialist skills, but these specialists had to become much more adept at sharing and combining their know-how. The orchestration of this exchange was the job of technology integrators, who played a role akin to that of producers in Hollywood, pulling together the talent required to get a project completed.

To make money from an idea, know-how has to be put into a form that allows its value to be appropriated. This is why intangible and tangible products will frequently be bundled together, even in the information age. A floppy disk is not worth much; we value it for the software and information it carries. But it is easier to charge people for software if it is put on a disk, rather than downloaded over the Internet. The US semi-conductor companies have recognized that coming up with bright ideas was not enough. Intel's success partly depends on its branding for its Pentium chips, which has allowed it to charge more for its products than it would have done as a commodity-chip producer.

To engage in radical innovation a company often has to be open to ideas from the outside and from unusual sources; quick to recognize and reward talent; open enough to be able to absorb counter-cultural ideas, able to combine know-how with other assets and skills, such as finance and marketing. The best companies combine radical and incremental innovation. They improve their productivity, quality and cost performance continually, while being open to radical, new ideas. They are good at unlearning as well as learning.

The Value of Unlearning

Creative companies are cannibals. Their ability to unlearn routines they have come to rely upon is as important as their ability to devise new ones. To make room for innovation, old ideas, products and processes have to be cleared away. That is what makes innovation so threatening: it challenges tried, tested and familiar activities that people rely upon. Think of the turmoil involved in moving house: vast quantities of stuff has to be sorted and thrown away. Deciding what to get rid of is as time-consuming as – and more upsetting than – decorating the new house. Competitive companies go through this upheaval the whole time. For a company the upheaval is more painful, because it means getting rid of people and challenging their ingrained habits, values and self-image.

Companies have to strike a balance between exploitation and exploration. If a company spends all its time exploring for new ideas, it will never earn a return on its knowledge. If the company concentrates on exploiting its current capabilities, it will not develop new ones. Successful companies which are rapid learners and which find a niche in the market create powerful incentives for themselves to give up learning. They fall into a trap set for them by their own success. Their core strengths become core rigidities. Their distinctive way of seeing the world eventually turns into tunnel vision. Companies usually seek to exploit established, valuable assets, rather than risk undermining them by investing in new generations of products. IBM ignored ideas that emerged from its own laboratories in the 1970s because it feared they would create simpler, faster computers which would undermine its trusty mainframes. Xerox was slow to respond to the threat of low-cost Japanese plain-paper copiers because it was apprehensive about cannibalizing the profits from its high-volume copiers. NCR clung to its electromechanical cash registers to protect apparently certain revenues from familiar products, and then lost 80 per cent of the market for cash registers to electronic machines in four years between 1972 and 1976. Companies invest to reward and reinforce success. In the process they often sow the seeds of future failure.

The most impressive companies avoid this trap. They excel at unlearning as well as learning. Minnesota Mining and Manufacture (3M) has a corporate policy which encourages scientists and engineers to spend 15 per cent of their time on their own projects. The company has a formal goal that 30 per cent of its sales should be derived from products that are new or which have been substantially modified in the past four years. Hewlett Packard claims that 70 per cent of its sales come from products substantially modified in the past two years. Its chief executive officer, Lewis Platt, told *Fortune* magazine in 1994:

> Most companies our size that have been very successful got themselves into deep difficulty – IBM, DEC, General Motors, Sears Roebuck. The only mistake they made is that they did whatever it was that made them leaders, a little too long. I worry every morning that I, too, will be party to holding on too long. We have to be willing to cannibalize what we are doing today in order to ensure our leadership in the future.

The Knowledge-Creating Company

There is an emerging consensus about what the knowledge-creating company of the future will look like. It will be good at learning and unlearning. It will be open to new ideas from a diverse network of contacts, but able to integrate them smoothly, with the financial, production and marketing skills needed to make money from them. Staff will have a large measure of autonomy to try and fail. Employees will be encouraged to challenge the status quo. Open communication and information-sharing with customers, staff and suppliers will encourage a flow of ideas. Teamwork and flexibility will be taken for granted. The company will rely on knowledge supply chains to link it into sources of know-how and expertise outside its boundaries. The knowledge-creating company will embrace eight principles.

1 *Cellular*

Know-how companies should be cellular. Cells are adaptive. They can act on their own to satisfy their basic needs and in concert to achieve more complex tasks. Companies need to be both networked and integrated to respond to an increasingly fluid, complex competitive environment. A rigid company will not be flexible enough to match the complexity of its environment. A virtual organization without a strong, strategic centre or a distinctive, thriving culture, will be unable to carve a route through the market. A cellular organization which is capable of devolving intelligence and initiative, but also bringing people together for major tasks, should be better able than either a hierarchy or a virtual network to access the right kind of knowledge when needed.

2 *Self-Management*
The cellular company practises self-management and self-organization of motivated, educated, ambitious workers. Self-management will make the cellular company more efficient but also unlock the initiative of staff. Self-management is only effective when people work within a clear set of values and general corporate goals to which they can commit themselves. This reduces the need for bureaucratic oversight. Self-management requires a flow of financial and other information to staff about corporate, team and individual performance. Self-organization will only work within a company with a rich, free flow of information.

A good example of a company which has successfully developed cellular self-organization is CMG, one of the fastest-growing software companies in the UK. Cornelius Stutterheim, the chairman of CMG, sums up his corporate philosophy thus:

> We have to realise and then act upon the realisation that our most important asset is our most mobile asset and it is not recorded on our balance sheet: it's our people. This asset fills up every morning and waters down each evening. The awareness of that means you have to treat people in the way that you would like to be treated yourself.

CMG was created in 1964 by three founders who were fed up with the stuffy bureaucracy of the large companies that employed them. In the early days CMG styled itself as a progressive but paternalistic company. It promoted an open culture of reward according to merit. Most of the share capital was held by its founders until the mid-1980s. When the founders decided to sell their stakes, the current management took the opportunity to create a broadly based employee-ownership culture through an employee buy-out.

Aspects of CMG's work culture are highly egalitarian. There are no executive offices. Every employee, regardless of status, has the same kind of desk. The company is open with information to the extent that anyone can read anyone else's personnel files, including how much they are paid. If someone wants to challenge another employee's salary, executives are obliged to respond to the query. Stutterheim believes an open flow of information is vital to create an environment in which people take responsibility for their actions with minimal interference from executives. He explained:

> People will tell you the truth and argue with you and hopefully they will also correct mistakes of their own accord. If people know why they are doing things they will do things better. If they are told the results of their actions that is better still. But ideally they should also have a stake in the outcome through employee ownership as well. Then the results are more rewarding still.

As well as being open, the company prides itself on being entrepreneurial and meritocratic. People are paid according to their performance. Pay is set by an annual open review of employee performance. Managers are demoted as well as promoted. CMG keeps work units small. No unit is allowed to grow beyond eighty people. If it does, it must be split into smaller units.

The shareholding of current employees has been reduced to about 30 per cent. The top 70 executives are required to own CMG shares worth a year's salary. The next 170 managers are required to hold shares worth six months' salary. The company runs a share-option scheme open to all employees, funded by payroll deductions. This share-option scheme is extremely popular. In general about 60 per cent of employees elected to take part. Pre-tax profits rose from £11.2 million in 1993 to £20.1 million in 1995 on revenues that grew from £128 million to £196 million.

3 Entrepreneurship

All organizations, large and small, public and private, will have to become more entrepreneurial. Cellular self-management should create space for initiative and entrepreneurship. Senior managers will have to become more entrepreneurial. Bill Gates, Andy Grove and Scott McNealy are all entrepreneurs running big businesses. Entrepreneurship, a capacity to spot and take opportunities in the face of uncertainty and flux, needs to be spread through an organization. Know-how companies need to be organizations of mass entrepreneurship.

4 *Equity Pay and Membership*
Self-management and entrepreneurship could fragment an organization. Organizations of the knowledge era will need to be held together by a sense of membership. Knowledge-creating companies will resemble clubs which have distinctive, self-regulating codes of behaviour and values. Membership has to be made tangible through equity pay and opportunities for people to pursue their own interests. The more a company can promote a sense of membership the more likely it is that self-management will succeed.

All staff who join Adobe, the software company based in San Jose, in the heart of Silicon Valley, are advised to get an accountant: with good reason. Within a few years of joining the company a large chunk of their pay will come in profit-sharing bonuses and stock options. For a majority of the staff at Adobe, the traditional pay packet is a thing of the past. Adobe's equity-pay approach is commonplace in Silicon Valley but still unusual in the rest of the US and the UK. That is almost bound to change in the next few years as the products, working practices and culture of the Silicon Valley industries spread into other industries and regions.

Adobe was founded in 1982 by Dr John Warnock and Dr Charles Geschke, who both came from the remarkable Xerox Palo Alto Research Center, which has spawned many of Silicon Valley's companies. Adobe is best known for its photoshop graphics software and its Acrobat programme widely used to download files from the Internet. Adobe went public in 1986. The company employs about 2,400 people. It is the world's third-largest personal-computer software company, with revenues of $762 million in 1996.

The two founders used stock options to reward staff when the company was small and cash was tight. Since then Adobe has developed an array of schemes to reward employees with equity.

Stock worth $156 million was issued under these employee stock programmes between 1993 and 1995. In that time 7.8 million options were granted to employees, and 7.4 million were exercised. All US employees are granted stock options when they join the company, regardless of their pay or rank. Each year staff are awarded additional stock options depending on their performance and whether there is a risk they might leave the company. In a typical year half the staff receive selective stock options. The company sells shares to any employee at 85 per cent of the share price when an employee enters the stock-purchase programme. An employee can buy shares at the discounted price, at any point in the two years after entering the scheme. Real stock, rather than options, can be granted at management's discretion to key staff to help to recruit or retain them. Team-based rewards recognize collaborative efforts at product development. At the start of a project, the team manager is given a pool of cash and stock, to award at his discretion, to team members as they hit milestones in the project. Adobe also operates a corporate profit-sharing scheme. Up to 10 per cent base salary can be paid as a profit-sharing bonus, depending on corporate performance.

As an example of what these schemes can mean to an average employee, take the notional example of a 28-year-old software developer who joined the company on a wage of $70,000 a year. By her third year with the company it is quite possible this employee's pay will be made up of a wage of $85,000 and exercisable options and bonuses worth in excess of $45,000. More than a third of her compensation might come in the form of equity pay.

5 Deep Knowledge Reservoirs
A strong company needs to be sustained by deep reservoirs of knowledge. All the most impressive companies are fundamental innovators, based on their ability to acquire and generate specialist expertise and know-how. A know-how company has to have a knowledgeable core, a capability it excels at. It cannot be a loose collection of generalists.

6 *Integration*

The ability to integrate diverse skills, different kinds of knowledge and complementary know-how will become more critical. Intel's know-how is realized by its ability to spend $3.5 billion on its next semi-conductor plant and the engineering expertise to make it work. Companies are knowledge integrators.

7 *The Holistic Company*

Public legitimacy is a vital intangible asset. A successful company has to reproduce its licence to operate. The knowledge economy will deepen the interdependence between the public and private sectors, between consumers and producers. Companies will be less like neatly bounded organizations. They will depend more on knowledge assets which lie outside them, in universities, for example, or the ideas of their consumers. The ability of life-sciences companies to exploit their new ideas – for example, for genetically modified crops – will depend on securing public legitimacy for these new products. Companies that want to marshal publicly provided knowledge for commercial use will need to show that they can be trusted. Companies are increasingly dependent upon assets such as knowledge which they cannot themselves own.

8 *Collaborative Leadership*

A knowledge-creating company needs to be an 'enterprise' rather than a business: an organization with a purpose and a project, not simply a way to make money. Too many large organizations appear to be assets in search of a purpose. Entrepreneurial companies are a purpose in search of assets. Creating that sense of enterprise is a vital job for corporate leadership. The cellular organization needs a smaller, more strategic, entrepreneurial and inspirational core. The centre will be less concerned with monitoring and checking, more with setting standards and goals, communicating values and threats, identifying challenges and risks, lifting ambitions to wider horizons and encouraging the company to see itself from the outside. The cellular company needs to be underwritten by a social contract. Creating and maintaining that social contract is the job of senior managers. Leadership in this organization is a constant search for creative collaboration, promoting a culture of curiosity and inquisitiveness, attacking complacency, encouraging dissent, dispute and creative abrasion.

In the knowledge economy, companies will need to become more like networks of intelligence. Instead of being modelled on machines, companies should be modelled on networks of intelligence, like the human brain.

CHAPTER SEVEN IF ORGANIZATIONS WERE LIKE BRAINS

My wife's grandmother, Ethel, was born and bred in London's East End. She lived into her 90s, in a tiny council flat in run-down Stepney. As Ethel got older, she got smaller and frailer. By the time she died her brain was incapable of any bouts of new learning. She lived in a dream-world, in which she and her doctor were about to elope to Southend. Despite these eccentricities, Ethel was able to live a reasonably ordered life by distributing her intelligence around her. She cooked, cleaned, washed, ironed, listened to the radio, by knowing where to find all the tools she needed to do these jobs. Ethel's flat was encrusted with little landmarks and rules of thumb that she had laid down over many years to help her get by. By picking up these markers and putting them back in the same place – the washing powder here, the ironing board there, the radio next to the toaster – she could get a lot done. Ethel's brain was addled, but she could appear mentally robust because so much of her intelligence had been sub-contracted to her environment. That was also her weakness. As soon as Ethel was taken out of her flat into a nursing home, she could not do a thing. All her rules of thumb and landmarks disappeared. Her worn-out brain was incapable of putting other landmarks in place in her new surroundings. She became utterly vulnerable. The same fate befalls many companies.

Companies rely upon rules of thumb and landmarks to navigate their environment: competitors are over there, customers come through that door, products are kept underneath the sink, marketing comes once a week to clean the windows. By relying on rules of thumb embedded in their environment companies can appear quite intelligent. The reality is that they become so dependent on these landmarks that their capacity to think, imagine, create and analyse becomes malnourished. When the environment suddenly changes

– new competitors arrive, customers stop coming, products change size and shape – rules of thumb are useless. Companies suddenly need to rethink but they find that task unfamiliar, testing and difficult. Like my wife's grandmother, they can go quickly from seeming to cope quite well, to being vulnerable and dependent.

Distribution is the key to human intelligence. Humans are more intelligent than other species in part because we have larger brains. But that is only part of the explanation. Our brains are not markedly larger than those of dolphins or whales for instance. An elephant's brain is five times bigger than a human brain: it weighs 8 kilograms. But then an elephant's brain is only 0.2 per cent of its body weight; compared to the human brain, which is 2.33 per cent of body weight. Yet brain-to-weight ratios are also misleading. The shrew's brain is about 3.33 per cent of body weight, yet no one would claim that the shrew is particularly intelligent. Brain size is no guide to intelligence. The distinguishing feature of human intelligence is that it does not rely on the brain. Human intelligence emerges from a more efficient division of intellectual labour. Human intelligence does not reside in a mind, housed somewhere inside the brain. It is distributed around the body, in the skin, at our fingertips and, beyond that, in the environment. The human ability to distribute, store and retrieve intelligence embedded in words and tools in our environment, leaves the brain free to take on more sophisticated tasks: speculating, choosing, deciding, analysing, learning. Human intelligence is not just in the central server, the brain, but distributed throughout the network of the body and its environment. The brain is just one organ among many which can intelligently interpret and respond to the environment.

We are used to thinking of the brain, the mind and intelligence as the same thing. The brain is most commonly thought of as a head office, where the captain of the ship sits like Captain Kirk in the *Enterprise*, scanning the horizon, setting course, issuing instructions, drawing on a vast internal library of memories and information. This traditional view of the nature of human intelligence is misleading. Human intelligence is networked. If companies want to become more intelligent they need to develop networked forms of intelligence. The brain is central to this network.

We are far more knowledgeable about the brain than we used

to be. In early 1998, for instance, French scientists claimed to have isolated the portion of the brain that controls nicotine addiction. Neuroscience will be a growth industry in the next century as scientists pinpoint which parts of the brain produce which emotions and feelings. That should allow researchers to develop drugs to target specific emotions and brain functions. Yet as we find out more about the human brain, the more bewildering it seems. We know that the brain is mainly neurons; there are as many neurons in the brain as there are trees in the Amazon rain forest. There are as many connections between the brain's neurons as there are leaves on the trees in the Amazon rain forest. The brain has perhaps 60,000 miles of intricate circuitry linking these neurons. They are not connected sequentially. The linkages are multiple and criss-crossing. There is no hierarchical organization: a thought might start from many parts of this dense network. Signals are transmitted through the neurons by electrical and chemical means. The junctions between neurons, known as synapses, are not like electrical plugs and sockets: they vary in strength, often changing in intensity during the day or in response to our consumption of drugs. If synapses were the same strength the brain might be akin to a computer. Evolution has wired up the human brain in a far more complex, subtle and refined way. The most perplexing aspect of our brains is why electrical and chemical signals in an organ with the consistency of trifle, can produce something as rich, extraordinary and ephemeral as a mental life. It is not just that consciousness gives us our experiences; it helps us to articulate and reflect upon them. Even more puzzling: these ephemeral mental states cause us to do things, by providing us with reasons and motives.

Companies that claim to be 'knowledge-creating' face a similar conundrum. It may be possible for an individual within an organization to be conscious, but how can a company become conscious? And if a company cannot exhibit the rudiments of consciousness, how can it claim to be intelligent or creative? Of course corporate consciousness might be quite rudimentary. As Daniel Dennett argues in *Kinds of Minds* there are many types of minds. Business organizations sometimes resemble animal minds: uncommunicative and capable only of focusing on survival and reproduction in a limited habitat. One approach to intelligence is what philosophers call dualism. Dualists argue the mind cannot be explained by physical sciences because it has an 'élan', a special substance, which produces consciousness. This dualism of mind and body is reflected in much business thinking: the thinking part of business is quite different from the doing part. Thinking, planning, analysing is done by men and women with sharp suits and flip charts at head office, who dream up strategies to be implemented by the unthinking, obedient organization. Creativity is a special skill, to be imported from young men and women in advertising, who show they are creative by wearing trainers and T-shirts. An alternative to dualism is materialism, which argues that the brain's mental events, such as thoughts and experiences, can be reduced to underlying physical events, such as electrical pulses. Materialism has many business advocates, mainly in the US, who urge companies to focus on the hard wiring of their information systems and Intranets. Companies can be re-engineered with technology to make them intelligent, materialists claim.

Dualism and materialism are misleading accounts of intelligence in people and organizations. Humans and organizations are at their most intelligent when they rely on distributed and networked intelligence, when they combine their own brains with the intelligence of others. Systems in which intelligence is ubiquitous and distributed are capable of a greater variety of more nimble responses than a system which relies upon a single, central, all-powerful intelligence. Senior managers who want to control the way a company thinks will render it stupid. The entire organization is constrained to move at the speed of the central intelligence. Intelligent organizations engage the intelligence of all their members. Our bodies harbour a great deal of accumulated wisdom, which is encoded in our reflexes, in our hands and feet, which do a great deal of our everyday thinking for us. In much the same way many companies become more intelligent the further away from head office one travels. One of Darwin's fundamental insights was that design from scratch is expensive and risky, but redesign through modification is cheaper and can be more effective. A system that modifies itself in response to changes in its environment will be more robust than one which has to re-invent itself from scratch, under central direction.

Humans store intelligence around our bodies and outside ourselves as well, in artefacts and tools that can be picked up and used as we need them. Humans became markedly more intelligent when they learned how to make tools, because tools store and transfer intelligence. As an example, take a pair of scissors. These embody the intelligence of the designers and the blade makers. Yet scissors do not just passively embody intelligence, they pass it on. The users of a pair of scissors become more intelligent, more able to achieve their aims, armed with the scissors. We have become much more intelligent because we have such a wide range of intelligent tools to call upon which add to the intelligence we carry around with us. The most important stores of intelligence are not physical tools but words and books, and especially recipes. Our ability to store and retrieve intelligence is growing exponentially with the combined power of computing and telecommunications. Modern companies are among the greatest creators and distributors of stored knowledge civilization has invented. They spread knowledge around society in the form of products and services, books and computers.

A system of distributed intelligence allows the brain to get on with the tasks it is good at: sophisticated intellectual activities such as interrogating our intentions, making bets about the future, testing assumptions that we rely upon, designing entirely new ways of behaving. The brain, freed from the humdrum task of information-processing, can focus on more complex tasks: creating plans, conceptual frameworks, and classifications. Our distributed intelligence engages in incremental innovation and adaptation to the environment, allowing the brain to pursue more radical and risky innovation. Humans are especially intelligent because they have evolved a potent intellectual division of labour, combining networked and centralized forms of intelligence. Creative companies distribute power and decision-making to match the intelligence of front-line staff and suppliers, to allow strategic thinkers throughout the organization, to focus on thinking their way into the future. This allows companies to engage in both incremental and radical innovation.

Yet distributed intelligence has weaknesses. Conflict between different sources of intelligence is commonplace. You bump into someone you find very attractive. Your mind tells you to play it cool, but your face can't help blushing, betraying your true feelings. The same conflicts between different kinds of intelligence occur in companies. The head office sets targets for customer service, but the telephone call centre doesn't answer the phone swiftly enough. The tensions between these different sources of intelligence, the centre going in one direction, the network in another, often only come to light at times of stress, when being co-ordinated matters most. You stand up to make a presentation. Your mind tells you to be calm but your voice quavers. That is one reason we admire great politicians or television performers. They keep calm under great stress, because they have the self-control to reconcile the conflicting signals that reduce most of us to jelly. Distributed intelligence tends to be robust, but that can be a drawback. It is embedded by constant use and often learned in a specific way, making it difficult to dislodge. Our great strength is that we have structured our environment to make it more productive and easier to cope with, which is fine as long as our environment is stable. But if our environment is subject to abrupt, significant and repeated change, then one can find oneself navigating by landmarks that lead nowhere.

Distributed systems of intelligence are capable of learning, often quite quickly: a child who burns his fingers on a hot tap will quickly learn not to do so again and may be able to generalize the lesson, to avoid similar taps. Yet this single-loop learning only goes so far because it draws on a narrow range of experiences. The most impressive acts of learning are those we complete in our heads, when we work out what to do without having to test it in practice. Imagine having to work out the best route from your home to a shop by trying out each route in turn. Learning through imagination involves working this out in one's head in advance. Brains excel at this kind of creative learning; fingers and toes do not. This is where the tacit knowledge praised by Nonaka and Takeuchi is next to useless; more formal, analytical and speculative techniques are required. Intelligent companies and organizations need to be capable of both kinds of learning.

CHAPTER EIGHT **THE RISE OF THE KNOWLEDGE ENTREPRENEUR**

This is the story of how patients all over the world will soon be brought the painless injection. Patients will be able to go into a doctor's surgery and ask to have a vaccine or other drug delivered without having to face a needle being stuck into them. It will be a bit like *Star Trek*: your doctor will simply wave a device over your arm and, without your noticing it, will give you your treatment in hundreds of microscopic particles. This device which does this is called a PowderJect and it was developed by a classic case of knowledge entrepreneurship.

Paul Drayson was unenthusiastic about going to university when he left school. He wanted to follow in his father's footsteps and become an engineer, working in the real world. That is what led him at the tender age of eighteen to join British Leyland, the state-owned car-maker, which was then in the throes of an industrial civil war which threatened its future. Drayson was studying for an engineering degree, sponsored by the company, at the same time as working in one of its car plants. He quickly realized he had made a mistake. His way out was to become involved in a research programme developing robots equipped with sensors to smell gas. That was a lucky break, because, as a result of that research, he was recruited by Trebor, a leading confectionary company, to apply the technology to food production. Eventually Drayson, still in his twenties, became managing director of a small biscuit company, Lambourne Foods. He acquired some business training, led a management buy-out of the company by remortgaging his house and borrowing from his parents, came within a day of losing the company to the recession of the early 1990s and then eventually sold it to a larger group. The buy-out had been financed by 3i, the venture capital fund, which asked Drayson to work as a consultant while he pondered what to do next.

Drayson was sure he wanted to create a company in a fast-growth, high-technology field. But he wasn't sure how. Then, in 1992 and quite by chance, he meet Brian Bellhouse, a scientist at Oxford University who had a vision which could revolutionize medicine: the painless injection. Bellhouse had been working for years on research funded by Rolls-Royce, the aero-engine maker, to examine how gases behaved at supersonic speeds. Bellhouse was highly inventive: some of his earlier inventions had been licensed to 3M and Johnson and Johnson. He was a serial academic entrepreneur. In the early 1990s, as Drayson was struggling with the recession in the food business, Bellhouse was grappling with a conundrum given to him by some geneticists at Oxford. They wanted to find a more effective way to put genetic material into plant cells and asked Bellhouse and a Ph.D. student, David Sarphie, to explore whether it could be done with a high-powered, gas-propelled gun, which would accelerate the tiny particles deep into the plant.

The gun worked for the geneticists and Bellhouse conjectured that it would also work for humans. He and Sarphie loaded the gun with tiny particles of salt. Bellhouse stuck his hand in front of the gas jet. The technicians pulled the trigger. The gun fired, the salt flew at high speed into Bellhouse's hand, but he felt nothing. They had found, in principle, a painless way to deliver medicines. The two scientists were excited by their discovery. Sarphie was due to unveil details of their experiment at a conference, when Bellhouse's daughter, Elspeth, insisted that they should patent the idea of the PowderJect. She also insisted they recruit an entrepreneur to develop the idea into a business, which is where Paul Drayson came in.

Drayson was lured by Bellhouse's vision of the PowderJect as a real-life version of *Star Trek*-style medical care. When he arrived at the Oxford labs, he found a gun the size of a bazooka. But Drayson was still impressed and inspired by the potential. Using the money he had made from his time in the food business, Drayson personally funded further development of the gun, organized for further patents to be issued and started negotiating with the university over ownership of the intellectual property rights. Drayson was not just inspired by the technology, he was also inspired by Elspeth. The two soon started having a relationship.

After nine months of haggling in 1994, Drayson persuaded the university to put its intellectual property into a company, along with Bellhouse and Sarphie, and to turn the PowderJect into a commercial proposition. Drayson realized that the key to the company was to develop and protect its intellectual property. Using his own money, the company developed worldwide patents on powder-injection techniques. Its financial independence was vital; had PowderJect had to turn to outside investors at that stage it probably would have had to give away much of its intellectual property too cheaply.

Yet Drayson's experience in the food business told him that strong patents would not be enough on their own. In the food business he had seen how powerful retailers had dominated smaller suppliers who had no brand reputation of their own. He decided PowderJect had to became a brand, not just a device. It had to aim to become the 'Intel Inside' of medicine, so that patients would go into a surgery and ask for a PowderJect rather than an injection.

However, Drayson quickly realized that that company would never have the resources or skill to exploit the PowderJect's potential to the full. He had no background in pharmaceuticals and was shocked to find it would take seven years to win regulatory approval for the device. PowderJect needed partners: the trick was to find partners who would help exploit the technology without dominating the tiny Oxford company with ten employees and a few thousand pounds in the bank.

Over the next four years Drayson negotiated a series of partnerships designed to turn the PowderJect into a global, mass-market product. To win regulatory approval and take the product out to doctors, PowderJect has formed partnerships with more than a dozen pharmaceutical companies, including Glaxo-Wellcome, Pfizer and Roche, who have done deals worth hundreds of millions of dollars to develop treatments delivered by the PowderJect. These deals gave PowderJect commercial credibility, just as Oxford University had given it scientific credibility.

To turn Bellhouse and Sarphie's bazooka into a hand-held device, Drayson signed a deal with BOC to manufacture tiny helium gas cylinders. In 1995, Drayson and Elspeth Bellhouse rejected a $15m bid for the company from Alza, a US maker of medical devices which may be one of PowderJect's main competitors. Instead, Drayson recruited two top executives from Alza and set up a plant in Fremont, California, part of the San Francisco-Bay Area biotech community, to make PowderJect products for the US. Later he forged a joint-venture with W R Grace, the US conglomerate, which was the parent of Orogen, a US Biotech company and the only other company in the world working on powder-injection techniques.

Seven years after Drayson and Bellhouse first met PowderJect has: dozens of partners each developing treatments using the technique; 150 employees in three locations; £82m in the bank after a stock market flotation and a market capitalization in 1999 of more than £600m, which has made Drayson and the other founders multi-millionaires and rightly proud of their achievement. Elspeth Bellhouse and Paul Drayson are married and in early 1999 were expecting their third child. PowderJect is still not home and dry. It is yet to make a profit or to win regulatory approval for its products, although the signs are that the PowderJect is not just painless but also a more effective way to deliver treatments.

PowderJect is an exemplary story of knowledge entrepreneurship. The heart of the company is the intellectual capital of Bellhouse and Sarphie, itself a product of a research programme into the behaviour of gases at supersonic speeds which goes back to World War II. Success in knowledge-intensive fields required deep reservoirs of know-how, which are themselves the product of long-term investment. The company's success has turned on the combination of its intellectual capital and technology, with Drayson's commercial skills, which brought in the financial, marketing and manufacturing capabilities it needed. PowderJect is a blend of knowledge and commerce: entrepreneurs in these knowledge-intensive fields create that blend. But that is not all. PowderJect has been carried along by a vision to transform something fundamental to all of us: how we take medicines. Knowledge entrepreneurs are often visionaries with a purpose in search of assets; in large companies it's usually the other way around, assets in search of a vision and purpose. And finally, Drayson was motivated by the prospect of making money. It is only by treating people like Drayson and

Bellhouse as heroes for creating wealth from knowledge that Britain will develop a fully fledged entrepreneurial culture.

There are more and more examples of this kind of knowledge entrepreneurship in the UK. David Potter founded Psion largely on the back of technology he developed at Imperial College London. In the course of the last decade Robin Saxby has taken a team of semi-conductor engineers from Acorn computer and created ARM, a specialized developer of semi-conductors, which now has a market capitalization of about £1bn and supplies the designs for chips in all Nokia mobile telephones, for example. At a small office near a farm outside Cambridge, Danny Chapchall has taken technology from the university to create Cambridge Display Technologies, which will be the brains behind screens for televisions and computers entirely made from a thin film of plastic. David Youlton, a former merchant seaman, has created Advanced Rendering Technologies, which provides much of the technology which will make digital broadcasting over the Web a reality. These are just some of the new breed of knowledge entrepreneur who have emerged in the UK, and more of them are on their way in software, the Internet and biosciences.

At a more mundane level, our travel agent, Philip Davies, is a knowledge entrepreneur. He runs Real Holidays, a thriving small business in north London. Our family loves holidays. We go to Real Holidays, not just because Philip and his staff are efficient and polite and they get us good deals on flights and hotels. We go to Real Holidays because we trust Philip's judgement and he comes up with ideas for where we might go mainly by borrowing tips from one client and retailing them to another. Real Holidays is successful because it is a knowledge-generating business. The skills of the staff and the experiences of the clients are combined to generate better ideas for holidays. When we go to Real Holidays we pay for judgement, insight and imagination. We go to Trailfinders to get the cheapest possible fare. Trailfinders is not a knowledge business, it's an information-brokering business.

Knowledge entrepreneurs like Phil Davies and Delia Smith create businesses that trade on their know-how and judgement, insight and ingenuity. Why should entrepreneurship be so central to the rise of the knowledge economy, when it seems global markets are spawning international corporations on a scale never before seen? In this world of corporate giants, what chance is there for the humble knowledge entrepreneur?

One answer is Bill Gates. Gates is the archetypal knowledge entrepreneur: someone who has built a global business from virtually nothing on the basis of a few good ideas and some ruthless commercial strategy. Thousands of people all over the world are at work in their metaphorical garages, hoping that they might become the next Gates or at least get bought out by him. Gates is first among equals in the global super class. Gates's wealth is so vast it is difficult to keep track. On one good day in July 1997 Gates made $2 billion between breakfast time and morning coffee. In that year Gates's net worth rose by $38,096 per minute. If Microsoft continues its astounding growth, Gates would become a trillionaire – with wealth equal to a thousand billionaires – in 2004, according to an analysis by the *New York Times*. If Microsoft simply makes a return equal to the average return on US stocks since 1926, Gates will become a trillionaire at the age of 73, in the year 2029. Gates has become the world's second-richest man, behind the Sultan of Brunei. The Sultan's wealth flows from the exploitation of oil which developed through millions of years of evolution. Gates's wealth stems from some very good ideas, which have taken little more than a couple of decades to develop.

Gates's fortune has been made from thin air. By the mid-1990s Microsoft stock was worth about $86 billion, yet the physical assets recorded on its balance sheet – buildings, real estate, equipment and the like – were worth only about $1 billion. The missing $85 billion of Microsoft's worth was entirely due to its intangible assets, its know-how, research capabilities, likely stream of new products, the Windows brand name and Gates himself. Gates is the best known and richest knowledge entrepreneur. But many more are following in his wake.

What is an Entrepreneur?
The knowledge economy will not be the sole preserve of global companies. It will breed a rich undergrowth of entrepreneurial high-growth companies that will be the source of many of the

brightest and best ideas. Entrepreneurship will flower in the knowledge economy.

The orthodox left and right have little room for entrepreneurs. Orthodox neo-classical economics, in which markets are open, information flows freely and economic agents are rational, reduces decision-making to mechanical calculation. There is very little people can do to buck the market, be they workers or entrepreneurs. Traditional economics regards the inner workings of a firm as simply a black box for processing inputs into outputs; it has little to say about why and how entrepreneurs create companies, enter new markets or take risks. The left has demonized entrepreneurs as profit-hungry exploiters who will be driven out of the market eventually by larger companies. Marx argued that market competition would drive down prices, favouring producers with lower costs and economies of scale: larger capitalists would drive out smaller capitalists.

The case for entrepreneurship has not been helped by its proponents, who described entrepreneurs in such subjective, mystical and emotive terms that they seemed to confirm that entrepreneurship did not belong with real-world economics. Even those who acknowledge that entrepreneurs are economic dynamos do not agree on how and why. Adam Smith said that an entrepreneur was a supplier of financial capital, while John Maynard Keynes argued that an entrepreneur employed capital and labour to make a profit for himself. John Stuart Mill and Alfred Marshall argued that an entrepreneur was a manager of production. None of these definitions is much use to us.

Jean Baptiste Say, writing in 1803, argued that an entrepreneur was an agent of change who shifted resources from sectors of low productivity, such as agriculture, to areas of higher productivity, such as manufacturing. That account was built on by the economist, Leon Walras, who argued that an entrepreneur orchestrated the complementary assets and skills, labour and capital, that an enterprise needed to succeed. Entrepreneurs excel at handling business risks that scare other people. Frank Knight, the Chicago economist, argued in his book *Risk, Uncertainty and Profit* (published in 1921) that the entrepreneur's main role was to decide what to do and how to do it without being certain how the future would turn out. An entrepreneur is confident and venturesome in the face of the timidity and caution of others who require more information and more security before taking action. Successful entrepreneurs hold their nerve in the face of an uncertain, turbulent market. The most impressive knowledge entrepreneurs are masters of precognition; they work out the emerging shape of new markets and industries and are confident enough to back their judgement.

Joseph Schumpeter's *Theory of Economic Development* (published in 1934) introduced the idea that industries are driven by creative destruction, with the entrepreneur destroying the old and building the modern in its place. The entrepreneur's role, according to the early Schumpeter, was not to invent products or technologies but to find ways to bring them to life. Often this meant combining existing technologies to create new uses for them. The modern economy abounds with entrepreneurs of this kind. Michael Dell combined personal-computer assembly with mail order to launch Dell Computer Corporation; Fred Smith combined the mail and airlines to create overnight delivery and Federal Express. For Schumpeter, the entrepreneur had to do more than manage risks. He had to be a leader, with 'the intuition to do the right things without analysing the situation; the power to create something new, and the power to overcome scepticism and hostility from his surroundings'. Entrepreneurs were in part motivated by an intrinsic sense of achievement: solving a puzzle, being independent, the joy of creation, the satisfaction from coming out on top.

The most impressive modern entrepreneurs are confident, sometimes inspiring, even charismatic and certainly ruthless in the face of uncertainty and risk. In addition, entrepreneurs are hungrily inquisitive, quick to absorb new ideas and restless to discover new opportunities. Israel Kirzner, in *Discovery and the Capitalist Process*, argues that entrepreneurship is a creative act of discovery and learning. Most often, entrepreneurs learn and discover how consumer demand may shift or how products could be produced more cheaply. Modern entrepreneurs sense and act upon opportunities to make money in the face of uncertainties and risks which put off the more cautious. Entrepreneurs spot value in ideas that most people overlook or ignore. An entrepreneur's confidence in the face of uncertainty comes from their distinctive view of the world, which carries their colleagues, suppliers and backers with them.

What is a Knowledge Entrepreneur?

All entrepreneurs trade on information and know-how about cheaper sources of supply for raw materials, market opportunities or unmet needs. What distinguishes knowledge entrepreneurs, like Delia Smith and Phil Davies, is the central role that know-how plays in their business. Knowledge entrepreneurs have four distinguishing characteristics.

First, the assets that they trade on are mainly intangible – know-how, skills, judgement, insight – not raw materials, land or machinery. Second, this know-how has to stand out to be the source of their distinctive, competitive advantage. Plenty of young computer programmers can design Web pages. But these independent producers are not knowledge entrepreneurs because their knowledge is not distinctive enough to create lasting value-added. Third, the know-how must be commercial as well as distinctive. The idea must either create new market demand or meet existing demand more effectively. The entrepreneur must devise a way to make money from it by turning it into a string of products that can sustain a business. Fourth, to turn an idea into a business the entrepreneur must bring in complementary business skill and resources. Many of the most successful knowledge businesses are run by partners – one with the ideas, the other, the business skills.

These are the characteristics of a new breed of knowledge entrepreneur emerging increasingly in the US and the UK.

Universities could become an important source of new companies exploiting academic research. As one example of how this will blur the line between academia and commerce, take the story of Amaze, a company that began its life as a research project into training methods at Liverpool's John Moores University. In 1989, researchers in the university's Learning Methods Unit developed interactive technologies to support teaching and learning. A programme for technicians learning how to conduct cervical smears won the unit a European Union award for multimedia development. That spurred the university to create a commercial strategy to exploit the technology. Amaze was set up as a wholly owned subsidiary of the university, with seven staff, in 1995. In its first year, the company had sales of about £400,000, which doubled the following year. The company became known for being able to repackage large, complex amounts of data into accessible, interactive programmes. It started working for retailers, such as Littlewoods, and computer groups such as IBM, to develop programmes to explain their products, systems and catalogues. Amaze now employs about fifty people. The company has just made its first profit on sales of about £1 million a year and it has a string of new customers, including the BBC and Cable & Wireless. Amaze hopes to float on the stock market in three years and has products under development which range from home shopping to theoretical physics. In 1997, the managers, mainly academics, bought the business from the university, with a £2-million buy-out funded by venture capitalists. The managers own 40 per cent of the business, the venture capitalists 55 per cent and the university the remainder.

Why Knowledge Entrepreneurs will be Vital

It is conventional wisdom that only global companies will have the resources and the economies of scale and scope to research and develop technologically sophisticated products, and market them across the world. It takes many failures to create a success. Large companies may not be creative but they have the financial clout to sustain the failure rate need for eventual success. In 1986 Malcolm Baldrige, the then US commerce secretary argued: 'We are simply living in a different world. Because of larger markets, the cost of research and developments, new product innovation, marketing and so forth . . . it takes larger companies to compete successfully.' This argument seems to be borne out by the wave of international mergers sparked by the downturn in the world economy at the end of the 1990s. Even Joseph Schumpeter, the advocate of entrepreneurship, eventually came round to the view that large companies, with market power and large research-and-development departments, would be the engines of technological change.

It is difficult to overstate how misguided a view this has become. As the economy becomes more knowledge-intensive smaller companies will be the most fertile sources of innovation. There is little evidence that large firms are better at innovation than small firms, although they are in some industries. There is mounting evidence that small firms are the engines of innovation in knowledge-intensive industries, even though these innovations might be legitimized and exploited by larger companies. George Symeondis, an economist at Essex University, conducted for the OECD (Organization for Economic Co-operation and Development) an exhaustive study of evidence on innovation in large firms. Symeonidis concluded that there was little correlation between company size and innovation. It is not company size that counts, but what managers do with it. Some industries favour large companies, others, smaller innovators. There is no iron law. Large firms seem to be more effective innovators in pharmaceuticals and aerospace, and other regulated, safety-sensitive industries. Smaller firms do better in computers, biotechnology and software. Large incumbents find it easier to hold on to their lead in industries with a slower pace of change, where there is greater consensus about the industry's future direction. In industries driven on by rapid and radical innovation and knowledge creation, large incumbents find life far less predictable and stable.

Large companies will find it hard to dominate sectors such as software, communications and biotechnology, which are being driven forward by rapid innovation. So much new knowledge about biotechnology, software and communications is spilling out of universities and research laboratories that large companies, with all their in-built learning deficiencies, are bound to overlook some of the most promising ideas. In the modern economy, dominated by global financial markets and driven by innovation, upheaval and entrepreneurship will go hand in hand. This process is not confined to high-tech sectors and service industries: a third of US manufacturing companies are less than six years old. In the 1980s it took five years for a third of the Fortune 500 to be replaced by new competitors. In the 1950s and 1960s, it took two decades for the Fortune 500 to turn over at that rate. Professor Baruch Lev and Professor Paul Zarowin, at the Stern School of Business at New York Unviersity, ranked 6,500 US companies by their financial performance between 1963 and 1995. Lev and Zarowin measured how frequently companies changed their rankings. In the 1960s the likelihood of a company changing its position in any year was generally 30–40 per cent; by the 1990s it had risen to 50–60 per cent. This upheaval creates opportunities for entrepreneurs as well as being driven by them. This is the persuasive theory of entrepreneurship, innovation and industrial upheaval, put forward by David Audretsch in *Innovation and Industry Evolution*. Audretsch's examination of why entrepreneurs take the risk to start a company and enter an already crowded industry draws on a unique database on small businesses held by the US Small Business Administration. Audretsch was interested not just in the way small businesses seemed to be generating jobs but in the capacity of some companies, in some industries, such as software, to enjoy rapid growth.

Audretsch explains the accelerating rate of industrial change by linking it to how fast the knowledge base for an industry develops. The rate of change will be determined by how frequently companies come up with radical innovations that change the nature of the industry. In industries where knowledge creation is rapid and dispersed, lots of new ideas for products and processes will be created. With lots of different ideas in the air, people are likely to disagree on their potential value. Which will be the right way to incorporate computing power into clothing? How should gene treatments be marketed? What will be the best way to hook a mass consumer market on to shopping on the Internet? These disagreements present entrepreneurs with opportunities to exploit an idea that other people might write off. The more rapid and discontinuous the nature of knowledge creation within an industry, the more conducive it is for entrepreneurship. In industries where knowledge does not move so fast – for example, more mature manufacturing industries – there will be fewer new ideas. When ideas emerge they are likely to be incremental additions to the industry's knowledge base. As a result opportunities for entrepreneurship will be limited.

The frenzy of knowledge creation in industries such as the media, communications, biotechnology and software could not be controlled by a single company or even a set of large companies. Knowledge entrepreneurs do not start firms because they are clearly on to a winner; they start firms because other, more powerful companies believe the entrepreneur is on to a loser. The best way to explain the process described by Audretsch is the story of Chester Carlsson.

Carlsson started Xerox after his proposal to create a copying machine was turned down by his employer, Kodak, which told Carlsson it was not in the copying business and anyway the machine would not make money. Decades later Xerox turned down a proposal from Steve Jobs to make a personal computer. Xerox said the computer would not make money. Seventeen other companies, including IBM and Hewlett Packard, rejected the idea before Jobs started Apple, which revolutionized the industry. IBM went on to turn down an offer to buy a chunk of Microsoft for a song in 1986, which would cost it more than $3 billion today. IBM did not think Gates and his computer operating system was up to much. IBM executives are reported to have said that neither Gates nor his thirty employees had the credentials, skill or intelligence to work for IBM. When Ted Hoff from Intel approached IBM and DEC in the late 1960s with an idea for a microprocessor, a programmable computer on a chip, they dismissed it. The two companies could not see the value in the idea because they could not believe that anyone would ever want to use a small computer. The success of Intel is now a legend. Entrepreneurs in new industries exploit gaps created by disagreements over the value of a new idea; they thrive on the short-sighted arrogance of large companies.

All this means that big companies will have to become more entrepreneurial themselves. Working for big companies will require more of the skills and attitudes of entrepreneurs. Big companies will have to make it more attractive for potential entrepreneurs to stay with them, by paying people with equity and stock options. Big companies in knowledge-intensive fields are becoming venture capitalists. Rather than be beaten by small, innovative start-ups, big companies are attempting to buy up the competition. Companies such as Microsoft, 3Com and Adobe were doing a deal a month in the mid-1990s with small start-ups, to buy their way into innovative ideas for the future. Big companies in knowledge-intensive fields will resemble a mother ship with a flotilla of smaller companies around it. To be creative a big company needs to be linked into a knowledge-creating network outside it, which gives it access to the places where counter-intuitive, unconventional ideas are being created.

Networks of Knowledge Entrepreneurs

Knowledge entrepreneurs rarely act alone. Entrepreneurs are traditionally seen as individualists. Knowledge entrepreneurs usually emerge from a network of complementary ideas and people. They are supported by a professional, personal and organizational network which provides them with information, opportunities, finance, technology and access to the market they need to make their business a success. Silicon Valley is home to so many entrepreneurs because venture capitalists and business advisers make sure that these complementary assets and skills quickly congeal to support a promising entrepreneur. Entrepreneurship is much riskier in the UK because it is so hard to get access to these complementary skills. In the knowledge economy the basic unit of innovation and entrepreneurship is not the firm or the individual but the knowledge-creating network which brings together entrepreneurs, venture capitalists and large companies able to take a new product to a global market. Entrepreneurship will become more of a feature of more people's working lives in the new economy. Whether they work for themselves or in a university, for a small or a large company, increasingly people will have to think of themselves as entrepreneurs: to make the most of their skills and know-how to carve their way through an uncertain labour market. Of course there is a large downside to this, which we explore in the penultimate chapter. Just as entrepreneurship and experimentation will be permanent features of life in the knowledge economy, so will be experiences of failure and rejection. Failure will become a ubiquitous and common feeling for workers in the knowledge economy. Entrepreneurial societies will be those that learn to prosper from failure by picking people up from a business failure and getting them to try again.

One thing is clear: policies to protect incumbent national champions in knowledge-intensive industries will be disastrous. As David Audretsch puts it: 'One has to wonder what would have happened to the US computer and semiconductor industry had IBM been selected as a "national interest" say around 1980 and promoted by favourable treatment and protection from threats from Apple, Microsoft and Intel.' When industrial structures were more static and stable, in the 1950s, what was good for General Motors might have been good for America. But in the turbulent and uncertain knowledge economy a better dictum would be: 'What is good for 25-year-old knowledge entrepreneurs will be good for America'. Knowledge entrepreneurship will only thrive within regions and companies with a culture of dissent, dispute, disrespect for authority, diversity and experimentation. California is bursting with knowledge entrepreneurs, not just because its universities conduct world-class research and because of its rich venture-capital funds, but because the culture and politics of California encourage creative dissent. That is just one reason why communitarian capitalism of the kind advocated by John Gray and Amitai Etzioni is a dead end. Communitarian capitalism would kill off knowledge entrepreneurship.

CHAPTER NINE BUILDING THE KNOWLEDGE SOCIETY

Many societies have excelled at producing knowledge, without making the most of their intellectual prowess. The water wheel, the first non-human, non-animal power source, was known to the Romans, but it did not flourish until the Middle Ages, a period in which progress was hardly a popular notion. The museum at Alexandria was the centre of technological innovation in the Roman Empire. By the first century BC, Alexandria had mechanical gears and a working steam engine. But the steam engine was never put to productive use; it opened and closed the doors of a temple. Roman society created neither the incentives nor the freedom to exploit its know-how commercially. Ancient China produced a stream of potentially revolutionary inventions, including paper, the water-clock and gunpowder. Yet Chinese inventiveness did not lead to a flowering of industry because there was no security for private enterprise, no legal foundation for rights outside the state, no method of investment other than in land, no social room for a class of entrepreneurs to emerge outside the state.

In our era, investments in our society's knowledge base will be essential but not enough to create a thriving knowledge economy. Someone with a decent education has a chance to make it in the knowledge economy; someone without an education has little hope. A society which tolerates its own educational failure is writing off a large part of its capital base. Yet education will not be enough on its own. We also need to excel at exploiting and applying our know-how, not just to make money but to make people better-off, to improve public services and satisfy unmet needs. A dynamic knowledge society must promote innovation and entrepreneurship alongside education and learning. Creating that mix is not just a job for narrow economic policies. As important will be the kind of economic culture we promote. Japan and Germany, for example, are outstanding knowledge economies because their education systems produce well-trained workers who are orchestrated within companies to deliver continual improvements to quality and productivity. Yet Japan and Germany also have weaknesses. Their companies excel at incremental innovation; they are less prolific at radical innovation.

Germany and Japan are inclusive, incremental innovators. California exemplifies a radical culture of knowledge creation. In the last decade California has spawned a string of innovative new companies in new industries, because it is conducive to radical free-thinking. California's laws promote diversity and experimentation. The downside is that California has a dreadful basic-education system which scores poorly in rankings of US states' performance. As the Californian economy boomed in the last decade, wage inequality widened and poverty grew. California makes up for the deficiency of its basic-education system by importing talent. The ideal would be a hybrid culture which combined the best of these worlds: a society which was inclusive and innovative, which gave everyone a chance through a world-class basic-education system, but which encouraged radical innovation, through an open, liberal, entrepreneurial culture. Let's start at the beginning with families and learning.

Families and Learning

The knowledge economy puts the connections between economic and social policy on a new footing. Learning and innovation will be vital to wealth creation in the new economy. Families are where children are first encouraged or discouraged to learn. Children learn skills within the family that will be vital in later life: the ability to compete and co-operate with siblings, for example. In the past the family was seen as an adjunct to economic policy, the place where 'labour power' was fed, clothed, refreshed and reproduced. Lately, family policies have mainly been designed to respond to the rising employment rate of mothers. We will need to go further. Families are the most basic economic unit of the knowledge economy: they create its raw material, human capital. No nation will have an adequate economic policy without a family learning policy. That does not mean turning the clock back to the 1950s, to recreate the traditional, nuclear family. On the contrary, it means devising a raft of policies to help families of all shapes and sizes to encourage their offspring to learn, through vastly expanded entitlements to child care, parental leave and pre-school education.

Demand for knowledge is rising from corporations and individuals. Our investment in knowledge creation and learning has to rise. To encourage this, education needs to leave behind organizational models inherited from the nineteenth century. The main response to demand for more investment in education has been to expand the role of schools and universities, extending the time students spend in these institutions and introducing performance targets to drive the system to higher levels of productivity. This process of modernization through institutional reform started in 1902 with the Balfour Act, which consolidated a national education system in England and Wales. The Butler Act in 1944 enforced participation in secondary education to the age of 14. The Robbins Report in 1963 and subsequent reforms in the 1980s opened higher education beyond an élite. Reforms in the 1990s drew three- and four-year-olds into the net of formal education. As educational institutions have extended their scope, central government has extended its power to set a core curriculum, accompanied by a panoply of targets, tests, restrictions and regulations.

This approach to modernization also reinforces a deeply conservative approach to education, as a body of knowledge imparted by organizations with strong hierarchies and demarcated professional disciplines. As Tom Bentley points out in *Learning Beyond the Classroom*, two traditions are reflected in this culture: the monasteries, which were closed repositories for knowledge in the form of precious manuscripts, and Taylor's factory, which encouraged standardized, easily replicated knowledge. The result is a system that is a curious hybrid of factory, sanctuary, library and prison. Educational institutions inherited from the industrial age provide a safe and supportive environment for children, but they also seek to control and contain children and standardize the knowledge they acquire. The reforms of the last two decades have intensified these tensions, rather than resolved them or created an education revival in the UK led by the creation of new kinds of learning institutions, tailored for their times.

A new educational system is slowly developing, in parallel and outside the traditional state and private school system. This evolving system operates with a different definition of learning and education. It delivers education through quite different mechanisms and funds it from private and public sources. Elements of this system include: the Open University; public investments in the National Grid for Learning and the University for Industry; home schooling, which involves 50,000 children in the UK and many more in the US; a plethora of corporate universities and a burgeoning self-help market involving books, digital television channels and interactive learning programmes. These new educational institutions are demand-led, use information technology as much as libraries and classrooms, and tailor learning to individual needs. They are frequently financed by shared investments between pupils, employers and the state.

How can the old and the new educational systems evolve together to mutual benefit? The starting point must be a redefinition of the purpose of education. We must move away from a view of education as a rite of passage involving the acquisition of enough knowledge and qualifications to acquire an adult station in life. The point of education should not be to inculcate a body of knowledge, but to develop capabilities: the basic ones of literacy and numeracy as well as the capability to act responsibly towards others, to take initiative and to work creatively and collaboratively. The most important capability, and one which traditional education is worst at creating, is the ability and yearning to carry on learning. Too much schooling kills off a desire to learn. The traditional institutions of education may be well suited to delivering basic core competencies, such as literacy and numeracy, but they fall down on many other counts: many people are turned off learning because they find school constraining, frustrating and patronizing. The new networked education system is more in tune with these modern goals, but it is designed for people with initiative who can afford to invest in their own learning. It is far from a national, inclusive system.

We need hybrid public and private institutions and funding structures. Schools and universities should become more like hubs of learning, within the community, capable of extending into the community. New primary schools, for example, should be set up as family learning centres, catering for adults and children. As far as secondary schools are concerned, we should follow Ivan Illich's inspirational advice thirty years ago to partially de-school society. More learning should be done at home, in offices and kitchens, in the contexts where knowledge is deployed to solve problems and add value to people's lives. With this must go changes in accreditation, to move away from a sole reliance on traditional entry qualifications, such as GCSEs. Instead we should provide people with a portfolio of continuous assessment and records of achievement. British universities have been able to survive in the middle ground between the old and the new economies. They do not fit neatly into either. In some respects universities are models for the new economy, particularly the way they encourage research, experimentation and knowledge-creation by autonomous, self-managing researchers and knowledge workers. Yet universities are hardly freewheeling, entrepreneurial places and academic communities are riven by professional, doctrinal and disciplinary disputes and demarcation lines which few outsiders can understand. Moreover, universities have their own protocols, hierarchies and procedures – especially the older universities – which make them slow-moving and resistant to change. In short, universities have cultures which seem to borrow from the library, the monastery, the gentleman's club and the laboratory but not the factory. British universities were able to survive as mutant-hybrids only so long as there was a social contract supporting them. For most of this century they have served only a niche market: the elite 5 per cent of the population. That meant that universities could be funded by taxation, which in turn meant that academics did not face rigorous market pressures to improve their performance. The academic community had its own social contract. High-flyers did not mind the poor pay and teaching load as long as they had the freedom to get on with their research. They did not worry that the poor performers among their colleagues were holding them back.

That social contract and everything that goes with it is falling apart. The proportion of the population going through universities has gone up to 35 per cent – one of the main achievements of Thatcherism was to drive the expansion of higher-education – and almost certainly will touch 50 per cent in the next two decades.

Demand for expansion, combined with growing state regulation to improve performance, is driving many universities to become mass-production degree machines. Meanwhile, elite institutions with international brand names are pulling away from the mass-production university designed to churn out the basic, commodity first degree. The same process of fragmentation is at work within the academic workforce. Top researchers and academic superstars are increasingly in an international market for their talent; academic scientists can often work in the private sector. These superstar academics can bid up their salaries terms and conditions. They operate in a quite different world from the mainstream, middle-ranking workforce, which is employed to do the basic teaching. And the top and the middle are far less tolerant of the under-performance of the worst academics who pull down the institution's rankings in research and teaching assessments. Add to all this the growth of new technologies to deliver learning and corporate universities, which will soon take students from outside their own companies, and it is easy to see why the cosy old order is falling apart. Universities and academics will become increasingly segmented. The elite will be involved in the 'knowledge-creation' business of research and experimentation; the mass will be involved in the 'knowledge-management' business of delivering degree modules. This segmentation means that the funding, organization, owner-ship, management and pay systems of universities will all become far more diverse.

It is not hard to see how far and how quickly this could go. Imagine that Rupert Murdoch were to set up the News International University, serving initially only his employees. After a while he might open up entry to the university to readers of his newspapers and viewers of his television programmes. News International University might grow very fast as one of the world's first truly global learning institutions. Armed with Murdoch's money, the university would acquire some star names as teachers. After ten years of development Murdoch might then decide the time was ripe to add some brand quality to his commodity business: he might bid for Oxford, or the London School of Economics. By that stage, of course, public funding for universities would be tightly constrained, tuition fees would be a fact of life and universities would be familiar with competing in a market. In those circumstances a lucrative offer from Murdoch will seem quite attractive. He might offer to pump billions of dollars into research and development, recruiting top stars from around the world. How many billion pounds would an international brand name like Oxford University or the London School of Economic be worth? Who would own the brand: the taxpayer, the academics? The accountants working for the vice-chancellors had better get cracking. Expanding university education should not be the Holy Grail. Bill Gates was a college drop-out. As the supply of graduates expands, the value of a college degree, on its own, will decline.

Innovation

Innovation is the central wealth-creating process in the knowledge economy: particularly the translation of ideas into products. The more radical and rapid the pace of innovation, the better off an economy is likely to be. Innovation in the knowledge economy will differ fundamentally from innovation in the industrial and service economy.

First, increasingly innovation does not take place within a single company, but through a network of companies, large and small, which are often linked into a knowledge base, such as a university. An innovative economy needs to breed these networks, which are often regional, based around a university, involving large companies which can provide access to global markets. Networks cannot be created by policy. They are organic and social. Yet there is a large potential role for public activism to help to promote collaborative networks and clusters, either along supply chains, or in regions.

Second, universities should become not just centres of teaching and research but hubs for innovation networks in local economies, helping to spin off companies, for example. Universities should be the open-cast mines of the knowledge economy.

Third, the knowledge economy requires a different approach to inward investment. Investment from the Far East, particularly from Japan, helped to rebuild much of the ailing British car and electronics industries. The Japanese transplants did not just provide jobs in manufacturing; they brought with them management and industrial-relations techniques which set new standards for productivity and quality. This wave of inward investment helped to make good some of British manufacturing's post-war deficiencies. In the knowledge economy we will need an inward investment policy designed to import talent and brains, rather than factories and machines. Silicon Valley has a *de facto* inward investment policy: it cream-skims the top talent, from the best universities in the world. Government restrictions on the employment of foreign workers are the most contentious industrial-policy issue in the US. The US research labs of Glaxo-Wellcome, the British pharmaceutical company, for example, are full of highly qualified Malaysian researchers; in the UK laboratories there are one or two foreign workers, at most. Britain has a relatively cosmopolitan culture, but it needs to be far more open to talent from abroad. A narrow nationalist culture will cut it off from ideas we need to import. A liberal, tolerant culture that is open to immigrants is vital to industrial policy in the modern era. The knowledge economy and multi-culturalism go hand in hand.

Fourth, competition policy, which was designed for a world of railways, breweries and steel barons, needs to be put on a new footing. Some economists, such as Brian Arthur, argue that knowledge-based industries create monopolies. They point to the way Microsoft has used its installed base in one product, personal-computer operating systems, to build an installed base in other products, Internet browsers, and so entrench its position. This argument persuades some people that governments should take a tougher anti-monopoly position to prevent Microsoft and its equivalents in genetics and neuroscience from dominating our lives. The menace of the monopolies is overstated. If knowledge-based industries tend to create monopolies, the government cannot alter that, other than to choose which monopolist we have. The pace of change in these new industries is so fast that monopolies will rarely last. One study of innovation in four US industries, including typewriters and lighting, found that only a handful of companies managed to maintain their industry position through periods of technological upheaval, such as the shift from manual to electric typewriters and from incandescent to fluorescent lamps. The computer industry has been through a major shift in technology in each of the last four decades. The leadership of the industry has changed hands with each shift. The best competition policy is not to restrict monopoly but to promote innovation. Indeed, the pace of change is moving so fast in these industries that law-makers, judges and regulators are too slow and their tools too cumbersome to keep pace.

Valuing Knowledge

We do not know how to value the economy we live in. In the 1980s the new right argued that the value of a product was the same as the price it would fetch on an open market. But markets work poorly with knowledge-intensive products. Market pricing and traditional accounting tell us less and less about how we should value what we produce and consume in a modern economy.

An everyday example of the problems this can create is bank lending. Banks lend to businesses against collateral, which serves as security for the loan. Usually this collateral is a tangible asset, such as property, which can be sold. Yet knowledge-based businesses have few physical assets and lots of intellectual capital. They may find it harder to get a loan from a bank than a less promising business that has more physical capital. Insider trading is another issue. It is relatively easy for an investor to assess the earnings and value of a traditional industrial company, such as an oil producer, based on its production capacity and the published oil price. In contrast the potential earnings of a biotechnology company are anyone's guess. A biotechnology company has more scope than an oil company to manipulate perceptions of its value, at least for a while. Events at British Biotech in 1997 and 1998 highlight the risks. Andrew Millar, British Biotech's clinical research director, had growing doubts about the progress in critical trials of new drugs. He passed on his doubts to other executives, but his reservations were not relayed in briefings the company gave to City analysts, which painted a rosy picture of the company's prospects. During 1997 the company's share price surged. Several senior executives cashed in share options worth millions of pounds. When news of the poor trial results leaked to the market the share price collapsed, from 200p to 30p. The executives walked away with piles of cash, while unwitting outside investors took a bath. The more a company depends upon esoteric knowledge, the more difficult it will be for average outside investors to assess its value.

In the new economy, returns to knowledge will go up, insider knowledge included.

Many of these problems lead back to the shortcomings of traditional financial accounting. All of the assets that are most valuable to a modern business – brands, people, ideas, technology – are not recorded on its balance sheet, which instead records all those things which are not a distinctive source of competitive advantage – buildings, furniture, computers. Accounting makes no attempt to measure that gap, which is entirely accounted for by intellectual capital and other intangible assets. These are the stealth assets of a business, hidden from financial view, yet vital to its competitiveness. Armies of accountants are paid to draw up balance sheets and yet they are next to useless as a guide to business performance. An entire industry – accountancy – is based on a fiction: that the flood of numbers auditors produce measure the sources of wealth and the value of the companies they audit. We have become so accustomed to accountancy's description of our world that we find it difficult to imagine life without it.

The creation of double-entry book-keeping is credited to a remarkable Franciscan monk and mathematician, Luca Paccioli, born in 1445. Paccioli taught mathematics in Perugia, Rome, Naples, Pisa and Venice and became a friend of Leonardo da Vinci, before settling down as a professor of mathematics in Milan in 1496. His masterwork *Summa de Arithmetica, Geometria Proportioni et Proportionalità*, which appeared in 1494, was the most comprehensive statement then published on double-entry book-keeping. We still speak the language that Paccioli created: assets and liabilities, profit and loss, the very notion of a balance sheet, in which debits and credit should line up. As Jamie Buchan puts it in his history of money *Frozen Desire*: 'Above all Luca laid the foundation of the modern conception of profit, not as some vague increase in possession, as in antiquity, but as something hard, even crystalline, mathematical and open to empirical test at any time whatever through an interlocking system of books.'

Luca's 550-year-old system has fared well. Every accountant, whether auditing a multi-national company or the local bowls club, walks in Luca's shadow. The robustness of traditional accounting is one reason to resist radical redesign. Traditional accounting is a standardized system for comparing the performance of very different businesses. Yet important parts of Luca's system have had their day. Published financial information is historic: it is one account, usually closed to revision, of what has happened to a company. Accounts shed little light on a company's prospects. Using financial measures alone to value a business is like driving a car by looking in the rear-view mirror. Most importantly, traditional accounting finds it difficult to measure the stealth assets which most matter to the competitiveness of a modern business.

One way to value an asset is to assess how much it would cost to replace it. This is a difficult calculation for an intangible asset, such as a skilled workforce or a brand value which may be difficult to separate from other assets and takes a long time to build up. Another way to value an asset is to estimate the income it will generate over its useful life. It is difficult to isolate the income attributable to an intangible asset, especially where it is bound up with a tangible product. A brand can be valuable in one context and worthless in another. Coca-Cola works on drinks cans but not on cars. A past income stream generated by an asset is often misleading for a product in an industry with rapid technological change. Perhaps the best guide to the value of an asset is how much a buyer would pay for it. In the US a market in R&D and know-how is developing. According to one recent study, R&D accounted for 73 per cent of the acquisition price of the average take-over in the US in the early 1990s. When IBM acquired Lotus for $3.2 billion, it estimated the R&D, mainly ideas in people's heads, to be worth $1.84 billion. In future it may well be that the best way to value intellectual assets will be through trading them on open markets designed for the task.

For example, it should be possible to create a futures market in intellectual capital. Neuroscience will become an explosive commercial field in the next 20 years. The future time of the world's top ten neuroscientists and their graduate students will become highly valuable. Imagine we invented a financial instrument, an option on the time of these top specialists. We would buy an option now – say £1,000 for a week of their time – and then trade it later to the highest bidder. That sounds far-fetched. Yet in effect this kind of market already operates in sports and entertainment, where talent

scouts attempt to buy up talent young. Talented players are transferred between teams in sports and in financial services. This
approach, to value intellectual assets through trading them on
markets designed for the task is far more promising than heading
down the cul-de-sac of collecting endless inventories of often irrelevant data suggested by new accounting tools such as the Skandia
navigator, an attempt to draw up an intellectual-assets balance
sheet.

Intangible Warfare

In the industrial era one of the main aims of warfare was to destroy
the physical assets upon which an economy depended: factories,
steel mills, chemical plants, power stations, railway yards, bridges.
The geography of the British aerospace industry, for example, is a
product of war. Aerospace factories are largely based in the west
of the country, around Bristol, Cheltenham and Preston, to be
beyond the range of Second World War German bombers. But if
the most important assets of the economy are intangible, how can
they be defended or destroyed?

Knowledge-based information warfare will increasingly concentrate the minds of defence experts. Our economies rely upon
information systems to control airports, power grids, telecommunications systems and the water supply. These systems can be disabled
by computer hackers working many thousands of miles away.
Information warfare will become as important as mechanized warfare. A recent report published by a defence think-tank in Washington warned: 'Information warfare has no front-line. Potential
battlefields are anywhere networked systems will allow access. The
US economy will increasingly rely on complex, interconnected
network control systems for necessities such as oil pipelines, electric
grids and communications. The vulnerability of these systems is
poorly understood. The US homeland may no longer provide a
sanctuary from outside attack.'

An enemy does not have to park a submarine off the east coast
of the US to launch missiles to knock out Miami's electricity supply,
Dallas's airport or Washington's subway system. Instead, all that
could be achieved from a basement in the Middle East, using some
sophisticated computers. Industrial-era warfare had high barriers

to entry. Only reasonably large maritime states could afford a nuclear submarine, for example. All you need to wage information warfare are some computers. All sorts of people, poverty-stricken states, terrorists, hackers, the Mafia even, could enter the warfare business, previously the preserve of established incumbents: nation states and their armed forces. When the Second World War began, radar was in its infancy, a magic tool to detect attacking aircraft and ships. Information warfare renders radar redundant. Forget the stealth bomber. The ultimate stealth weapon may be a computer connected to the Internet.

As former CIA deputy director William Studeman put it: 'Massive networking makes the US the world's most vulnerable target.' A nation like China, which is largely rural and has few computer networks, is far less vulnerable to information warfare than the US. This is no idle speculation.

After the Gulf War, when everyone was looking forward to eternal peace, a new military revolution emerged. This revolution is essentially a transformation from the mechanised warfare of the industrial age, to the information warfare of the information age. Information warfare is a war of decisions and control, a war of knowledge, and a war of intellect. The aim of information warfare will be gradually changed from 'preserving oneself and wiping out the enemy' to 'preserving oneself and controlling the opponent'. Information warfare includes electronic warfare, tactical deception, strategic deterrence, propaganda warfare, psychological warfare, network warfare and structural sabotage. Under today's technological conditions, the all conquering stratagems of Sun Tzu more than two millennia ago 'vanquishing the enemy without fighting' and subduing the enemy by 'soft-strike' could finally be truly realised.

This is a summary of the speeches delivered at the founding ceremony for Beijing's new Military Strategies Research Centre in May 1996, published in *Jiefangjun Bao*, the Chinese army newspaper.

CHAPTER TEN IS KNOWLEDGE ALWAYS GOOD?

The most fundamental questions posed by the rise of the knowledge economy will be about the morality of discovery: is all knowledge necessarily good? In some circumstances might ignorance make us better-off? The assumption that knowledge is good is embedded in modern culture. Knowledge helps us get a purchase on the world and achieve our ends. Knowledge reduces uncertainty and confusion; it liberates people from superstition and tradition. That is the dominant, optimistic account of how society has become richer through the accumulation of knowledge. Yet there is a quite different account of scientific knowledge as the creator of new hazards, risks and uncertainties.

Genetic engineering, for example, could create new cures for disease and make food production more efficient. Yet because genetic engineering is so potent it also creates unprecedented risks: for instance, viruses that might jump across species. Industrialization created acute risks but before we recognized the threat of global warming they were generally either local or occupational: cancer among workers in an asbestos factory; lung disease among miners; and pollution on housing estates near a chemical factory. Knowledge-based industries could create new generations of global products; in the process they could also create global risks. If something goes wrong at a water-bottling plant, the relevant batch of bottles can be recalled from the shops. If something goes wrong with a mutant gene released into the food supply, it may be impossible to organize a product recall. Knowledge-based products, like software programmes, are infinitely expansible. The risks they create are as infinitely expansible as the benefits. A bug in an early release of Microsoft '98 is inconvenient and temporary; a genetic bug in a new strain of fast-growing crop could be far more troubling.

The risks bred by industrialization weighed heaviest on the working classes. The risks generated by the new economy will be global and not class-specific.

Our ability to understand the risks our innovation creates has not improved markedly. The explosion of knowledge threatens to make us more ignorant. As every day the products become more technologically complex, we rely more on specialists to make judgements for us about our safety. Many of the risks created by modern science – risks from radiation, for example – are invisible, difficult to calculate and hard to explain. The weightless economy creates not just wealth from thin air but risks as well. A classic example is the dispute over the safety of British beef in 1996 and 1997 that rested on the role of a rogue protein called a prion, which helped to produce BSE. The public yearned for a neat explanation of when and why the prion made beef unsafe. The more the scientists were exposed to publicity the more aware the public became of how little they really knew. Scientific knowledge has become more powerful but, as a result, it is more contested and controversial.

Genetics will produce our most troubling dilemmas. Take, for example, the impact of genetics on a traditional industry such as insurance. Quite soon it may be possible to buy a do-it-yourself gene-testing kit or to visit a 'gene shop' to establish your genetic predisposition towards illnesses such as Parkinson's disease. What should we do with this new knowledge? Imagine you discover you are at high risk of developing a brain disease. If there were no requirement that the results of your genetic test should be disclosed, then you could join a life-insurance scheme and claim large sums from it by withholding your genetic information from the other contributors to the scheme. The honest, relatively healthy contributors to the scheme would be disadvantaged. Yet to make it mandatory that someone should disclose this information would also have troubling consequences. The 'healthy' members of an insurance scheme might protect themselves by excluding high-risk applicants known to be in danger of developing brain disease. Mandatory disclosure of the genetic information might create an insurance underclass. New knowledge, the ability to read our genes, will create new awareness of risk as well as well-being. We may be able to devise ways to pool and share genetic information to create the basis for a new kind of solidarity. If not, it might be better for us to remain in ignorance rather than gain knowledge that we cannot be sure to use beneficially.

Advances in knowledge improve our lives but only at the cost of creating uncertainties, risks and dilemmas. Knowledge is a social resource, not something that can be owned, partitioned, protected by guards, fenced off or acquired by conquest. It cannot be valued using simple standard measures of unit costs or market prices, volume or weight of output. The value of knowledge lies in the eyes of the beholder, the context in which it is used and the purpose to which it is put. The value of radical innovations, which threaten convention and tradition, will always be contested. Public debate about the value of knowledge has a direct bearing on the conduct of companies in the knowledge economy. In *Competing for the Future*, Gary Hamel and C. K. Prahalad argue companies need to shape future markets by getting in first with innovations, which set the terms of competition for others to follow. *Competing for the Future* was a much-needed antidote to the downsizing and re-engineering fashion of the early 1990s. Yet its triumphalist tone creates the impression that companies only need to worry about the speed at which they can translate new ideas into new products. Yet as they compete to create new products, companies in science-based industries in particular, are creating new risks and fears. If companies are not adept at managing the public risks which their innovations generate, they will find it harder to win public trust in their new products. Companies need public trust to persuade consumers to trust innovations: trust and legitimacy is another critical intangible asset.

CHAPTER ELEVEN

THE NETWORKED ECONOMY

You probably will not have heard of Li Fung, Hong Kong's leading export trading house, but you may be wearing something it has made, a T-shirt, a pair of boxer shorts, a cotton jacket. The label will tell you it is made for a retailer. It was actually made by sub-contractors working for Li Fung. The label will say the garment was made in a single country, Thailand perhaps. In reality Thailand was probably the last stage in a regional production process spanning several countries in South East Asia. Li Fung is a microcosm for how the global economy is being organized around dispersed networks of suppliers and retailers, rather than through integrated, hierarchical companies or alternatively through open markets.

Li Fung is a family business. Like many large Chinese businesses it is underpinned by a family network. The company was founded in 1906 by the grandfather of Victor Fung, the current chief executive, who runs the business with his brother. When Victor Fung's grandfather founded the business his value-added was that he spoke English. In those days, it took three months to get to China by boat from the West; even a letter took a month to arrive. No one at the Chinese factories spoke English; the American merchants spoke no Chinese. Victor Fung's grandfather charged a commission of 15 per cent as a commercial interpreter. Li Fung continued in this business, acting as a broker, putting buyers and sellers together, until the 1980s, when Victor Fung took over, after a spell at the Harvard Business School.

Victor and his brother have transformed the company. They opened offices in Taiwan, Korea and Singapore, to turn Li Fung into a regional sourcing agent for large Western retailers seeking Far Eastern supplies. Most big buyers could source their own products if they were just buying from Hong Kong. But Li Fung can organize sourcing from the best factories across the region. As the Asian Tigers developed in the 1980s and China opened to trade, so Hong Kong became a relatively high-cost manufacturing base. As manufacturing has moved to China, so Hong Kong has become a vast service economy and Li Fung now manages what it calls 'dispersed manufacturing'. The company will organize the entire manufacturing process for a wide range of commodity items – particularly textiles – which Western retailers ask to be made.

Victor Fung explained:

Say we get an order from a European retailer to produce 10,000 garments. It is not a simple matter of our Korean office sourcing Korean products or our Indonesian office sourcing Indonesian products. For this customer we might decide to buy yarn from a Korean producer but have it woven and dyed in Taiwan. So we pick up the yarn and ship it to Taiwan. The Japanese have the best zippers and buttons, but they manufacture them in China. Okay, so we go to YKK, a big Japanese zipper manufacturer and order their best zippers from China. Then we determine that because of quotas and labour conditions the best place to make the garments is in Thailand. So we ship everything there. And because the customer wants quick delivery we may divide the order across five factories in Thailand. Effectively, we are customizing the value chain to suit the customer's needs. Five weeks after we have received the order the garments arrive on shelves in Europe, all looking as if they were made in the same factory.

Hong Kong is one of the junction boxes for South East Asia's borderless manufacturing network. Networked manufacturing has several advantages. It's faster and more flexible for retailers than working with dedicated suppliers. Retailers can order products later and so get closer to shifts in consumer demand. Victor Fung explained: 'If you can shorten your buying cycle from three months to five weeks, for example, you can gain eight weeks to develop a better sense of where the market is heading.' The Li Fung network combines the advantages of scale and flexibility. The company is a smokeless factory. It designs products, buys and inspects raw materials and finished goods. But it does not manage any production workers nor own any factories. Li Fung works with 7,500 suppliers, in more than twenty-six countries. At least 1 million workers are engaged on behalf of Li Fung's customers. Managing a million workers would be a colossal undertaking.

There are three keys to Li Fung's success: information, knowledge and relationships. Li Fung is an information-switching box between its 350 customers in Europe and the US and its 7,500 suppliers. This information is exchanged by telephone and fax. Soon the information will be available through a vast data warehouse. Yet information, on its own, is not enough. What Li Fung needs is what the US Army calls ground-level knowledge about the quality of different suppliers. As Victor Fung put it:

> Of course we have a lot of hard data about performance and about the work we do with each factory. But what we really want is difficult to pin down; a lot of the most valuable information resides in people's heads. What kind of attitude does the factory owner have? Do we work well together? How good is their internal management? That kind of organizational memory is harder to retain and share. Capturing that kind of know-how is the next frontier.

That know-how is bred and shared by the relationships that underpin the vast Li Fung network.

Networks of the kind run by Li Fung, rather than companies or markets, will be the most dynamic parts of the new economy. The twentieth century was dominated by the rise of public and private bureaucracies that displaced smaller social units of production based on families or clans. To many people it seems that global markets, in which only global companies can prosper, rule the world. Yet as the century draws to its close we are increasingly aware of the limitations of both markets and large organizations. Markets can be ill-informed and short-sighted; they are excellent at trading goods but poor at trading knowledge. Large organizations can be cumbersome, slow-moving and inward-looking. These shortcomings mean the twenty-first century will develop a richer ecology of economic institutions: modern versions of clans, fiefs and guilds. The basic unit of competitiveness and growth within the modern economy will not be 'the market' or 'the company' but 'the network'. Networks are not held together by hierarchy or structure but by relationships and social capital.

The Networked Company

Air Nikes became one of the most fashionable shoes to wear in the 1990s. In the course of twenty years Nike went from being an upstart running-shoe maker to become the leading sports-fashion brand. Not only did Nike change an entire industry, it changed our lifestyles. Trainers, which were once only to be worn for sports, became a ubiquitous fashion item, worn by young and middle-aged alike, for work and pleasure, sport and relaxation. Nike's rise was made possible by a radically new approach to designing and making shoes, which combined sophisticated design with low-cost global production. Nike is the archetypal networked company of the 1990s. Much-vaunted Nike exemplifies some of the downsides to the networked corporation: it has attracted sustained criticism for the use of child labour in its sub-contractors' factories in South East Asia.

Nike concentrates on pre-production, the design of shoes and research into new materials, and post-production, the marketing and branding of its products. Everything in between – the production of the shoes – is done by others. No one from Nike touches the shoes it makes. Nike sub-contracts production to a tiered network of sub-contractors. At the top are Nike's 'developed partners', who produce the company's most expensive fashion-statement products. These companies usually produce relatively low volumes, perhaps 20,000 to 25,000 units a day. These partners co-develop products with Nike and co-invest in new technologies. The bulk of production is handled by Nike's 'volume producers', who make about 70,000 to 85,000 shoes a day, mainly of one sort – for example, football boots or basketball shoes. Nike does no development work with these suppliers, who may also supply competitors such as Puma and Adidas. 'Developing partners' are sub-contractors in emerging low-cost economies who might in time become developed partners. Nike encourages its long-standing partners to form joint-ventures with these developing companies, to provide them with training, finance and production advice.

An even larger web of second-tier suppliers who make materials, components and sub-assemblies, such as inner-soles and laces, supports this network of assemblers. And beyond that lies a third tier of specialized component makers, which Nike often controls directly through ownership. These specialists make Nike's patented features such as its Nike Airsole, which are critical to the technical distinctiveness of Nike shoes. This network of component makers and assemblers is managed through a Nike 'expatriate' programme, in which Nike's staff act as commercial ambassadors stationed in supplier companies. This expatriate network is like Nike's Intelligence Agency, constantly scanning for new ideas, cheaper techniques and design improvements.

Nike is not alone. Examples of networked companies abound. Visa, the credit-card company, is not really a company at all but an alliance of banks, brought together into an international settlements system. Visa is a service owned by 20,000 financial institutions, which offer credit-card services. Yet, in itself, Visa is just a skeletal co-ordinating body, which oversees transactions, brokers relationships and pulls together the network as a whole. Visa handles 7 billion consumer transactions a year, worth more than $650 billion. This is the largest consumer purchasing block in the world. And yet Visa has no assets more durable than its brand and a set of relationships: a network. Increasingly competition is not between single companies but between networks of companies, supply chains and collaborators (a point stressed repeatedly by Rosabeth Moss-Kanter). A company's competitiveness will depend not just on its internal capabilities, but on its ability to exploit these to greatest advantage through the right kinds of networks. Does this mean that more companies will become hollowed out, virtual corporations in which most activities are outsourced to a floating army of independent contractors? The short answer is: probably yes. The slightly longer answer is: and in the process a lot of companies will make a lot of mistakes.

Corporate networks, such as joint-ventures and alliances, are formed for all sorts of reasons. The oldest reason is to collude in rigging a market. Critics argue this motive is alive and well in global airline alliances or Microsoft's relationship with Intel. Alliances and joint-ventures are often used to open up markets that are difficult to penetrate because of regulatory or cultural barriers. It is difficult for a non-Italian company to do business in Italy without a domestic partner, for example. In mature industries such as bulk chemicals, joint-ventures and alliances allow companies to beat an orderly retreat from a declining market. Yet, in the last decade, companies have increasingly turned to networks of suppliers and partners for a variety of other reasons, in particular to cut costs, by shifting more of the burden of risk on to the shoulders of suppliers who have to absorb rises and falls in demand. Nike and Li Fung do not lay off thousands of workers when demand falls; their sub-contractors do.

Outsourcing started as a drive to cut costs. But in the course of the 1990s it has developed more strategic goals. James Brian Quinn, Professor of Management at Amos Tuck School of Business at Dartmouth College, puts the case for, this way: 'Concentrate the firm's resources on its core competencies where it can achieve pre-eminence and provide unique value for customers. Strategically outsource other activities – including many traditionally considered integral to any company for which the firm neither has a critical need, nor special capabilities.' Quinn argues that a company can reap four main advantages by combining a focus on core competencies with strategic outsourcing. First, they concentrate their investment and energies on what the enterprise does best. Second, well developed core competencies erect formidable barriers against competitors. Third, a company can mobilize the ideas, innovations and specialist skills of suppliers, which it would never be able to replicate itself. Fourth, in rapidly changing markets, with shifting technologies, this collaborative strategy reduces risk, shares know-how, speeds learning and shortens product-development cycles.

Take three examples of what this is likely to mean. J. P. Morgan, the US investment bank, has signed a seven-year, $2-billion agreement for four of its computer suppliers to take over a third of the bank's spending on technology and development. About 700 J. P. Morgan staff have been transferred to these suppliers. Technology has become so critical to financial services that companies cannot afford to go it alone. J. P. Morgan has decided it needs to engage the know-how of its suppliers more fully to succeed. Sara Lee, the US branded-goods maker which makes Kiwi shoe polish and Douwe Egberts coffee, announced in 1998 it was to sell off most of its manufacturing activities, in textiles, meat-processing and lingerie. John Bryan, its chief executive, told the *Financial Times*: 'Trade liberalization means that you can produce and ship to anywhere in the world. Production will move to the lowest-cost point of manufacture. We are better-off focusing on those business functions we do best, marketing and branding, not manufacturing.' British Airways has not gone that far, yet the airline is being driven in that direction. British Airways cannot distinguish itself from its competitors on the basis of its physical assets: airlines generally fly the same planes supplied by Boeing and Airbus, they use the same airports and depend on the same air-traffic control systems. British Airways stands out on the basis of its soft assets: the quality of its service; the sophistication of its computer programmes, which allow it to maximize capacity on the planes; its branding and marketing. There is no reason why the physical aspects of the service – maintaining and flying the planes – should not be contracted out. That would allow British Airways to concentrate on what it does best: providing service and seating people efficiently.

It is not just back-room functions that are being outsourced. Many companies are outsourcing the first line of customer contact as well. That is why telephone call centres have spread so rapidly in the UK and the US. Production in traditional industries such as car manufacturing is increasingly networked. Take the case of the Micro Compact Car, the joint venture between Daimler-Benz and Switzerland's SMH watch-making group which has just brought out its new micro car, the Smart. Most of the Smart is made by a small group of suppliers, called 'systems partners', who have teams working on the production line at the assembly plant near Hambach, in eastern France. Magna International, the Canadian body and interiors group, welds the car's structural shell. Eisenmann, a German coatings specialist, paints the shell and passes it on to VDO, a German instrument specialist, which installs the cockpit. Only at this point, 3 hours into the 7½-hour assembly process, does MCC lay its hands on the car. Even then, MCC workers assemble sub-systems which arrive from other companies, the motor and axles from Krupp-Hoesch, doors from Ymos, lighting and electricals from Bosch. This is a high-tech version of nineteenth-century manufacturing: combining independent producers in collaborative networks, to milk the benefits of self-interest and co-operation.

The production networks created in the last decade are designed to help companies economize on knowledge, by relying on specialist suppliers. Yet increasingly companies are turning to collaborative networks to learn and innovate, design and develop products. These are networks to create knowledge. A collaborative network should provide companies with distributed intelligence, sensing new opportunities, combining different skills and sharing ideas to create and exploit new knowledge. To understand why collaboration has become so vital to innovation, take the case of EMI's ill-fated innovation of the CT scanner in the 1970s.

EMI pioneered the CT scanner, widely regarded as the greatest advance in radiology since the X-ray (the inventor, Geoffrey Hounsfield, received the Nobel prize in medicine), EMI excelled at knowledge generation and acquisition, but it was dreadful at knowledge application and exploitation. While EMI had hugely valuable technology, it lacked manufacturing capability in medical equipment and had no knowledge of the largest market, the US, where it was best known as the company which created the Beatles. Moreover, the CT scanner was relatively easy to imitate. The first competing products were on the market three years after EMI had launched its scanner. Instead of teaming up with partners who could provide manufacturing and marketing clout, EMI tried to go it alone. It soon lost its lead to a highly capable competitor, the US giant General Electric. By the early 1980s, EMI was forced to exit a market it had created. EMI had been the first mover and it had the best technology but, because it attempted to exploit its knowledge base unilaterally, it failed. Had EMI engaged in a collaborative network, with a group of partners to set the standard for this new industry, it might have succeeded.

Collaboration is becoming increasingly important at all stages of the innovation process. Companies need to pool resources to finance and market products for global markets. Collaboration of this kind is increasingly common in the car and drugs industries. Most 'people carriers' on sale in Britain, for example, have been jointly developed by several companies. It is striking that younger knowledge-based companies such as ARM, CDT and PowderJect have learned from EMI's failure and decided to exploit their know-how through partnerships and licensing agreements. Products and services are becoming more technologically interdependent and complex. The personal computer took off as a domestic product when its price came down and it could be combined with complementary products: printers, scanners, modems and software. Networks of companies are more likely to bring together the complementary products needed to set standards for new product markets.

Companies will increasingly turn to external knowledge creating networks – involving not just large and small companies, but universities, research laboratories and other non-profit institutions – to come up with radical innovations, especially in fields such as biotechnology. Walter Powell, Professor of Sociology at the University of Arizona and the pre-eminent analyst of the development of the biotechnology industry, puts it this way: 'In the rapidly developing field of biotechnology, the knowledge base is both complex and expanding and the sources of expertise are widely dispersed. When uncertainty is high, organizations interact more, not less, with external parties to access both knowledge and resources. Hence, the locus of innovation is found in networks of learning, rather than in individual firms.'

The knowledge base underlying biotechnology developed in university research laboratories in the 1970s. Since 1980, when the US Supreme Court ruled that genetically engineered life-forms could be patented, the industry has exploded, creating a new species of biotechnology firm. The initial research into recombinant DNA methods and monoclonal antibodies, drew primarily on molecular biology and immunology. It took only a few years for these radical breakthroughs to become standard science. Genetic engineering, monoclonal antibodies, polymerase chain-reaction amplification and gene sequencing are all part of the standard toolkit of microbiology graduate students. The field's technologies and sciences – genetics, biochemistry, cell biology, general medicine, computer analysis, optical sciences – have become entangled. Biotechnology is not an industry nor even a single technology, but a set of inter-linked sciences, each with its own formal knowledge base, with relevance to a wide range of industries, including food and health. The field is not just multi-disciplinary but multi-institutional, with several sources of knowledge and different channels to exploit it. In addition to research universities, start-ups and established firms, there are government agencies, non-profit research institutes, regulators, leading research hospitals, specialist research companies and others involved in generating new ideas.

The biotechnology industry rests on a web of inter-relationships. The implications for how companies need to organize themselves are profound. As Powell explained: 'The skills and organizational capabilities needed to compete in biotechnology are not readily found under a single roof. In a field such as biotech, where knowledge is advancing rapidly and the sources of knowledge are widely dispersed, organizations enter into a wide array of alliances to gain access to different competencies and knowledge.' Alliances have been central to the industry from the outset. Recombinant Capital, the San Francisco based research group which tracks the biotechnology sector, estimates that there are 3,500 alliances and collaborative agreements within the US industry. Established pharmaceutical companies invested $4.5 billion in alliances with biotech companies in 1996 alone.

Collaborative networks of the kind that abound in newer industries such as biotechnology will provide the industrial structures of the future. What matters will be how companies use networks to develop and exploit their capabilities to the full. As Powell puts it:

Internal capability and external collaboration are complementary. Internal capability is indispensable in evaluating ideas or external suppliers, while collaboration with outsiders provides more access to news and resources that cannot be generated internally. A network serves as the locus of innovation in many high-tech fields because it provides timely access to knowledge and resources that are otherwise unavailable, while also testing internal expertise and sharpening learning. Regardless of whether collaboration is driven by strategic motives, to fill in missing pieces in the value chain, by learning considerations, to gain access to new knowledge, or by embeddedness in a community of practice, connectivity to an inter-organizational network and competence at managing collaborations have become key drivers of a new logic of organizing. Networks are vehicles for producing, synthesizing and distributing ideas.

Does this mean, then, that the corporations of the future will all be virtual networks? Far from it.

The Rise and Fall of the Virtual Corporation

In October 1991, Linus Torvalds, a 21-year-old computer-science student at the University of Helsinki, made available through the Internet the kernel of a computer operating system he had written. The Linux system was a version of the Unix operating system widely used on large corporate and academic computers. Torvalds invited fellow programmers to download his programme, test it and improve it. At first only a few took up his offer. Yet as the programme improved and word spread, so the community using and developing it grew to thousands. The Linux club eventually turned the programme into one of the best Unix operating systems in the world entirely through collaborative self-help. The Linux story is cited by Thomas W. Malone and Robert Laubacher, from the Massachusetts Instititute of Technology, as a model for how a great deal of work could be done in future. The Linux community, a temporary, self-managed gathering of diverse individuals engaged in a common task, could be a model for a new kind of organization and even a new economy, they argue.

Their case for the 'E-Lance' economy goes like this. Business organizations co-ordinate flows of work, materials, ideas and money. Until a hundred years ago the technologies available to co-ordinate these flows were rudimentary. Co-ordination of dispersed activities was difficult. People tended to work close to their homes, often as independent producers. The business organizations that did exist – farms, shops, foundries, workshops – were small. When their products had to reach distant consumers, they did so through a long series of transactions involving wholesalers, jobbers, shippers, storekeepers and pedlars. The co-ordination mechanisms made available by the Industrial Revolution – the train, the telegraph, the automobile and the telephone – changed all that. An array of activities could be centrally managed by a single company, which could exploit economies of scale in manufacturing, marketing and distribution. Malone and Laubacher, and many others, argue that powerful personal computers and electronic networks will be the co-ordination technologies of the twenty-first century. Information will be shared instantly and inexpensively among many people in many locations. The value of centralized decision-making and expensive bureaucracies will decline. Self-motivated workers will be able to co-ordinate themselves. Virtual teams will become commonplace. Yet the spread of electronic networks will allow these teams to act globally, procuring and marketing products around the world. This new production system will combine the density and small scale of independent producers of the nineteenth century with the global reach of modern corporations.

Malone and Laubacher conclude:

> The dominant business organisation of the future may not be a stable, permanent corporation but rather an elastic network that sometimes may exist for no more than a day or two. When a project needs to be undertaken, requests for proposals will be transmitted or electronic want ads will be posted, individuals or small teams will respond, a network will be formed and new workers will be brought on as their skills are needed. Once the project is complete, the network will disband.

Malone and Laubacher are profoundly mistaken, if they believe anything like this will happen soon, on any scale. Companies are becoming more like networks – mutual clubs of collaboration among producers – but they are unlikely to dissolve entirely into virtual teams. Companies will still be important for two reasons. First, they are reservoirs of knowledge and organizational memory, which virtual teams lack. Second, companies are a vehicle to make money from know-how, something virtual networks of the kind created by Linus Torvalds find very hard. The virtual company, contrasted with the ungainly hierarchical organization, seems attractive. Networked organizations seem to have lower costs because they have fewer middle managers. They are more responsive because they are closer to customers and decision-making is devolved to self-managing front-line staff. Networked organizations are able to pull together a diversity of talent from outside the company. That's the theory. The reality is quite different. Companies should beware of becoming fashion victims of the virtual-company fad.

Dispersed, networked organizations take a great deal of patient management. They only work with a strong sense of common values and rules. If an organization becomes too decentralized it will find it difficult to take concerted action when needed. A virtual organization often needs a smaller yet stronger centre. The best organizations are both networked and integrated. The key corporate skill is not simply to network but to integrate the diverse sources of knowledge and input provided by a network. If a company does not have strong core capabilities it will find itself dissolving into its network.

There is no 'one size fits all' solution. A company needs different networks at different stages of a business life-cycle. A good analogy is to think of the networks a person needs as they grow up. When someone is very young they need a close, supportive network of parents, siblings and grandparents. As a child grows, this network gradually expands to take in nannies, teachers, friends and the extended family. Once a child becomes a teenager he or she will want to develop an independent network of friends to allow them to break away from dependence upon their family. This adolescent transition from a closed tight network to an open, diffuse network is often extremely painful, for parent and child. In the middle years of their lives people often need several networks: a dense close network of family, friends and nannies to help rear children, an expansive network for work opportunities and friendship. People are at their most productive when these networks are developed and synchronized. When people reach old age, they once again rely increasingly on a tightly knit network of neighbours and family to look after them. People have to recreate closer, more domestic ties.

People and businesses need different networks at different stages of their development and they are at their most vulnerable during 'network transitions' – for instance, when a product plan moves from inception, in a close-knit team, into development, which may require pulling together a wider set of skills and resources. Large companies should not aim to become 'networked' as if this was the solution to all their problems. They need to be able to call up different networks, as and when they need them.

Networks are only as strong as the capabilities of the companies that make them up. Collaborative networks help to develop and exploit corporate capabilities; but networks are rarely a way to create a capability in the first place. To understand why, take the case of Toyota, the Japanese car manufacturer, credited with creating the networked model of lean production. Supplier networks are not designed to spread knowledge but to concentrate the right knowledge where it is most needed. The lean production network links stripped-down companies, each focused on their core competency, to deliver components just-in-time to the Toyota assembly plant. Such a network may economize on knowledge but it is less effective at creating knowledge.

That is why Toyota is radically revising its production network, at least as far as electronics is concerned. At the heart of Toyota's production network is Denso, the electronics supplier. Electronic components were so far from Toyota's expertise that it entrusted their development and supply to Denso. The two companies share sensitive financial and product information without fear of it leaking. Yet in the late 1980s Toyota realized that its ignorance of electronics and its reliance on Denso would eventually make it vulnerable to losing control of the highest value-added parts of a car. Electronics accounts for about 10 per cent of the value of the average Toyota car. That is likely to rise to 30 per cent within the next five years. Electronic systems are so integral to a car's design that they cannot be treated as separate components, to be sourced externally as black boxes to be plugged into the car. To be good at buying electronics components from outside suppliers Toyota had to understand more about electronics. In recent years 30 per cent of Toyota's graduate recruits have been electronics engineers. The company has built up an electronics division at its Hirose plant as an alternative to external suppliers. The company could not acquire the knowledge it needed from the network.

Conclusion

Companies will not dissolve into a floating set of temporary virtual teams. But they will become more networked. Internally, they will increasingly rely on cellular, self-managed teams. Externally, they will increasingly follow the model of the biotechnology and software industries, in which innovation emerges from collaborative networks. This shift towards more networked forms of organization will have far-reaching consequences for how we work, and for how organizations are managed and owned. Networks are sets of relationships between independent producers; they cannot prosper unless they have a fund of social capital to call upon – mutual trust, reciprocity, co-operative self-help. Networks can be enabled by technology but they are held together by social ties. So, as networks become increasingly important to competitiveness in the modern economy, so will social capital. The most successful organizations and regions will not just have deep pockets, good technology and innovative ideas; they will have a fund of social capital and trust which allows all these ingredients to be combined and recombined fluidly.

CHAPTER TWELVE SILICON VALLEY: THE INTELLIGENT REGION

Each valley in the corrugated landscape of northern California has a distinct microclimate, suited to growing a different crop. Napa is renowned for its wine, Castroville for its artichokes, and Gilroy proudly proclaims itself the garlic capital of America. The walnuts and apricots of Paradise Valley, just south of San Francisco, were once famous across America. These days Paradise Valley is even more famous but it goes under a different name: Silicon Valley. Silicon Valley is a congested industrial strip reminiscent of the industrial belt that stretches from Tokyo to Osaka, the heart of the Japanese economy. Silicon Valley as a region mirrors the product for which it is best known, the computer chip: more and more intelligence has been packed into layer upon layer in a very confined space, making it the largest agglomeration of knowledge capital in the world. But it also has financial capital in abundance, with the world's largest concentration of venture capitalists. The region's economy is orchestrated by social ties and networks that stretch from universities to companies, from venture capitalists to lawyers, from large companies to small. Entrepreneurship thrives in Silicon Valley because when an entrepreneur – often someone straight out of university – emerges with a good idea, they are immediately embraced by a network of venture capitalists, lawyers and advisers, who help to bring in companies and managers with complementary skills and assets. It is almost an organic process, like cells reproducing and growing.

Silicon Valley is impressive and instructive, not simply because of its record of growth since the 1950s but because of its recent spectacular recovery from the recession of the early 1990s, which, combined with mounting competition from Far Eastern electronics companies, seemed to threaten most of the Valley's large companies.

Yet despite losing its way and being written off by many people in the early 1990s, California has rebounded, with Silicon Valley at the heart of its recovery.

California has dramatically expanded its share of high-tech jobs in the US. In 1975 about 15 per cent of all high-tech jobs (computing, communications equipment, electronic components, medical instruments, electronic controls) were in California. In 1997 the state was home to about 22 per cent of US high-tech jobs, many of them in Silicon Valley. In 1996, venture capitalists invested more than $2 billion dollars in small companies in Silicon Valley. The 2 million inhabitants of the Valley have a GDP of about $65 billion, about the same as Chile's 15 million inhabitants, according to the Centre for the Continuing Study of the Californian Economy. The Valley is home to about 6,000 high-tech companies. The computing and electronics jobs in Silicon Valley are increasingly high-value-added, occupying the high-skill portion of the industries it competes in. In 1994, California accounted for 22 per cent of high-tech jobs, but 26 per cent of US high-tech value-added. In the Californian computer industry value-added was $196,300 per worker in 1994, about 45 per cent above the national average. In most other high-tech industries California's lead in value added is between 10 and 20 per cent. In 1997, California was creating 2,000 jobs a month in computer services: the equivalent of building a major new car plant every month. In 1972, there were more than ten jobs in metal products for every job in computer services, but by the late 1990s computer services far outweighed metal products as a source of employment. Average pay in computer services in California in 1996 was $60,000 a year, compared with $31,700 in metal products. By 1996 there were 355 Internet hosts (computers permanently connected to the Internet) per 1,000 people in Silicon Valley, a far higher ratio than anywhere else in the US, with new hosts being added the whole time. If the Internet becomes a familiar way of doing business and shopping, Silicon Valley will play the role that Detroit played in the evolution of the motor car. The stock-market capitalization of Microsoft (which is based in Seattle), Intel and Cisco Computers is almost three times that of Detroit's big-three car companies, even though the car firms' sales are more than ten times greater than those of the high-tech companies.

Silicon Valley has managed to side-step repeated structural threats to its competitiveness largely because of the way its economy is networked together. The character of these networks explains why Silicon Valley recovered from recession in the early 1990s while Route 128 in Massachusetts – another high-tech, industrial region – floundered. As Annalee Saxenian shows in *Regional Advantage*, her study of the two areas, Silicon Valley's networks helped to revive established companies such as Intel and Hewlett Packard, as well as creating a new generation that were hardly more than a glint in an entrepreneur's eye in the 1980s. Route 128 was heavily dependent upon large companies, such as Digital Equipment Corporation, which insisted on quite hierarchical relationships with suppliers. Although many companies were spun out of the Massachusetts Institute of Technology, MIT's approach was more government-focused and less entrepreneurial than Silicon Valley's.

Silicon Valley is a network-based industrial system which promotes rapid collective learning and flexible adjustment among specialist producers of complex and related technologies. The Valley is based on dense social networks. Ideas travel with people in a mobile labour market. A colleague today might be your customer tomorrow and your boss next year. Three years is a long time to hold a job in Silicon Valley. Yet Silicon Valley combines this social density with cosmopolitan openness: many of its biggest companies are run by post-war immigrants. Andy Grove, the co-founder of Intel, only arrived in the US in 1950 from Hungary. Women and young people prosper in Silicon Valley; they would be stifled in big bureaucracies in Germany and Japan. The bars and restaurants of Palo Alto and Menlo Park echo to a diversity of languages – Mandarin, Bengali, Russian, German. There are so many Indian computer programmers in Silicon Valley that cricket is one of the fastest-growing sports in the region.

The intensity of the relationships promotes competition, as well as collaboration. Continuous, rapid innovation is essential to stay in the game and to command respect. Companies cannot innovate on their own. Traditional boundaries between and within firms have broken down in Silicon Valley. The key units of innovation and competition in Silicon Valley are not companies but teams within companies and networks beyond them. The company is like a junction box where these internal and external relationships are brought together.

Silicon Valley's adaptive strengths were only fully revealed by the recession of the 1990s, yet their roots lie in the region's postwar development. Much of the Valley's vitality stems from its founding educational institution: Stanford University. Hundreds of businesses have spun off from Stanford, many into its own industrial park. The line between academic and commercial knowledge creation has been blurred. Even more important was Fairchild Semiconductor, the region's founding company. The semiconductor industry had taken root in California with the founding of Shockley Transistor in Palo Alto. William Shockley, a Stanford graduate, and one of the inventors of the transistor, left AT&T's Bell Laboratories in 1954 to commercialize his invention. After an unsuccessful attempt to do so in Massachusetts he turned to Palo Alto. The venture ran into the sand, but eight of its leading engineers formed Fairchild Semiconductor, with the help of legendary investment banker Arthur Rock. Fairchild prospered, but not thanks to the market economy. Its growth was almost entirely driven by orders from the Air Force and later NASA. Silicon Valley may now represent red-blooded capitalism, but its inception turned on public spending.

Within a decade of Fairchild's creation, the eight founders had left to start new ventures, among them Andy Grove, Gordon Moore and Robert Noyce, who persuaded Arthur Rock to invest $2.5 million in Intel without anything resembling a business plan. Thirty-one semi-conductor firms were created in Silicon Valley in the 1960s, all were the offspring of Fairchild. This constant fracturing, with large companies splitting into smaller start-ups, has driven Silicon Valley's growth. This process constantly recycles talent out of large companies into start-ups. Money and greed are vital lubricants. In the 1970s, as Silicon Valley reduced its dependence upon defence orders, venture capitalists became the most important source of finance for start-ups. The Sand Hill Road – home to the most powerful venture capitalists in the Valley – runs down the side of the Stanford University campus. This is where the intellectual and financial circuits of Silicon Valley overlap. One Silicon Valley venture-capital firm, Kleiner, Perkins Caulfield & Byers, has invested about $1 billion to help start 250 companies, which in 1995 had revenues of $4 billion and a stock-market value of about $85 billion. The 1996 *Fortune* magazine list of the 100 fastest-growing companies in the US included twenty-five from California, nineteen of them producing high-tech products or services. One in five public companies in Silicon Valley is counted as a 'gazelle', a small firm which has seen its revenue grow by at least 20 per cent in each of the past four years. The national average is one in thirty-five.

Silicon Valley's prospects are promising. Even though the bubble will burst on the extraordinary growth it enjoyed in the late 1990s, the high-tech components of Silicon Valley's economic base may cross-fertilize. Larry Ellison, the founder of Oracle computers, recently took a stake in a leading biotechnology firm. Other high-tech companies are demanding consumers of advanced software. The multi-media companies will feed into the Los Angeles-based entertainment industry. Both will find new outlets through the Internet. What makes Silicon Valley so dynamic is the velocity at which people and ideas move from universities to commerce, small to large businesses, the drawing board to product launch. Silicon Valley, by chance and culture, rather than policy or plan, has created networks which are open enough to rapidly absorb new ideas from around the world, yet cohesive enough to pull people together to create streams of new products. As a consequence, the Silicon Valley model is being imitated all over the world. There is a Silicon Valley clone in Bangalore and in both Russia and China. New York has its Silicon Alley and there is a biotech Silicon Valley in Iowa. There are Silicon Prairies at nine locations in the Midwest. Ireland has a Silicon Bog, Austin, Texas a Silicon Gulch and Israel a Silicon Wadi. Silicon Valley's growth has been metaphorical as well as meteoric. It is a state of mind, a commitment to entrepreneurial, knowledge networks, as much as a location.

Public policy cannot create new Silicon Valleys around the world. Yet many of the constraints which will hold back Silicon Valley will only be removed through public policy. Innovation in public policy will be essential to match the rate of innovation in the economy. Property taxes are so low that there is not enough money to fund a decent basic-education system. Zoning restrictions will not allow the construction of high-rise apartments. Housing is so scarce that new immigrants to Silicon Valley often have to drive for two hours to get to work. Traffic congestion is endemic and as a result the physical environment is degrading. The place is ugly, overcrowded, overheated. The way to solve these problems lies in public initiatives, to sort out education, transport and the environment. Yet Silicon Valley lacks a political machinery to address these regional concerns. The business community has realized it needs a public policy machine to address the problems the region's growth is throwing up. Through the Joint Venture Silicon Valley initiative business leaders are getting together with local government and community leaders to address common concerns.

Silicon Valley exemplifies the connection between innovation, collaboration, relationships and social capital. The connections between social ties and knowledge-sharing, which is the source of so much innovation, explain why knowledge-creating networks are not threaded across the world but clustered in regions and cities. Knowledge-creating networks depend upon the transmission of ideas and tacit knowledge. This is best done through regular face-to-face contact. Innovation involves risk-taking. That requires trust and co-operation, between those providing the financial capital and those with the ideas, the knowledge capitalists. In the most innovative regional economies in the world these transactions are underpinned by social relationships. Innovative trust emerges from quite intense relationships, which themselves depend on frequent contact, shared values and proximity. Ideas flow between companies and organizations most fluently if people do as well. In the most impressive knowledge-creating networks, people are constantly on the move, crossing the boundaries between universities, research labs, venture capital, large companies and start-ups. This kind of exchange is much more feasible at the level of a city or region.

The global economy is evolving into a patchwork of regions and urban agglomerations. Globalization has dislocated the communities created around traditional industries, such as shipbuilding and coal, but it is creating new industrial localities around new industries which depend on knowledge-sharing and collaborative innovation. The rise of the global economy does not mean the death of distance or the end of geography. The nation state is less powerful as a basic unit of economic organization, while regions and cities are more powerful. As a result the social and political communities fostered by the new economy are likely to be regional and city-based rather than national. The advance of industry in the nineteenth century meant that geographically bounded nation states became central to economic management. This was because industrialization helped to integrate nations, through the telegraph, the railway and the radio, but also because the state became the ultimate guarantor, through monetary and fiscal policy, policing and education, of the institutional underpinnings which a modern economy required.

As finance and trade has gone global, so innovation and knowledge creation has become localized. This is perhaps best borne out by the growth of large cities around the world, places where people mingle and meet, ideas and insights are shared. Cities are vast, dense knowledge-sharing organisms. In 1950 the fifteen largest metropolitan areas in the world had a population of about 82.5 million. By 1970 their populations had grown to 140.2 million and by 1990 it was 189.6 million. These large urban centres, regional economies of great scale, are becoming more concentrated in poorer countries. In 1950, ten of the fifteen largest cities were in developed economies. In 1990, only five were. Dense, knowledge-rich regions are the basic building blocks of the new economy. Increasingly the global economy is a mosaic of regions, overlaid by increasingly unproductive national and international organizations.

The most impressive regional network economies create a virtuous circle of high trust, rapid learning and international competitiveness, which brings together knowledge capital, financial capital and social capital. Intelligent regions are becoming the junction boxes of the modern economy. Regional, knowledge-creating networks combine: knowledge production, from universities and research labs; knowledge distribution and exploitation, through start-ups backed by venture capital and large companies to market products; knowledge regulation and validation, through the setting of technical and industry standards. Having these elements within a region is not enough. The critical factor is how these ingredients are combined. In Silicon Valley, in the 1990s at least, these elements have been combined in a dynamic and creative cycle which is producing waves of radical innovation. By contrast, Baden-Württemberg, Germany's most successful industrial region, has produced fewer radical innovations, in part because the process is more regulated and consensual. It's solid but slower-moving.

A regional, knowledge-creating network will only generate radical innovation if it has strong tendencies towards creative dissent and destruction. Without a tendency to question and challenge convention, the network will become introverted and defensive. Closed, inbred networks can prosper but often only in relatively small niches. The north Holland flower industry, which has spawned supporting engineering industries in refrigeration, humidity control and glasshouse construction, is now 'locked in' to its position as a global producer of flowers. That does not matter too much because innovation in the flower business is slow. Yet incest can become a significant drawback for a region if its firms compete in industries such as electronics, which are subject to rapid technological change. Different social milieux create different capacities for innovation. Silicon Valley's fluid and open social structure creates more dynamic relationships and so more radical innovations. Baden-Württemberg's reliance upon consensual institutions and long-term relationships tends to produce incremental innovation.

Baden-Württemberg was widely regarded as a model economy in the 1980s. It is famous, not just for its large, Swabian companies, Daimler-Benz, Audi, Porsche and Robert Bosch – each renowned for high-quality products – but also for its impressive small and medium-sized companies, the *Mittelstand*. Baden-Württemberg seemed to have hit upon a model of consensual capitalism, in which firms and banks, employers and employees, co-operated to improve productivity, backed by a rich infrastructure of research institutes, universities and technology-transfer agencies, as well as regional credit banks and a strong regional government. This co-operative ingenuity and skill helped the region to retain a stronger manufacturing base than for instance the UK. Yet Baden-Württemberg's performance in the last decade shows how hard it is to maintain the pace of innovation. The region stands as a warning for the currently fashionable Silicon Valley that the seeds of its future malaise may well have been sown, in all likelihood by its very success.

There was nothing predestined about Baden-Württemberg's prosperity. At the turn of the century the region was so poor that tens of thousands of its farmers migrated to Texas, Minnesota, Ohio and the Missouri Valley. Yet at the same time the area was home to some of Germany's most impressive engineering entrepreneurs: Karl Benz, Gottlieb Daimler, Robert Bosch, Claudius Dornier and Ferdinand Porsche. The region's post-war economic success was less to do with entrepreneurship, and more to do with the way its institutions have underpinned a co-operative approach to innovation. Baden-Württemberg only became a *Land* in 1952 after it emerged from the centralized control of the Nazi regime and the confusion of Allied occupation. In those days Baden-Württemberg's economy largely relied on textiles and agriculture. Yet in the following decades it developed one of the most powerful agglomerations of engineering and electronics companies in Europe. The large and small firms, in engineering, electronics and automotive products, work hand in glove. Large Baden-Württemberg companies outsource far less than their US or Japanese counterparts, and when they do, they employ locals. These relationships are underpinned by local institutions such as the *Verbände*, business associations, Max Planck research institutions and the Stenbeis Foundation, which promotes local technology transfers. These self-regulating, co-operative business associations are supported by the strong regional government and a loyal local banking community.

This co-operative but regulated approach to innovation helped Baden-Württemberg to defy economic gravity. While manufacturing employment and output has declined dramatically in the UK and the US, in Baden-Württemberg it has been maintained, thanks to the quality of local producers. In 1957 about 50 per cent of jobs in Baden-Württemberg were in manufacturing, with about 18 per cent in agriculture. By 1995, agriculture's share of employment had fallen to 2 per cent, the region's population had expanded by about 4 million, unemployment was low and about 43 per cent of the workforce was still employed in manufacturing. Yet all is not well in this apparently model region. Baden-Württemberg's Future Commission reported in 1993 that local companies faced three challenges. One was intense, low-cost, high-quality competition from the Far East. Another was the level of social costs, which were threatening to price local products out of global markets. The most important was the region's innovation deficit. The Baden-Württemberg model was good at producing incremental innovation but not the radical innovations that would propel its firms and industries into growth industries such as biotechnology and multimedia. The region's strengths had become its weaknesses. It was locked into automotive and engineering industries, organizationally and culturally.

Baden-Württemberg is a case study of how a once entrepreneurial and innovative regional economy, built upon knowledge-creating networks, has become closed and introverted. Its strength – the intimacy of the ties between its companies, banks, research institutes and public bodies – has become its weakness.

Our economies are developing a far richer ecology of institutions to co-ordinate economic activity, to generate ideas and translate them into products. In this new ecology a range of corporate, regional and personal networks will organize the most critical process: generating new knowledge that can be translated into products and services. Durable and dynamic networks are underpinned by reciprocity and mutual trust, which allow members to share information, risks and opportunities with ease. Networks are made up of complex competing and co-operative relations, akin to those between class mates or members of a football squad all trying to make it into the manager's first-choice team. Networks thrive with repeated, continual negotiation and re-negotiation of mutual expectations, commitments and actions to deliver on those commitments. The more that modern economies come to rely upon networks to generate and exploit knowledge, the more they will also rely on trust. For trust is an essential lubricant of creativity in the knowledge economy.

CHAPTER THIRTEEN TRUST: THE ETHICS OF THE NEW ECONOMY

Tony Blair led New Labour to a stunning election victory in May 1997 largely because he understood the value of trust. When Blair launched Labour's election campaign in a gilded hall in London's Whitehall he announced that the election was just that, an issue of trust. Labour won because Blair and his colleagues had a well worked strategy to convince the British public that Labour could again be trusted and that the Conservatives could not. This is how they did it.

Experience and familiarity are the most usual reasons for trusting someone. Yet New Labour had no recent track record in government: it could not build up trust based on people's experience of the party in power. Instead Blair set out to build a record for competence by modernizing his party. The message was: 'I am a competent manager; look what I have achieved with my own party. That is what I could do with the country.' As well as acquiring an image of competence, Blair tried to acquire a reputation that would inspire public trust – for example, by winning endorsements from leading businessmen. In other words: 'You can trust me because of the kind of company I keep.' New Labour also offered the electorate a quasi-contract, as a symbol that it could be trusted. Labour promised not to raise the burden of personal taxation in the life of a parliament and set out its policy targets in five pledges. By mimicking a contract, the party was trying to show that it was willing to be judged on its performance, against clear commitments. This was reinforced by a series of important symbolic gestures, to stress New Labour's intimacy with the concerns of the disenchanted Tory voters the party was wooing. The party ditched Clause Four of its constitution, on nationalization and common ownership, to symbolize its change of direction. Tony Blair presented himself and his family as the epitome of middle England, respectable, thrifty, hard-working, Ford-driving. His pitch was: 'Trust me, I am one of you.' People do not trust politicians. They regard them as venal, cynical and potentially corrupt. At his most impressive, Tony Blair was able to stand outside politics. Labour won in 1997 because the Conservatives had so spectacularly lost public trust on so many counts. They were seen as incompetent, corrupt, divided and uncaring. The Tories lost because they suffered a compounded fracture of trust. Blair won because he was so skilful at acquiring trust on several fronts at the same time, using several different approaches.

Trust will be vital as a lubricant for knowledge creation: people share and act on ideas when they trust one another. Trust and co-operation are as critical to success in the modern economy as self-interest. Yet many of our traditional bases for trust have been eroded by social and economic change: class, community, family, religion. Established institutions are suffering from a malaise, if not a crisis, of trust. The political system is rightly treated with widespread cynicism. Large companies, which have ruthlessly downsized their workforces, cannot be relied upon to deliver security. Just as trust has become so vital, so it is more difficult to produce. That is one reason why we need to embark on a wave of innovation in our institutions – both public and private – to reform them to inspire and reproduce trust, among their workers, consumers and financiers. We cannot hope to repair our trust deficit by retreating into older, more homely bases for trust, based on nostalgia for the comfort blanket of community. We need to match the pace of economic and scientific innovation, with innovation in our social and public institutions to put trust on a new footing.

The significance of trust has been highlighted by a range of recent writers, from Francis Fukuyama's *Trust*, his account of the role of trust in economic development, to Will Hutton, in *The State We're In*, his attack on the short-termism of financially driven market economies, and a string of communitarian writers such as Amitai Etzioni and John Gray, who argue that individuals can only realize themselves within strong communities which provide security against outside shocks and clear rules for co-operation. Hutton, Fukuyama and the communitarians are right to identify the critical role trust plays in modern economies. Much of the rest of their analysis is simplistic and crude. At their most sentimental they seem to see trust as an unalloyed good, a substance akin to honey, which spreads well-being wherever it flows. A simplistic account of trust as community leads to the assumption that the more trust there is within an economy, the more innovative it will become. That is mistaken on several counts. Trust and social capital come in different forms, which serve different purposes. Just as it is possible to have too little trust, it is possible to have too much.

In our everyday language exchange, co-operation, promise-keeping and trust are all bound up together. We teach our children that trust and exchange go hand in hand to produce virtue and economy. The rebuke, 'You promised', is often interchangeable with 'You owe me'. When two people trust one another, they make a judgement about how likely it is that they will be able to co-operate with one another reliably. As trust declines, so does a willingness to share information and pool risks. People demand greater protection against the threat of betrayal and insist on costly sanctions to defend their interests. The more people trust one another the more they are able to combine their different expertise and resources, without relying on contracts, lawyers or rules to make sure no one is cheating. The neo-liberal new right presented self-interest, private property, free markets and choice as the main ingredients of economic success. That is wrong. As Matt Ridley puts it in *The Origins of Virtue*: 'Trust is as vital a form of social capital as money is a form of actual capital.'

The economic value of trust has been recognized for centuries. Adam Smith, in his *Theories of Moral Sentiments* (published in 1759), argued that if a common bond between a group of people was strong enough, they would combine to suppress the activities of free-riders or parasites. John Stuart Mill remarked in the nineteenth century: 'The advantage to mankind of being able to trust one another penetrates into every crevice and cranny of human life.' Twenty-five years ago Kenneth Arrow, the US Nobel prize-winning economist, pointed out: 'Virtually every commercial transaction has within itself an element of trust, certainly any transaction conducted over a period of time. It can be plausibly argued that much of the economic backwardness in the world can be explained by the lack of mutual confidence.'

Why should trust be of particular value in the knowledge-driven economy? Trust has become so valuable because we need it more and yet it has become more elusive: demand has gone up while traditional sources of supply have contracted. Trust has become more important because it fosters the co-operation and risk-sharing that promote innovation and flexible responses to change in a global economy. Yet trust has become harder to sustain, precisely because there is so much upheaval and change, which threatens the settled relationships which breed trust in the first place.

Trust in Demand

As the character of the economy continues to shift towards the global production and trade of intangible services made using intangible assets, so trust will become more important. Trust is a vital component in most exchanges between buyers and sellers. The buyer of a computer takes it on trust that the machine will do what the seller says when he gets it home and plugs it in. It is not always possible for a consumer to check the quality and performance of a product at the time of purchase. As the international division of labour expands, so we depend on goods we barely understand, made by strangers in factories many thousands of miles away. Trust is going to become ever more important to trade as products become more knowledge-intensive and globalization extends its reach. We will buy more goods by telephone or over the Internet and take it on trust that the people on the other end of the line will supply what we have paid for. Knowledge-intensive products, akin to specialist services, are difficult to test in advance. You cannot test-drive a divorce lawyer. Trade in intangible services and know-how is particularly dependent on trust. That is one reason why corporate brands will become ever more important. Consumers will use brands as short cuts to decide whether a product can be trusted.

Trust is increasingly important to the culture of work, in theory at least. Companies will seek to create new products by unlocking the tacit knowledge of their employees. People share ideas when they feel uninhibited enough to take risks. Creative work is a fragile, insecure process: ideas have to be proposed, put to the test, justified and rejected. An atmosphere of trust is vital to persuade people to open up and share ideas which may be rejected. Creative work will increasingly involve people working in teams which combine members with different skills and backgrounds. These teams are more effective when people can trust fellow team members to play their part. In low-trust organizations, people will tend to hoard knowledge, and only share ideas formally, through memos and only when requested. In high-trust organizations people are more likely to bestow their knowledge on one another and develop joint understandings of problems and their solutions. Trust and co-operation will be vital to the work cultures of the future.

Entrepreneurial cultures, for example, thrive when there is a high tolerance for well intentioned failure: when people are trusted enough to be given a second and third chance. Entrepreneurs are risk takers. They need to be backed by goodwill. That is why trust plays such an important role in the finance of innovation. Often young entrepreneurs have little more than a good idea. They depend at the outset on the trust and goodwill of investors, who will have to wait before the business delivers financial results.

Companies will only be able to exploit the benefits of flatter-networked organizations, in which authority is devolved to front-line staff, if they create high-trust cultures. Hierarchical companies rely upon command, control and constant checking to make sure orders issued from on high are followed on the ground. Most large companies have large 'Corporate Distrust' departments, which spend their time checking up on people, to make sure they have done what they are supposed to have done. Low trust is a recipe for high-cost management and administration. Self-management and initiative thrive on trust. Companies need to win public trust to secure their licence to operate and innovate, particularly if innovation involves potential public risks. A prime example is Monsanto's recent failed campaign to establish that it could be trusted to develop and exploit genetically modified food. Monsanto's ability to innovate genetically modified foods is determined by its scientific know-how. The company's ability to appropriate the value from its innovations depends on it winning public trust to press ahead with commercial exploitation. Companies have to renew their licence to operate. That means renewing public trust in their operations.

The theoretical case that trust is a central ingredient in economic development is more impressive than the evidence, which is still scanty. One of the few efforts to measure the value of trust in economies was made by a team of economists from Harvard and Chicago Universities. They used the World Values Survey, which polled 1,000 people in each of forty countries, to test the link between levels of trust between people, co-operation within companies, and confidence in the effectiveness and fairness of public institutions. The survey asked respondents whether they thought people could generally be trusted or whether they needed to 'take care' dealing with other people. It found the highest-trust countries were in Scandinavia, where two-thirds of people said they could trust strangers. The lowest-trust countries were in Latin America and in societies dominated by hierarchical religions. The higher the level of trust the more likely the country was to have large, international companies, effective government, an impartial judiciary, low tax evasion and little corruption. High trust was linked, albeit weakly, to lower inflation and higher GNP as well as social outcomes such as lower infant mortality and higher educational achievement. The authors concluded: 'Trust promotes cooperation, especially in large organizations. Despite economists' skepticism, theories of trust hold up remarkably well.' Mari Sako, from Oxford University, came to similar conclusions when she looked at relationships between suppliers and customers in the world's automotive industry. Sako found that suppliers in a high-trust relationship were significantly better at just-in-time delivery and were more committed to joint problem-solving with their customers. Trust was created and reproduced by a kind of gift exchange in the relationship, with the suppliers and customers voluntarily sharing information and ideas, above and beyond the terms of their contract.

Perhaps the best way to value trust is to work out how much it would cost to repair trust once it was lost. Trust is a quality most of us take for granted. We only understand trust's true worth when we lose it. Companies lose trust in as many ways as they acquire it. At one extreme, companies and industries can lose trust gradually, by repeatedly letting people down. This was the problem of the British car industry in the 1960s. Chronic distrust between the workforce and managers, produced products which people could not trust either. Trust has been restored in the quality and reliability of cars made in the UK but the process took almost two decades and an overhaul of the industry's industrial relations, ownership, technology and management. At the end of the process the industry is much smaller and no major manufacturer is British-owned. The turmoil the British car industry went through to restore its reputation is one measure of how costly its loss of trust was.

The BSE crisis that hit the British beef industry in the mid-1990s shows how a specific crisis can become a chronic malaise. Trust in Britain's food-producing industries has been damaged in the 1990s by a string of scandals which have highlighted poor management and weak quality assurance. The BSE crisis, the product of contaminated feed being fed to cattle, has been linked to twenty-seven human deaths and 171,548 cases of BSE among cattle. The cost of restoring public trust in the industry, and getting the world-wide ban on British beef exports lifted, will be about £4 billion by the year 2000 according to a study by the National Audit Office. That will be mainly spent on the slaughter and disposal of 8 million cattle. A cow is a remarkable milk-making machine, a chemical refinery that automatically converts grass, water and air into a nearly perfect, liquid-protein dietary supplement. This refinery operates with almost no human supervision, is mobile so it can search out its own inputs, can heal almost all its own mechanical failures and can detect and neutralize pathogens which enter its system and threaten the quality of its output. And it can build several replacement refineries out of basically the same raw materials: grass, water and air. The BSE crisis has meant that most of Britain's milk refineries have had to be destroyed and replaced. The asset base for an entire industry has been wiped out. The public cost of this crisis – £4 billion – is an underestimate of the total cost in terms of jobs and lives lost.

So far, so good. But, taken much further, this appealingly simple link between trust and economic performance starts to break down. Trust, like knowledge, is a vital resource because it is complex. This complexity is largely unrecognized by the likes of Fukuyama, Hutton and communitarians, who seem attracted by a simple, pre-modern account of trust in settled communities. The first problem with this simple 'community trust' approach is that it fails to recognize that we want open societies which promote experimentation and change as well as a sense of community. The second problem is that trust comes in different shapes and sizes, it is produced by different mechanisms. The value of trust depends on context and circumstance. We might want more of some kinds of trust and less of others. Personally, I am not in the slightest interested in living in a settled, unchanging, closed community, which has strong common bonds at the expense of learning new skills or giving young people new opportunities. I want to be able to trust more in modern institutions and communities, not to retreat to old ones. The third problem is that too much trust can be bad for you. High-trust, long-term relationships do not always lead to improved efficiency. On the contrary, sometimes they lead to corruption and abuse.

The Trust Deficit

In close-knit, slow-moving, pre-modern societies, people could have confidence in one another, based on strong common bonds and their frequent interaction, in families, clans and tribes. As Matt Ridley puts it: 'In the conditions in which human beings evolved, in small tribes where to meet a stranger must have been an extremely rare event, this sense of reciprocal obligation must have been palpable – it still is among rural people of all kinds.' These closed, agrarian societies encouraged respect for order and hierarchy, in which people's sense of identity was wrapped up with tightly defined roles. Trust, according to Adam Seligman in *The Problem of Trust*, only became the glue for social relations when people broke free from the shackles of these older, settled communities.

As people came to see themselves as free agents, society was no longer held together by bonds of blood and belonging. Free agents cannot be forced to co-operate by tradition or hierarchy, but only if they choose to make binding commitments to keep their word. Modern societies, which prize freedom, autonomy and choice, need trust to produce co-operation, because the traditional sources of co-operation – family, tribe, religion, hierarchy – are less potent. Several factors, which make trust more valuable, also make it more difficult to sustain. This tension is evident in modern economies.

As companies have extended their global reach, for example,

they have run into the difficulty of establishing trust across cultures – for example, between employees in the same global corporation. According to one study, 40–50 per cent of international joint-ventures collapse within five years, mainly because the partners do not trust one another. The more international trade expands, the more companies will run up against these differing cultures of trust and fairness. Companies have become increasingly ruthless in looking for cheaper sources of supply. Aggressive outsourcing has unsettled traditional relationships with suppliers and employees. Companies facing global competition have found it increasingly difficult to maintain a social contract with their own employees, to protect them against economic upheavals. Brutal downsizing in the early 1990s at large, formerly paternalistic employers such as AT&T and BP has left behind a lasting legacy of mistrust among the remaining employees. Performance-related pay systems in many of these companies encourage people to act individualistically. The pace of technological change and innovation, driven on by advances in science, is bringing new products on to the market the whole time, leaving older technologies, products, companies and workers stranded in their wake. The process which drives modern economies forward – innovation and knowledge creation – means there is a risk in relying on the tried, tested and trusted.

The dilemma facing modern societies is that they need to generate stronger bonds of trust, to make people feel more secure, only because so much of modern life, especially economic life, is so volatile and uncertain. We want innovation and change which brings us new products and more opportunities. Yet we also want to feel more secure and settled. This is one version of the trap described in the opening chapter: we do not want to go backwards but we do not know how to move forwards. The way to resolve this dilemma is to understand that trust comes in several guises, from several sources. Modern societies need distinctively open, modern forms of trust, not a return to the past. We need to develop ways to establish trust and common bonds in a fluid society which is open to change. To work out how to square this circle we have to go back to first principles and examine the nature of trust.

Trust is so valuable to us because it is multi-faceted, linked to, but distinct from, reliability, mutuality, faith and co-operation. We trust someone when we rely upon him or her. Yet trust is not the same as routine or predictability. We may rely on a bus turning up, but few of us would say we trust the bus to come. In contrast, we rely on a friend to collect us from the railway station because he or she has promised to do so. We trust the friend and feel let down, betrayed even, when the person fails to do what was promised; this is a different order of feeling from the disappointment we feel when the bus does not turn up on time. Trust involves our relying on other people when there is a risk that we might be let down or disappointed. When we trust someone we make ourselves vulnerable to that person. Trusting involves taking a risk that one might be let down.

At its strongest and most intimate, trust is mutual and reciprocal. I trust my wife and she trusts me. We've known one another a long time and been through a lot together. But trust does not have to be mutual, as the likes of Hutton and Fukuyama seem to suggest. I trust my financial adviser to give me prudent advice about pensions. This is dependent trust. I have to trust her because I am dependent upon her. Trust lubricates relationships of dependency and power; it is not always reciprocal. Nor is trust the same as faith, even though the religious will say they 'trust in God'. Faith does not normally involve a calculation of self-interest, trust often does. Often we choose to trust someone after we have made a calculation of the likelihood that that person will let us down and the benefits that will flow to us from trusting them. Trust is one way to achieve co-operation but it is not the same as co-operation. People can combine and co-operate – for instance, in army regiments or bureaucracies – without trusting one another very much. Trust is only one way among many, and not necessarily the most effective way, to promote co-operation.

Trust has properties akin to knowledge. Just as it is difficult to specify how know-how and expertise should be exchanged in a contract, so it is difficult to specify in a contract how much people should trust one another. Trust, like knowledge, has tacit and explicit components. I trust my lawyer to do some specific tasks for me – handling the purchase of my house – based on his explicit qualifications and my contract with him. I do not trust him to go further than that or to become my analyst or confidant. My trust in my lawyer is explicit, specific and limited. My trust in my closest colleagues, with whom I have worked for a long time, is largely unspoken, tacit and open-ended. Trust, like knowledge, is a renewable resource: it atrophies when not used but it can multiply with frequent use. Trust frequently enjoys increasing returns: the more you use it, the more you get. That is how companies such as Tesco, Wal-Mart and Intel built up such momentum behind their brands; success breeds success, reputation feeds reputation, trust begets trust.

Trust can be embodied in a relationship with a person, or disembodied – when we trust rules, policies or procedures. I first grew to trust my local Toyota garage thanks to the efforts of the salesman who sold me my first Toyota. After I went back to have the car serviced I got to know other people at the garage. I began to realize that Toyota provides high-quality service because of the way the business is organized and managed. Now I trust Toyota because of the policies and procedures it employs, not just the individual salesman. My trust, which was embodied in a salesman, has become invested in the organization as a whole. This process can work the other way. One can lose trust in a company because one loses trust in a person who represents it. I was never particularly dissatisfied with the quality of service provided by British Gas until it started paying ridiculously generous sums to its then chief executive, Cedric Brown. Trust takes a long time to build up but it can be lost in a moment's indiscretion or betrayal.

There is a mistaken tendency to identify strong trust with long-term relationships. The 'trust as community' school of thought praises the long-term relationships between banks, manufacturers and suppliers in Japan because they help to build trust. Yet the most creative and innovative relationships are often based on intense, short-term trust. This is the kind of trust that the film, advertising and entertainment industries thrive upon. When a crew comes together to make a film, for example, they may not know one another, but will work hand in glove for a few weeks very intensively. Film crews generate intense trust very quickly. This capacity is one that companies will have to develop as they seek to respond to change by reconfiguring themselves. The 'trust as community' school argues that the more trusting relationships become the more open and mutually supportive they are. Yet film crews generate lots of intense trust precisely because they know the relationships are formed around a project with a limited life and in which they will all play quite specific roles. Long-term trusting relationships can create their own problems. They can lead to corruption and insider dealing – the problems which have beset the Japanese financial system – where trust, mutual back-scratching and public lying about the scale of losses faced by overextended Japanese banks have gone hand in hand. It is a mistake to associate the most creative and innovative relationships exclusively with long-term, mutual trust.

Trust varies in its intensity, scope and duration. At its most limited, trust is guarded, qualified and conditional, limited in duration, open to review and related to a specific task. At its broadest, trust is like goodwill, an open-ended, reciprocal, emotional quality to a relationship, in which people do not simply solve problems and keep promises, but jointly set out to create something together. In between goodwill and prudent trust lies a range of kinds of trust. We engage in role-based trust when we give someone considerable licence to act on our behalf because we trust their integrity or their competence. This is the kind of trust we have in doctors, lawyers, police officers and nannies. Problem-solving trust involves greater intimacy and joint understanding of the kind colleagues generate when they work creatively together in a team.

Really impressive companies and organizations are not just trusted; they combine different kinds of trust just as they combine different kinds of knowledge. Often a company only reaches its potential if it moves between different kinds of trust in its relations with employees and customers. International joint-ventures, for example, often start with the partners making limited commitments to one another. They often insist on being able to check on the trustworthiness of their partner. In this formative stage of the relationship, trust is based on calculation and judged against yardsticks. As a joint-venture develops, the partners should start to trust one another more, based on their experience of one another. If a joint-venture succeeds, the parties start to bond and share values.

They start to identify with the joint-venture rather than with their separate companies. In most joint-ventures, trust starts with small steps, develops momentum and eventually becomes like goodwill, open-ended and mutual.

In many start-ups the story works the other way around. When Gordon Moore and Andy Grove launched Intel, they had neither products nor a business plan. The venture capitalist that backed them was making a leap of faith, backing the people as much as the business. Intel would never have got going with small steps. It took off with one big leap. As Intel developed, however, it generated trust by delivering on its promises and establishing a track record for trustworthiness.

Intel, Wal-Mart, Hewlett Packard, and BMW are all good at acquiring trust on several counts at the same time, not just on the basis of one attribute. Intel and BMW both make products with strong technical characteristics, yet they also have powerful and emotive brands. The organizations that impress us most, inspire our trust on the basis of their performance, procedures and brand image. They do not rely on one single kind of trust. The same is true of successful economies.

In the early 1990s it was fashionable to argue that for an economy to be successful it needed to follow Japan and Germany by being 'high-trust'. That is too simplistic. The most impressive economies of the future will combine different kinds of trust. They will have laws and institutions, for example, which will promote trust that contracts will be honoured and adhered to. The weakness of 'background' trust in contracts is one reason why investors are so nervous about China and Russia. Successful economies will also need strong background social trust: to assure people that there will be a co-operative, common safety net to help them through periods of change and volatility.

In addition to background trust, there is mounting evidence from California and other high-tech regions around the world that successful economies are built on collaborative innovation. Successful economies, like Silicon Valley, excel at trusting in the unfamiliar, the untested, the novel as well as the familiar and long-standing. This kind of opened-ended trust is bred by openness with information, transparency in transactions, and commitment to test and justify ideas rather than rely on tradition. Successful economies will be 'multi-trust'. They must create trust and co-operation in conditions that make long-term relationships difficult to sustain.

Prospecting for New Sources of Trust

Each Sunday our family goes to a market in London to buy our vegetables for the week. Each Sunday we park our car and leave the keys with the blokes who run the car park. The men know us well. We have no idea who they are, or whether they run a drugs business from their little hut. But we trust them with our car because they have never let us down. This tit-for-tat trust, built on repeated exchange, is the most basic way that we establish trust. Yet there is a limit to how much trust experience can generate. Familiarity only breeds trust when people can form repetitive, stable relationships. The more casual and fleeting the encounters in an economy, the harder it is to establish a track record and build trust on familiarity. In a global economy, with rapid technological change, we do not have that many close familiar relations. We want to shop around. We have to get used to the fact that we and our colleagues will change jobs. We need to base trust on something other than experience and long-term relationships. There are four ways to square this circle of producing more trust in a society which is in constant flux.

First, the role of contracts could be extended from commerce into other areas of life such as government and politics, to set clear yardsticks for acceptable performance. Second, to win public trust for innovation we need to establish a transparent, publicly account-able system of 'trusted, expert, third parties' who will assess risk on our behalf. Third, we need improved procedures to make sure injured parties – for example, consumers or workers who feel they have been treated unfairly by a company – can have redress and appeal to arbitration and independent review. Fourth, open trust can only flourish in a society in which information is open and accessible.

Contracts seem to be the opposite of trust. If one can trust someone, why would one need a formal contract to safeguard your interests? In Japan, it would be an insult to insist on a formal, written contract before entering into a business relationship. Yet contracts can help to provide the platform for a trusting relationship. People who work for a large employer sign a contract of employment, which covers their pay, holidays and disciplinary procedures. Most people never refer to this contract once they start work, but they would not start work without it. The contract provides them with a platform of security, a baseline for acceptable behaviour. A willingness to enter into a contract can be a commitment to trustworthy behaviour; the first test of a new relationship. A contract provides a yardstick by which people can assess one another's behaviour, whether work is carried out as specified and on time. It should be no surprise to see contracts or quasi-contracts, such as New Labour's five campaign pledges, spreading from commerce into other areas of life, such as politics, public service and even marriage and family life. Contracts create a baseline for trustworthy behaviour in a fluid society in which relationships are rarely long-term.

Procedures for treating people fairly – employees, colleagues, customers, suppliers, neighbours – will be vital to establish an organization's trustworthiness. One way we all assess the quality of people who manage us is to ask whether they are fair in dispensing the power they have over us. Any organization or manager with a reputation for deciding issues such as pay, promotion and dismissal on a whim of arbitrary power, will not be seen as fair. This is perhaps particularly true of skilled, mobile, independent employees – knowledge workers – who are more likely to want to work in organizations which are seen to be fair, reputable and respect their employees. Often we trust people and companies because someone else we already trust has recommended them. That is why 'trusted third parties' will be so vital to trade on the Internet. These 'trusted third parties' will be akin to regulators who will assure electronic consumers that they can trust a company selling its services across the Internet. They will provide quality control in a networked world. In science we will increasingly rely on 'trusted third parties' to review for us whether genetically modified food should be licensed for human consumption. Trust in qualified third parties will become more important as society's division of labour multiplies and our dependence upon specialist knowledge increases. That is one of the downsides of a society in which specialist knowledge proliferates. Consumers become increasingly dependent upon the credentials of other people as a guide to their competence, but we are rarely in a position to check the relevance of those credentials.

The final general measure to promote trust in a fluid society is to force companies and the government to commit to share information with consumers and workers. A society that wants to encourage trust and radical innovation has to support a radical approach to freedom of information. This should be the first test of trustworthiness in a modern society: is an organization prepared to be open with information that could be used to judge its performance? We live in an era in which information is cheap and plentiful. All organizations should be willing to commit themselves to be judged on open information about their performance and impact on society. That commitment should be a measure of whether they are genuinely part of a democratic, open society. Consumers of NHS hospitals, for example, should have far more information about the comparative costs and performance of different doctors and operating theatres, to know which are under-performing. Companies should be under an obligation to provide far more information on the impact of their activities on the environment, both social and environmental. As far as banks are concerned, for example, this should include information on their lending policies and performance in poorer areas of our cities and to ethnic minorities. A willingness to be open with information in an era when there are few technological constraints on acquiring and distributing information should be the first and most fundamental mark of a trustworthy organization. Companies are closed, secretive organizations in a democratic era awash with information. If they are to inspire our trust in future, as they acquire even more power they have to be more open with information we can use to hold them to account.

Can You Have Too Much of a Good Thing?

There is a dangerous tendency to regard trust as an unalloyed good: you can never have too much of it. Yet just as it is possible to have too little trust, having too much trust can also create economic problems. The current problems of the Japanese and German economies have been compounded – if not created – by their surfeit of the wrong kind of trust. Openness with information and preparedness to be judged by public yardsticks and contracts is vital to avoid the problems created by exclusive, closed systems of trust. Germany and Japan are not just high-trust societies but closed-trust societies. Our aim should be to create an open, high-trust society.

Start with a very mundane example from the German mining-equipment industry: Christel Lane, from the University of Cambridge, has studied relations between customers and suppliers of mining machinery in Britain and Germany. She found that industry trade associations played a vital role in Germany, promoting the stability, consistency and mutual trust that underpinned long-term relationships and intimate technical collaboration between suppliers and customers. Opportunism and risk were reduced. The German mining-equipment industry was regarded as top-class. Yet Lane's research uncovered a downside to the German model. 'Greater conformity to rules among German managers leaves less room for autonomous decision-making and may stifle managerial initiative,' she concluded. Technical norms for products were imposed by industry trade associations, which left little scope or incentive for innovation. The dense, closed-trust nature of German industrial relations means that German companies will continue to excel at producing incremental innovations and products of high quality. Yet German companies are less well placed to exploit the radical innovations of the future. That is because German industry has too much of the wrong kind of trust. Britain has a trust deficit; Germany has a trust surfeit.

At the heart of the high-trust German economy are stakeholder companies that are communities of mutual obligations between employees, managers and shareholders. Shareholders are involved and patient, employees are skilled and co-operative, and managers are consensual and inclusive. The German model of innovation through trust faces two challenges. The most obvious threat comes from the way that background trust in the 'German system' is being undermined as companies come under pressure from global competition to cut costs. They are less able to keep to the terms of their historic bargain to provide workers with security. With unemployment high, the background trust between companies and workers is being weakened and with it workers' willingness to engage in co-operative efforts at innovation that might do them out of a job.

As important in the long run is a second, largely unnoticed challenge to Germany's industrial future. German industry is held back by its trust in inherited institutions which sanctions incremental improvements to established bodies of knowledge. It discourages people from taking risks to create entirely new families of products, by exploiting novel ideas. Radical innovation usually involves combining different kinds of knowledge, from different professions, companies and cultures. Yet the German vocational training system, the backbone of the German knowledge-production machine, is not as good at fostering this capacity for dynamic, creative combination. Skilled knowledge workers in Germany are craftworkers, *Berufsarbeiter*, and their training is geared to their trade. Knowledge creation in German industry comes from the strength of these communities which provide support, advice, approved methods and best practice for an entire trade. A *Berufsarbeiter* is never alone: he always has his professional community to fall back on. The high trust within a trade allows its knowledge to be shared fluently and as a result knowledge multiplies by exchange. The weakness is that each worker has to fit into an ordered community. To win the community's support one must accept one's place within it. This community of practice is difficult to challenge or question, let alone to break out of. That discourages radical thinking, especially by young people, women and outsiders of all kinds.

The lessons from Germany and Japan are that trust needs to be tested regularly to establish that it is still appropriate and warranted. Trust is stronger if it is open to revision. The closed, inward-looking trust that promotes stability and cohesion is often at odds with the open, questioning trust that promotes creativity and change.

Which Way is Forward?

Trust and mutuality should become stronger organizing principles in our societies as they become more dependent upon knowledge creation. Self-interest produces only limited supplies of trust. To generate more creative collaboration and joint-risk-sharing we need higher levels of trust. Yet we live in an era when the market has cut deeply into the fabric of trust we inherited from earlier times. The market undermines familiarity as a source of trust by corroding the bonds of community and family. With traditional sources of trust and co-operation undermined, perhaps fatally, our societies often seem incapable of generating enough trust to sustain the level of collaboration they need. Society has become more individualized and diverse, less bound by tradition and social order, which most of us like; but it has also become more fragmented and anonymous, which we do not like.

How can we move forward? The answer is that we need to create a society that fosters modern rather than traditional, open rather than closed, forms of trust. The Soviet Union was a good example of a closed, low-trust society, dominated by a corrupt hierarchy. Wall Street is a good example of an open, low-trust economy, dominated by highly fluid, short-term markets. Japan generates high trust by being closed to change which threatens traditional bonds of family, community and hierarchy. None of these is a good social model. Silicon Valley is perhaps the closest to an economy which is both innovative and open while being capable of generating high degrees of co-operation and trust. But Silicon Valley has a weak civic culture and it is a highly unequal society. What would be the guiding principles for a society that was open and innovative, and yet inclusive and co-operative?

Such a utopian post-capitalist society would be sceptical of tradition but also of narrow self-interest and hierarchies, even if they came in modernized garb. This post-capitalist utopia would embody the principles of radical democracy: self-management and self-organization, not just in political life but increasingly in the economic sphere as well. Ownership of economic assets would be spread much more widely, including a renewed role for innovative forms of social and public ownership of knowledge assets. This society would be inclusive and make the most of its reserves of human capital but it would richly reward achievement and entrepreneurship. Such a post-capitalist society would depend on civic institutions that could produce a distinctively modern form of trust. Modern trust will not come from a retreat into tradition or nostalgic community. Modern trust is based on people choosing to trust one another and to collaborate, after open debate informed by free flows of information. The ethic of the day should be self-organization and co-operative self-help, in pursuit of innovation and change, in economics, welfare and politics. The values of a modern, open, high-trust society are: universalism, open debate, disinterestedness, scepticism, conjectures judged by evidence, inquisitiveness, pursuit of continual improvement.

Most people want to live in a society that is not tightly bound by tradition. They want the opportunities and well-being which science and technology bring us, despite the upheavals. Yet most people do not want to live in a narrowly self-interested society in which co-operation is rare. We need to embrace modernity by creating distinctively modern ways to generate greater trust, co-operation and collaboration. Modernization does not necessarily mean privatization, individualism and markets. It could mean a society organized around a revived ethic of collaboration and mutual trust. For that to be possible we need to be far more radical than we have been with our civic, social and public institutions. We need to embark on a period of sustained and intense innovation in our civic institutions, to create a new civic culture to accompany the dynamism of the new economy. It is that task that we address in the final chapters of this book.

CHAPTER FOURTEEN WHO SHOULD OWN KNOWLEDGE?

Each night the computers at the Sanger research centre near Cambridge come to life to talk to the Internet, spelling out long strings of four letters, A, C, G and T. The strings of letters are unreadable to anyone but an expert. Yet they spell out the story of human heredity encoded in our DNA. Researchers at the Sanger centre are part of an international collaborative effort to read the entire human 'genome' – that is, every one of the roughly 100,000 genes that make up a human being. The book of man, as it has been called, should be complete by the year 2005, at a cost of $3 billion, mainly provided by governments and public bodies. This genetic manual could allow us to treat a much wider range of diseases, including perhaps forms of cancer, heart disease and neurological disorders. The Human Genome Project is a testimony to the power of collective human intelligence to improve our well-being. Of course it also spells big money for biotechnology and pharmaceutical companies keen to develop the new treatments that genetics will make possible. In May 1998, a US scientist, Craig Venter, broke ranks with the project by announcing a deal with Perkin-Elmer, a US company that makes gene-sequencing machines, to compile a private account of the human genome. Perkin-Elmer's share price leapt. Other commercial exploiters of this stock of public knowledge are not far behind.

Who should own the human genome and the rights, if any, to exploit it for commercial purposes? If the rights to exploitation were vested in governments and the public sector, many people would be alarmed. There might be potential threats to civil liberties. Earlier this century, governments in Sweden and the US engaged in forms of eugenics. A dictator or a crazed bureaucrat armed with the human genome could wield enormous power. More prosaically, the public sector would almost certainly be less efficient than the private sector in turning this know-how into widely disseminated commercial products. Yet the idea that private companies should be given ownership over our genes is also disturbing. Human genes are like recipes: they issue instructions to cells to grow hair, digest food or fight off bacteria. These recipes were developed through millions of years of evolution: a shared human heritage of trial, error and adaptation. Unravelling what these genes do is a collaborative effort. The scientist who puts the last piece of a genetic jig-saw puzzle together succeeds only thanks to the work of tens of others who have gone before him. Everything suggests ownership of human genes is fuzzy and shared, if indeed they can be owned at all. Private ownership of genes is as morally and economically disturbing as public ownership.

The human genome is a perfect example of why the issue of ownership will be at the heart of the new economy. Ownership used to be one of the sharpest dividing lines in politics. The traditional, state-socialist left favoured collective, public ownership of at least the 'commanding heights' of the economy, to make sure that workers who created wealth had control over the companies they helped to build. While the left stressed equity, the new right argued that private ownership, combined with market competition, was the key to economic growth. In the 1980s, this argument seemed to be settled, quite decisively, in favour of the right. Communist regimes collapsed and across the world state-owned enterprises were privatized, often with huge gains in efficiency. These days ownership is hardly an issue. No one mentions it. Tony Blair's New Labour won power in 1997 after ditching Clause Four of the party's constitution on nationalization. Politicians are far more likely to dispute how markets should be regulated than how organizations should be owned. Yet ownership will be an increasingly controversial issue in the new economy. Conventional public and private forms of ownership will be inappropriate to and inefficient in the new economy. We need to innovate new forms of ownership, which are both post-capitalist and post-socialist. To understand why, take the example of the human genome a little further.

Who Owns Our Genes?

There are few better examples of the power of the new economy than genetics. DNA was first isolated in 1869 by Johann Miescher, a Swiss biochemist working with pus-saturated bandages at the university hospital in Tübingen in Germany. DNA was virtually neglected for 70 years, but in a period of 15 years, while the rest of the world was distracted by the Second World War and the triumph of radar and the atomic bomb, molecular biologists laid the foundations for modern genetics. In the next century, genetics will overshadow physics in its social and commercial significance. This period of intense scientific inventiveness culminated in 1953, when James Watson and Francis Crick announced that the molecule of DNA – deoxyribonucleic acid – was a double helix. The helix, however, is less interesting than the links that hold the two spirals together. These links, like steps on a spiral staircase, are formed from four chemicals: adenine (A), guanine (G), cytosine (C) and thymine (T). A, C, G, T are the letters of the genetic alphabet which the computers at the Sanger institute tap out each night like a genetic morse code. The particular sequence of these letters determines our genetic inheritance. Thus genetic analysis is known as gene-sequencing.

It was not until the 1970s that the next big steps were made. In 1970 Hamilton Smith, a US scientist, discovered an enzyme which was like a molecular pair of scissors: it could recognize a sequence of DNA and then cut it at the same place every time. That opened the way to create strings of the same sequence of DNA that would be long enough to allow experimentation. That allowed a British scientist, Fred Sanger, to discover a way to read the code of A, C, G and T. In the early 1980s, scientists realized that variations in this code between individuals also helped to explain their suscepti-bility to disease. In 1983, a group led by an American, Nancy Wexler, showed that Huntington's disease, a fatal brain disorder, was due to an inherited defect in the fourth of our forty-six chromo-somes. The discovery allowed predictive testing and a decade later the gene in question was isolated and replicated for study. In 1986 the gene which, when damaged, is responsible for Duchenne Muscular Dystrophy was identified; the one for cystic fibrosis, in 1989. Hardly a month goes by without a geneticist claiming some new breakthrough.

This effort to unravel our genetic inheritance is a huge collective achievement, driven by a highly competitive scientific community. Most of the research has been publicly funded. The inquiry has proceeded by scientists sharing their findings and techniques. In 1990 James Watson extended the appealing metaphor of the double helix. 'I have come to see DNA as the common thread that runs through all of us on the planet Earth,' Watson said. 'The Human Genome Project is not about one gene or another, one disease or another. It is about the thread that binds us all.'

Yet this explosion of genetic knowledge also creates huge opportunities for people to make money by exploiting their know-how. The case for the commercial exploitation of biotechnology is persuasive. It would be a huge mistake to give the job of exploiting this knowledge to government, which has neither the skills nor the incentives to spread innovations efficiently. Private companies will do the job much more efficiently and creatively. The job of turning a genetic discovery into a treatment for a disease is time-consuming and costly. Innovators should be given some incentives and rewards for success. Since the late 1970s the biotechnology industry has grown fastest in the US, not just because the US is home to most of the research and the richest venture capitalists, but because the US has allowed companies to own patents on genes. This appears to have been a deliberate act of industrial policy. Ownership has been its main tool.

In 1980, the US Supreme Court overturned decades of legal precedents that said that naturally occurring phenomena, such as bacteria, could not be patented because they were discoveries rather than inventions. Yet that year the Court decided that a biologist called Chakrabarty could patent a hybridized bacteria because 'his discovery was his handiwork, not that of nature'. A majority of the judges reiterated that 'a new mineral discovered in the earth or a new plant discovered in the wild is not patentable'. Yet they believed that Chakrabarty had concocted something new, thanks to his ingenuity. Even Chakrabarty was surprised. He had simply cultured different strains of bacteria together in the belief that they would exchange genetic material in a laboratory soup. The embryonic biotechnology industry used the case to argue that patents should be issued on genes, proteins and other materials of commercial value. By the late 1980s, the US patent office had embarked on a far-reaching change of policy to propel the US industry forward, routinely issuing patents on products of nature, including genes, fragments of genes, sequences of genes and human proteins. In 1987, for example, Genetics Institute Inc., was awarded a patent on erythropoietin, a protein of 165 amino acids which stimulates the production of red blood cells. It did not claim to have invented the protein; it had extracted small amounts of the naturally occurring substance from thousands of gallons of urine. Erythropoietin is now a multi-billion-dollar-a-year treatment.

The industry's case is that innovation prospers when it is rewarded. Without rewards, innovation will not take place. The barriers to entry in biotechnology are relatively low. Biotechnology companies do not have to build costly factories or high-street retail outlets. The basic units of production are bacteria manipulated to deliver therapeutically and commercially valuable substances. Without the protection of a patent, an innovative biotechnology company would find its discoveries quickly copied and ripped off by later entrants. If ownership of the right to exploit a genetic discovery were left unclear, there would be far less innovation in the economy as a whole. We would all be worse off. The US biotechnology industry is much larger than anywhere else because innovators there have been allowed to patent their 'inventions'. In 1998 there were almost 1,500 patents claiming rights to exploit human gene sequences.

The ownership regime for industries and products spawned by genetics is far from settled. Critics of a purely private-sector approach appeal to a linked set of moral, practical and economic arguments in support of their case against private exploitation. The moral case was put most powerfully by religious leaders. In May 1995, a group of 200 religious leaders, representing eighty faiths, gathered in Washington, DC to call for a moratorium on the patenting of genes and genetically engineered creatures. They said: 'We are disturbed by the US Patent Office's recent decision to patent body parts and genetically engineered animals. We believe that humans and animals are creations of God, not humans, and as such should not be patented as human inventions.' This point of view is not confined to the religious. A deeply ingrained assumption in our culture is that patents establish a moral claim that someone should own an idea because he invented it. Yet even the biotechnology industry does not claim to have invented its products, merely to have discovered and engineered them. These patents offend deeply held assumptions about the moral rights of ownership and authorship.

The practical argument is about what should be owned: the gene itself or the treatments. Most people would regard a drug developed from knowledge of a gene sequence as a patentable invention. Far more problematic is the right to own the gene itself. The cystic-fibrosis gene, for example, is patented and anyone who makes or uses a diagnostic kit that uses knowledge of the gene sequence has to pay royalties to the patent holder. This is surely too broad a patent. It is not so much a patent as a monopoly franchise. Innovation is spurred by competition and people may well be put off developing competing treatments for cystic fibrosis by the rents they would have to pay the monopolist. The patent system is creating a series of genetic monopolies when it should be promoting innovation and competition. We should encourage patenting of biotechnology products and treatments but not genes: they are social products, which should be socially owned.

The moral and economic cases against a purely private-sector-led approach converge. The argument was made most powerfully in 1994 by Pope John Paul II, who hailed progress in genetics but warned, in terms reminiscent of the Christian socialists: 'We rejoice that numerous researchers have refused to allow discoveries made about the genome to be patented. Since the human body is not an object that can be disposed of at will, the results of research should be made available to the whole scientific community and cannot be the property of a small group.' Patents create strong incentives for private companies to protect and exploit the knowledge they control, without disclosing it. That undermines the equally important incentive to share knowledge in pursuit of scientific inquiry. We are lucky that Watson and Crick did not work for Genentech or Glaxo-Wellcome because every genetic researcher would now be paying them a royalty to use their discovery. Genetics, like most sciences, is built on a bedrock of shared knowledge. The more basic the knowledge the more inappropriate private ownership becomes.

Privatization of research may make the process of sharing research and know-how less likely. Perkin-Elmer will publish its research on the human genome but only once every three months and the company will reserve at least 300 genes for patenting. Publicly funded researchers share their results more openly and more frequently.

The science of biotechnology is inspiring. It offers us huge potential benefits. Yet central to its development will be a new political economy of ownership as well as scientific endeavour. We may never understand the science, but we need to get a better grip on the issues of who should own our genetic inheritance and how. In biotechnology, as in many other knowledge-intensive industries, we need to develop a new mixed economy which should involve creating new forms of social ownership and hybrid institutions which bring together the public and the private. The public sector plays a central role in the industry: funding much of the basic research and training; regulating consumer markets; and overseeing the patent regime. The private sector's role is also vital. Civil servants, academics and regulators will not create new products and businesses; entrepreneurs will. Yet a purely private-sector-led development of the industry would alarm many people on moral grounds and may not be efficient in the long run because it would undermine basic knowledge-sharing and research. The human genome is part of our common heritage, it is the genetic equivalent of the Great Plains of North America. We are in danger of allowing 'genetic farmers' to carve it up, laying fences across it and charging us excessively high prices for access to it. This genetic heritage does not belong to them, nor even to us. We are no more than bearers of a common stock of genetic code created by millions of years of evolution. The manufacturing industries of the twentieth century developed through the institutional innovation of the joint-stock, shareholding company. The knowledge-intensive industries of the new economy will require similarly radical innovation in the way our basic economic institutions are owned. At the heart of this will be a new constitution for the ownership of companies.

A New Constitution for the Company

The traditional idea of company ownership is a myth. All over the world, managers justify decisions on the grounds that they have to deliver value to the ultimate owners of the business, the shareholders. Yet it is difficult to work out in exactly what sense shareholders own a company. The traditional idea is that a firm is founded on a set of assets – land, raw materials, buildings and machinery – that are owned by the shareholders. These are the residual assets of the business, which would be sold if it went bust. The shareholders appoint a board of directors who appoint managers to run the business and to employ labour and other factors of production to work on the capital. A firm structured in this way runs into tricky issues about how authority can be delegated from shareholders to directors and then to managers, who need to be controlled, monitored, rewarded and held to account. All power flows down from the shareholders, in theory at least.

This account of shareholder ownership is one of the most powerful fantasies of corporate life. Yet ownership is not a simple concept. When someone owns an object – a car, for example – they can use it, stop others from using it, lend it, sell it or dispose of it. Ownership confers the right to possess, use and manage an asset, to earn income from it and to claim an increase in its capital value. Ownership also confers responsibilities on the owners to refrain from harmful use. Owners can pass on any of these rights to other people. As John Kay, the director of the Said Business School at Oxford University points out, when we say 'I own that umbrella', that usually means we can put it up, take it down, sell it, rent it or throw it away. If the umbrella was stolen we could appeal to the police and the law courts for its return. Yet it is far from clear that shareholders own a corporation in the way that you and I own our umbrellas. Take a shareholder in Microsoft. Their shareholding does not give them any right to use Microsoft assets or products. They cannot turn up in Seattle and demand admittance to the offices. Microsoft shareholders are not held accountable for its anti-competitive behaviour: the managers are. If a Microsoft shareholder went bankrupt, Microsoft assets could not be used to pay off his debts. Shareholders in Microsoft have a largely theoretical right to appoint managers to run the business. They have some claims on the company's income and capital value, but these rights are conditioned by the claims others make. Shareholders have specific claims upon the corporation which are constantly balanced against potentially competing claims made by staff, suppliers and managers. The modern corporation is shaped by a shifting balance of power between the parties who have a claim upon it.

A knowledge-based firm differs markedly, in theory and in practice, from that traditional model of the company. The core of a knowledge-based company is the know-how of the people who work there. The critical issue is how these people are combined. In its purest form – a business consultant's, for example – a know-how company is created when people pool their intangible assets, including their knowledge, expertise and customer relationships. A know-how business is created when people come together, give up their individual property rights over their work and jointly invest these rights, temporarily in the enterprise. The traditional company is based on an assertion of shareholder property rights. The know-how firm is created when property rights are pooled, by a social contract among peers, not by the top–down delegation of power from shareholders to managers. That fundamental distinction, between social contract and hierarchy, has far-reaching implications for the way that knowledge-based companies will be organized and owned.

The central issue facing a know-how firm is how to promote the co-operative pooling of knowledge: devising the social contract. In the traditional company the central issue is nominally about how much power can be delegated from the top down and how shareholders can monitor senior managers and senior managers can monitor their juniors. In the know-how firm the key issue is how to maintain a sense of membership, joint commitment and how to prevent costly defections or people free-riding on the efforts of others. A know-how company is not established upon a set of defined assets which can be clearly owned or disposed of. A know-how company is created by an agreement between people to forgo their claim upon their work for the sake of a joint enterprise. This means the question of who owns the company becomes even harder to answer. A traditional company is founded on the assertion of the shareholders' property rights. A know-how company is founded on an agreement among producers to relinquish their rights to their work and to combine together. Property rights are inherently fuzzy and shared in a know-how company.

In traditional companies, managers are the shareholders' agents on earth. In a know-how company, the managers have to earn respect and authority on their ability to promote co-operation and collaboration among the providers of know-how. Managers in a know-how firm have to be collaborative leaders who gain their authority by their ability to devise, revise and enforce the social contract, in order to maximize the returns to the combined knowledge of the partners in the enterprise. When managers fail they will suffer defections, free-riders and declining co-operation. In a know-how company, decisions need to made by the people who have the relevant knowledge, rather than the appropriate people within a hierarchy. This implies a much more distributed, networked structure and style in know-how firms, where power – and responsibility – should go with know-how rather than with hierarchy.

This contrast between the traditional firm and the know-how firm is a caricature. The real world is nowhere near so cut and dried. Most companies will be an uncomfortable mixture of these two models. What does this mean for the ownership of companies in the future?

As economies become more knowledge-intensive, there will be more know-how-based companies, owned through social contracts between knowledge workers rather than by traditional shareholders. Partnerships and employee ownership will become more common. Knowledge assets often reside in, or stem from, people. People cannot be owned, unless we return to a form of slavery. Companies cannot own the source of one of their most important assets: human capital. Companies will have to develop innovative ways to involve workers, the providers of knowledge capital, with opportunities to share in the financial wealth they create.

It is difficult to convert traditional, hierarchical organizations into free-wheeling, knowledge-creating partnerships. In traditional companies change will be evolutionary. These large organizations need a measure of structure and hierarchy to work efficiently. Global companies, operating in global-product markets, will need large financial resources to compete. Knowledge capital on its own will not be enough. It has to be combined with financial resources to count. Most companies will find themselves in this middle ground. If they were designed to satisfy the interests of knowledge workers, they would not deliver the financial performance to succeed. If they were organized as machines to deliver shareholder value, they would not encourage the innovation they need to renew themselves. The task for companies will be to develop ownership structures which dynamically combine knowledge capital and financial capital. This tension between financial and knowledge capital underlies Goldman Sachs' debate in 1998 about turning its partnership into a public limited company. Those in Goldman Sachs that wanted the change argued that the partnership structure constrained the company's ability to raise financial capital, weakened its balance sheet and undermined its ability to compete with better-capitalized competitors. Those partners that did not want to become a public limited company argued that the partnership made Goldman Sachs uniquely able to attract and motivate the brightest and the best, because the partnership was designed to reward knowledge capitalists.

Most managers, in most companies, are searching for structures which combine financial and knowledge capital. They will manage neither pure know-how companies, nor traditional hierarchical companies, but hybrids. The most creative and successful companies will be combinations of intellectual and financial capital.

Social Ownership: the New Case

The rise of the knowledge economy will encourage hybrid ownership which combines public and private. In the 1980s, neo-classical economics swept all before it, largely thanks to a central insight about ownership: when there are many buyers and sellers of ordinary traded goods, such as cars and hi-fi systems, open markets combined with strong property rights are the most efficient way to organize the economy. If producers have clear, strong rights to their property, they will have an incentive to make the most of what they own. In the 1980s not only did private ownership and the market win out over public ownership and state planning, but a particular form of private ownership, the public limited company, became dominant. It would be stupid to ignore the good reasons why the public limited company has emerged triumphant. Private ownership creates a set of incentives for managers that should promote efficiency. Tinkering with ownership in the economy would be hugely controversial for any government and yield dubious economic benefits. Public ownership was a rallying cry for socialists, in the early part of the twentieth century, when the economy was largely nationally regulated and owned. These days most large companies are international in their operations and ownership. Taking them into public ownership would be enormously contentious, not to say costly.

Changes to the distribution of ownership are blunt tools for redistributing income and wealth; tax changes would be far more effective. Employee share ownership is far riskier than traditional pooled schemes as a form of saving, for example.

The knowledge economy may require a quite different mix of property rights and ownership forms throughout society. Private ownership may not be the more efficient way for large swathes of a knowledge economy to be owned. Large advances in economic growth are due to the discovery of 'non-rival goods', products which can be used simultaneously by many people, possibly millions, without anyone being worse off. Knowledge makes us better-off not just because it can be shared and spread so easily.

To improve living standards an economy needs to be good at producing non-rival goods which can spread valuable knowledge quickly. How should such an economy be organized? Here is the rub for conventional economics: market exchange and private property are not the ideal way to produce such goods and so they will not necessarily be the best institutions to promote economic growth in future. Markets and private property are a good way to organize an economy largely made up of physical objects. They may not be the best way to organize an economy driven by knowledge.

When an economy is largely made up of ordinary rival goods, the most efficient way to organize it is for many self-interested buyers and sellers to be brought together in decentralized markets which recognize property rights. The case for strong private property rights is best made by considering what the world would look like without them: chaotic and a lot poorer. The classic case is the 'tragedy of the commons': a piece of land which no one owns nor has a responsibility to look after will be over-used and under-invested in. The case for strong private property rights might be fine for an agrarian economy, in which land was the vital resource, or even an industrial economy, which used large quantities of raw materials to produce consumer goods. But this approach will fare less well for the twenty-first-century economy built on non-rival goods such as knowledge. Non-rival goods are hard to measure and hard to control. Once a piece of software is published it can used over and again, replicated at virtually zero cost. Non-rival goods, especially those that embody fundamental advances in knowledge, are often jointly and incrementally produced by teams of people.

Some intangible goods can be protected by traditional property rights. A satellite television broadcast of a football game is a non-rival good: I could tap into my neighbour's satellite receiver and watch the game without diminishing his enjoyment. That is why satellite broadcasters such as BSkyB put so much effort into encrypting and protecting their broadcasts. Musical recording and videos are more difficult to protect from illegal copying. The principles behind chemical engineering or the window-based graphical user interface for computer programmes, are more difficult to protect. Companies with strong private property rights are not the best way to produce these fundamental knowledge goods. Imagine for a moment that Bell Labs had been given a non-expiring, iron-clad patent on the discovery of the transistor, that meant that it could charge anyone a fee for using its design. (As it was, the company was required to allow wide use of the patent.) Prices would have been higher, but in addition the rate of discovery would have been markedly slower because this fundamental knowledge would have been controlled by a monopoly.

Public ownership of basic inventions may be no better. They could lead to a lot of wasted effort and misuse of knowledge by unscrupulous, incompetent or corrupt bureaucrats and politicians. So we may need an entirely new system to produce and own the most basic knowledge goods of the economy. Private property and state ownership may have provided viable alternatives for an industrial economy in which the basic goods were iron, coal and steel. In the knowledge economy we will need hybrid organizations to combine the skills of the private sector in dissemination and exploitation of knowledge with the public sector's ability to spread and share basic knowledge broadly.

The old capitalism triumphed over socialism in large part because it was founded on strong property rights (combined with and protected by the institutions of liberal democracy). The new capitalism, the knowledge economy, will be driven by the discovery and distribution of non-rival intangible goods – information and knowledge – created by largely intangible assets – human and social capital. These knowledge goods are best produced through collaboration and competition, partnerships and networks which bring together the public and private. The old capitalism was founded on strong property rights, the new capitalism will be founded on fuzzy, pooled property rights. The new economy will only come to life with new forms of ownership.

CHAPTER FIFTEEN FINANCING SOCIAL CAPITAL

Financiers in the City of London do not find it difficult to create sophisticated financial products, like derivatives, options and swaps, which are traded in billions of pounds a day. Why do these financiers find it so hard to come up with ways to lend a few hundred pounds to poor people with no credit rating, or a few thousand to budding entrepreneurs with no track record in business? If Long Term Capital Management, the hedge fund, can lose hundreds of millions of dollars and be bailed out by government, why is it so hard to channel money, through the financial system, to the poorest parts of our society?

Popular development banks in India and Latin America do it, involving hundreds of thousands of lenders and borrowers in vast schemes of self-help. In the US and Ireland, credit unions, mutually owned savings-and-loan organizations, play such a role. To fully realize its potential, a knowledge economy has to be inclusive. It has to draw in people and ideas from all social settings. To invest in human capital we have to invest in the social capital of our most disadvantaged communities. What would it take for the UK to develop an approach which shifted more of our social spending, on benefits and subsidies, into social investment, to create lasting social capital?

A place to start is Shorebank, one of the most impressive community banks in the world, based in Chicago, which has broken through the superficial and outmoded divide between charity and commerce, social purpose and profits. Shorebank invests in social-capital creation and by doing that well it makes a financial return to compare with any bank in the US. Shorebank's remarkable story began in 1973 when four Chicago bankers who had specialized in community-development banking decided to buy the ailing South

Shore Bank, the last bank in one of Chicago's poorest areas. South Shore Bank served a community of about 80,000 mainly African-Americans. It was trying to leave the neighbourhood. Ron Grzywinski and three partners bought the bank, with $800,000 of equity and a $2.5-million loan.

Their colleagues thought they were mad. Commercial life was draining from South Shore. Grzywinski explained:

> We viewed a disinvested community as a failing market. Capital was flowing out of the area. Homes were falling into disrepair. Property values were falling. Store-owners were quitting. Community residents saw fewer opportunities for work and improvement and so stopped investing in education and work skills. Revitalizing such a community requires recognition that disinvestment is a market phenomenon and consequently, can only be reversed by reinvigorating local markets. Permanent, self-sustaining community renewal results from creating an environment in which private investors inside and outside the community are confident that their investments will be rewarded as healthy community dynamics are restored.

That is what Grzywinski and his team set out to achieve in South Shore.

They started with five core principles. First, they believed that most people in distressed communities like South Shore wanted to improve their lives. They had the same aspirations as everyone else. They lacked conventional collateral or credit histories, but they were creditworthy. Second, renewal would only be self-sustaining if it were supported in a disciplined and business-like fashion. Charity would not work in the long run. Third, local markets for jobs, property and retailers could only be restored if there were strong, local institutions. Fourth, communities declined through a complex, compounded process which required an equally complex and comprehensive response. Renewal needed to be holistic, improving the apartments people lived in, the stores they shopped in, the quality of their schools and transport. Fifth, revitalization needs to be focused on a defined area with potential to create a self-sustaining cycle of renewal.

Grzywinski is not a conventional banker. During the 1960s, when he set up one of the most successful minority-community lending programmes in Chicago, he realized that banks could become commercially successful by becoming community institutions. At just the time when many commercial banks were heading in the opposite direction, leaving distressed districts, Grzywinski realized there was a huge opportunity to be successful by moving into such neighbourhoods, with a different kind of banking. Banks were seen as legitimate, trustworthy and strong, in communities where pretty much everything else seemed to be collapsing. Through its lending a bank could become highly knowledgeable about the state of a community: spotting opportunities, sharing ideas, bringing people together. Grzywinski's idea was that a bank should be a community broker, bringing lenders and borrowers together to find mutually beneficial opportunities which have a social and a financial pay-off. Of course, that was easier said than done, which is where Jim Bringley came in.

Bringley was Shorebank's chief lender when the bank started up. Bringley realized that the area had two assets in abundant supply: derelict properties and people willing to put in their 'sweat equity' to refurbish the property. Bringley started small, with a programme organized with local savings-and-loans companies to lend money to people who wanted to rehabilitate 300 units scattered over the area. The scheme's success convinced Bringley to go ahead with a more ambitious programme. Largely thanks to him a 'rehab' movement was born in South Shore: a local industry, in which local people bought, renovated and sold apartment blocks to local people. The 'rehabbers', as they became known, provided the effort and skill; South Shore provided the financial capital and business advice. Local rehabbers had their ears to the ground. They could acquire run-down buildings for a good price, helped by South Shore. Many of them had jobs during the day – for example, as maintenance men for the city council – and did their rehab work at night. They were skilled at acquiring materials cheaply. Bringley realized the rehabbers could learn from one another. He offered the rehabbers the use of the bank's boardroom on a Saturday morning so they could give one another advice. The group started a cycle of learning, with the experienced rehabbers acting as mentors to novices. Bringley realized that the development movement could be a success but only if he disposed of the rules of conventional banking.

Bringley, in common with other lenders at the bank, despised paperwork and bureaucracy. He thrived on direct, intense contact with customers. Most of the people who have borrowed from Shorebank would find it difficult to get past the technical, impersonal credit checks imposed by a conventional bank. Bringley realized that each loan needed to be structured to meet the ability of the lender to pay it back. Lending to poor people is a knowledge-intensive business, which relies more on local, tacit know-how and judgement than computerized credit checks. He made judgements about the trustworthiness and intentions of people he was lending to. South Shore is lending to people most conventional commercial banks would not let through their doors. Yet less than 1 per cent of the bank's loans have turned sour. That is because South Shore realized that poor borrowers needed bespoke, handcrafted banking. The person making the loan stayed with the customer throughout the process, whereas in most banks the borrower is passed from department to department. The lender and the borrower built up a relationship, a quality almost completely absent from modern banking other than for the very rich.

Through a mixture of Grzywinski's vision, Bringley's entrepreneurship and the commitment of the rehabbers, the rehab movement took off. Without a penny of subsidy the rehabbers have provided thousands of affordable, safe, modernized properties in South Shore. Since its start more than 20 years ago, Shorebank has lent more than $500 million to rehabbers. The main residents for the apartments the rehabbers provide are single mothers with young children. These days, two loan officers are making $20-million worth of loans a year, covering more than 100 buildings in the area. As the buildings improved so the neighbourhood became more attractive. The rehabbers and the property owners become more wealthy. Rehabbing created jobs. Business started to revive as stores reopened. Family life became more stable. The community and its markets recovered in tandem.

Shorebank has since moved into mortgages and finance for new construction. The bank has expanded into thirteen other distressed areas of Chicago as well as other US cities such as Cleveland. The bank also lends to small businesses, which are often under-capitalized. In common with Silicon Valley venture capitalists, Shorebank has learned how to spot a good entrepreneur who has no track record or conventional collateral. The bank lends to an entrepreneur on the basis of his character and the projected cash-flow of a business. All the business owners Shorebank finances have to put up personal guarantees. They face financial ruin if the venture goes wrong.

To cut short a long and inspiring story, Shorebank has a capital base of $77 million, and assets of $725 million. Its total assets have grown fifteen times and total capital by ninety-five times over the past twenty-five years. Shorebank made a record profit last year of more than $5 million and its return on equity has averaged more than 25 per cent for most of the last twenty years. Last year Shorebank lent more than $61 million to thirteen distressed neighbourhoods in Chicago. And the bank has done this without calling on direct subsidies to its borrowers. Why is there no equivalent of Shorebank in the UK?

The reasons are complex. The banking industry in the UK is far more concentrated and centralized. There is less scope for local banks. The regulatory regime in the US, in particular the Community Reinvestment Act, has forced banks to think more strategically about their lending to distressed communities. Shorebank relies on local knowledge to make its lending profitable, precisely the kind of knowledge which is being cleansed from the UK banking system, driven by technology and capital ratios and automated credit checks. Yet there surely is scope in the UK for new kinds of financial institutions, which, like Shorebank, can move beyond the false dichotomy of charity and commerce. At the end of this chapter, we will come back to a proposal to create a new kind of bank: the Social Capital Bank, as a central institution in promoting social investment to create social capital.

Shorebank has shown that community development is good business. Financial and social capital can grow together, under the right conditions and in the process create human capital in the form of new skills and know-how. Shorebank's work has a wider significance because it shows how we can engage in social investment, to bring a lasting social return, rather than simply financing social spending, which provides people with a flow of benefits. Shorebank shows how social investment can help people to solve problems, rather than simply ameliorating them or processing them, which is what state social spending does too much of the time. It has done so by bringing social, financial and knowledge capital together. The other important lesson of the Shorebank model is that finance for social investment can come from many sources. Taxes and charitable donation do not exhaust the possible sources for social-capital investment. Not only do we need more innovative and imaginative ways to invest socially, we need more ingenious ways to raise funds for social investment.

The End of 'Tax and Spend'

The welfare state, designed by William Beveridge, was meant to rid us of Want, Disease, Ignorance, Squalor and Idleness. There were three main ingredients. First, a developed system of state social insurance, to protect people against the loss of earnings power: retirement pensions and unemployment benefit; disability and sickness allowances; special tax privileges and benefits for birth and marriage. Second, the creation of tax-financed health and education systems, which nationalized much of the voluntary sector and created a system that was 'free' at the point of delivery. Third, full-employment policies to put an end to idleness and create the economic basis for a healthy flow of contributions to the social-insurance fund, and a tax base to finance the new health and education systems.

Five decades later this interlocking system of welfare is collapsing, in large part because the social and economic assumptions on which it was based have fallen apart. Mass joblessness and exclusion have been a feature of our societies for almost two decades. The traditional family is no longer the dominant model, with the rise of more single and single-parent households. The proportion of elderly in the population is rising fast, beyond the capacity of the traditional social-insurance system to keep pace. Technological advances in healthcare have opened up new demands. The costs of the system are rising as its productivity continues to lag behind that of the private sector. The quality of many public institutions can create a dependency culture among recipients which disempowers them.

The case for welfare reform is irresistible and yet it is hugely controversial. Across Europe, governments are chipping away at entitlements built up since the war, in the face of fierce opposition. Virtually everyone is wrapped into the welfare state, as a recipient or contributor. The big budgets of health, social security and education are difficult to keep in check, let alone reduce. Demand-side reform, large-scale reductions in entitlements to benefits, are difficult to achieve. Most reform plans focus on the supply side: making services more efficient through measures such as contracting out and privatization. Yet even that has met with often understandable scepticism: the internal market in the health service just seems to have created more jobs for managers and administrators. People recognize the severe limitations of the traditional welfare state but fear the consequences of far-reaching reform. Most taxpayers do not want to pay more in tax but nor do they support unduly harsh policies against the poor. It is widely accepted that we need to move to a new form of social finance – other than tax or traditional social insurance – to mobilize resources for welfare. Yet coming up with a viable alternative, even in an area such as pensions, where everyone agrees it is needed, is politically controversial.

So, as a society, we are stuck. We shoulder an extremely ineffective and cumbersome welfare state, which is not good at generating a sense of social cohesion, promoting self-reliance or delivering services with an efficiency to match the private sector. We know it needs sweeping reform. Yet we fear losing our own entitlements, paying more or being accessories to policies that will punish the poor. We cannot find a way forward.

Indeed, the demands on social insurance are rising. In Germany, for example, the over-60s share of the population is forecast to rise from 21 per cent in 1998 to about 36 per cent in the year 2035. The cost of Japanese state pensions is projected to quadruple by 2030. Healthcare will be another burden as the population ages. The healthcare costs of a US citizen over the age of 65 are three times that of someone below that age. Once someone passes the age of 85, the costs triple again. In Germany, contributions to healthcare are set to rise from 12.5 per cent of gross income to 17.5 per cent at the peak of the grey wave. There is little sign that other demands upon public spending are likely to fall dramatically. Demand for education will rise. Unemployment is likely to remain a persistent problem. The implications are alarming. On current trends, healthcare could double to account for 10 per cent of American GDP by 2030. In Germany, social-security contributions could account for 30 per cent of the average employee's wage by the year 2035. The pressures to spend more on pensions, healthcare and education will rise. Yet at the same time the stable tax-paying population, in secure jobs, with good incomes, may well contract. The tax system of the old, ordered capitalism is being undermined by the new capitalism.

We are in the midst of a chronic crisis in 'tax and spend' politics. Too much social spending delivers too little lasting benefit. Our tax systems will find it increasingly difficult to raise finance to meet these growing demands. The reason we need to move beyond traditional 'tax and spend' policies is not just that they are politically unpopular. The real reason is that they are no longer sustainable. The new economy will make it far more difficult to raise money for public spending through the old tax system. Taxpayers will be increasingly unwilling to pay more in tax, or other social contributions, unless they can see lasting benefits. More social spending needs to become social investment. But that will require radical changes to the structure, culture and organization of the public sector. We need a public sector which does not just deliver social services more efficiently, but one which can create lasting social value. The tax system must become a system to finance social investment. The remainder of this chapter examines the pressures to create a new social investment system for the new economy. The next chapter explores how we can use that social investment to create lasting social value.

The Death of Tax

It used to be said that only death and taxes were certain. In future, that may be true only of death. The growth of the Internet and electronic commerce, combined with globalization of trade and production, and shifts in the job market towards self-employment and contract work, spell the end for the twentieth century's tax system. One of our most fundamental connections to government, and implicitly to one another – how we pay our taxes – is set to change for ever. Tax avoidance used to be the preserve of the rich. In the next century it will become a national pastime.

Take a step back for a moment. The most important property of a tax is that it can be collected. Taxes are charged on easy-to-observe activities. To be effective the tax system has to feed on the way an economy generates wealth. In the 990s Anglo-Saxon England had an efficient tax system, designed to pay 'Danegeld' to the invading Vikings, based on a fixed rate per 'hide', as units of land were then known. Not only was land easy to observe and record, it was also the source of income and wealth. Such a land tax made sense for a primarily agrarian society. In the 1890s, Britain was primarily a manufacturing economy. Many people were employed by large companies; taxes on their wages became feasible, thanks to the emergence of the modern corporation and its wages department. Capital and labour rather than land was the source of wealth. Estate Duty, a tax on bequests, was introduced in 1884 to rationalize capital taxes. The tax system was evolving to suit an industrialized economy.

Now look forward, not even 100 years, but ten or twenty. Perhaps 70 per cent of the British economy will be made up of services. Most of the economy's output will be immaterial. A growing share of transactions will be conducted over the Internet and will leave no physical trail. Experiments with electronic cash will be well under way. Virtual currencies, modelled on air miles and loyalty-card schemes, could be proliferating. Advances in information technology and communications will allow production to be ever more international. Capital, and skilled labour, will be more internationally mobile. At the other end of society, more people living on the margins of employment will be paid in cash; their earnings will go unrecorded. A tax system designed for an industrial world, will be outmoded by the rise of the dematerialized, new economy. Industrialization shifted the tax base from land to capital and labour. The new economy will require an equally fundamental transformation.

Our tax system, like so many other economic institutions, is designed for a post-war industrial order. Two features of that old economy which were vital to the state's ability to collect taxes are fading fast.

First, large companies, employers, building societies and banks, were akin to sub-contractors to the Inland Revenue, collecting taxes on its behalf by docking our wages and income on our savings. Most of the tax collected in the UK came through these large, intermediary organizations. This private-sector, tax-collection machine will not exist in future, in quite the same way. More employment will be in smaller companies. Between 1979 and 1997, self-employment grew from 1.9 million to 3.3 million. There were 3.7 million enterprises in the UK at the start of 1996, an increase of 1.3 million since 1980. Of these, 2.5 million had no employees. Micro-enterprises employing fewer than five people accounted for 89 per cent of all enterprises in 1994. Collecting taxes from this sea of small businesses will be increasingly costly. The line between self-employment and employment will be difficult to maintain. The Inland Revenue – a large, bureaucratic organization – was at its most effective when it was collecting taxes from other large bureaucratic organizations. It may find life harder in future.

Second, the post-war tax system was built on a stable social base: the traditional family. A variety of forces, including divorce and the rise in women's employment, is creating an increasingly diverse and individualized tax base which is more complex and costly to police. More important, the old tax system relied heavily on the very large, stable middle class created by the old capitalism. People in stable jobs, with stable incomes, were the tax system's equivalent of the agricultural plains of the US Midwest, ripe for a tax farmer to cut through with a combine harvester. This large, stable middle class is disappearing fast. Employment is becoming more insecure and uncertain. Many people in the formerly prosperous middle class have seen their incomes stagnate, in real terms, and their prospects become more uncertain.

The darkest clouds hovering over the old tax system are the globalization of trade and production, combined with the growing dematerialization of the economy. Take globalization first.

Capital and skilled labour is increasingly mobile. Financial capital, your and my savings, can be shifted within seconds around the world, often several times a day. Industrial capital is also increasingly mobile. The social, political and financial connections between a company, its historic home and its tax base are unravelling. A couple of years ago Jürgen Schremp, the chairman of Daimler Benz, warned members of the German upper house of parliament that the price of keeping the company's factories in the country would be a tax bill of zero. In the 1970s large US corporations earned only about 15 per cent of their revenues from abroad; now it's close to 50 per cent. Production networks of the kind that Nike has made famous, threaded across the world, linking sub-contractors, are also complex financial networks of transfer-pricing and tax arrangements. Globalization makes corporate tax collection vastly more complex: tax competition between countries to attract investment exerts permanent downward pressure on corporate tax rates. Skilled labour is also increasingly mobile. Swedish companies such as Ericsson recently complained to their government that high marginal tax rates were to blame for an outflow of top technologists to the US. Globalization has been eroding the tax base at least since the 1970s, when capital controls were removed. The impact of globalization will be even stronger when it is combined with the growth of electronic commerce and the rise of the intangible economy. Start by considering the impact electronic commerce, buying and selling things over the Internet, will have on taxes.

As yet, the Internet has been mainly used as a way to trade in tangible products. Instead of buying a CD or video from a shop, one can go on to the Internet and buy from an on-line mail-order service based in the US which will mail the product to the consumer. The purchase on the high street would attract VAT, the same purchase over the Internet almost certainly would not. This leakage of VAT could turn from a trickle to a torrent as more products become intangible. Computer bits and digital information, sounds and images, do not have to travel in containers or pass through ports, where they can be scrutinized by customs officers. They can be transmitted down telephone lines and by satellites, to personal computers. Increasingly our homes will be equipped to replicate software, download videos, reprint books and make compact discs. This trade will escape the tax man unless he were installed on a semi-conductor put in every computer sold in the UK, a prospect which would alarm civil libertarians.

The Internet should give many smaller traders direct access to international markets. A small record label – based in Sheffield, for instance – providing on-line music world-wide, cannot be expected to remit taxes to scores of tax authorities across the world. A growing amount of trade will be conducted over private Intranets, run by large corporations to organize their suppliers and distributors. It will be ever more difficult for the tax authorities to work out where and when these Intranet transactions take place. It is difficult to establish which country should tax an international company dealing in products that can be transmitted electronically. A consumer in Essex could download software made in Seattle, marketed via a Web-site in California, delivered by a server located in the Bahamas. Where should this transaction be taxed?

The dematerialization of trade will remove one of the tax authority's most useful cross-checks on tax assessments: inputs and outputs. Take the example of software. When a company distributes software on floppy disks, the tax authorities might check the number of blank floppy disks the company purchased as a guide to how much software it sells. But when a software programme can be downloaded in seconds over the Internet, like Adobe Acrobat or Netscape Navigator, there is no physical cross-check. Tax collection will become even tougher when money becomes electronic. At the very least, tax havens and offshore banking facilities will be used more readily in future. Tax havens, once the preserve of the rich and sophisticated, will soon be within reach for the average taxpayer armed with a personal computer and a modem. According to Jeffrey Owens, Head of the Fiscal Affairs Division of the OECD:

> Internet banking will offer simple access, 24 hours a day, low transaction costs, a degree of anonymity and immediacy of transferability of funds – all attributes which are not available today. If they can be combined with well run offshore institutions, in an environment which provides security, it can be reasonably expected that a much wider clientele will be attracted to these services than uses them today.

That is the near future. Slightly further away, but perhaps only just over the horizon, the future of money, as a form of payment, is in doubt. Tax authorities can check on reported incomes and expenditures by monitoring data on payments – for example, bank statements and cheque-stubs. That may become more difficult in future. Computers and telecommunications networks have already replaced money as the main form of payment between banks. Real-time gross-settlement systems handle wholesale payments among banks in several countries. As computers and telecommunications systems become more powerful, there is no reason why these systems should not be extended from financial markets to other companies and consumers. Using such a system, a consumer could make a transaction by transferring assets from his or her 'account' to the corresponding account of the company from whom the services were to be purchased. At the moment these two flows are separate: payments are usually made after the services have been provided. With a powerful enough computer and communications system the two flows could be simultaneous. The finance director of British Airways would click an icon on his computer screen and assets would be automatically transferred from a low-tax savings base into the UK, to be switched in an instant into the electronic accounts of his employees. The employees may well have computers clever enough to automatically transfer some of these assets back into offshore tax havens. In a world where high-street banks, money and paper still loom large, transactions such as this are not hard to track. In future, the audit trails may disappear into cyberspace.

Our industrial-age tax system is clearly in trouble. The question is, how much trouble? On the face of it the tax authorities do not seem to find it difficult to collect more taxes. Taxes accounted for 38 per cent of GDP among OECD countries in 1996, up from 34 per cent in 1980. The theoretical threats to the tax system from electronic commerce pale, compared with the massive expansion of the tax system, and the public sector it funds, in the twentieth century. Yet even if electronic commerce, social change and new technology only eat away at the margins of the tax system, the impact could be considerable. The public sector finds it difficult to respond to change because so much spending goes on programmes politicians are committed to. France collects about 50 per cent of its GDP in taxes. If it were to lose about 10 per cent of that, about 5 per cent of GDP, the French budget deficit would have to double to fund public services or, to keep public spending stable, funding for health would be halved. California, home to the digital economy and the Proposition 13 tax revolt, offers a glimpse of one possible future. California's higher-education system, the knowledge base for its booming economy, is severely under-funded. On current trends, there will be a $6 billion-a-year shortfall in the state's university funding by the year 2015. California is prospering because it is drawing on the infrastructure of universities, roads and schools, built in the two decades after the Second World War, using tax dollars collected by the old tax system from the old tax base. But the state is not renewing these assets. California's tax base is dominated by older, white, voters whose incomes have stagnated in the last few years, while most of the recipients of public services are poor, young and often angry minorities. Silicon Valley has created thousands of millionaires but the Californian tax revolt of the 1980s, which put a cap on property taxes, means councils in the area cannot fund improvements in education, the environment, transport and housing.

An Intelligent Tax System

Five principles should govern a twenty-first-century system for raising funds for social investment.

First, the system must be able to adapt at the speed of the society around it. One of the biggest problems with public spending is how hard it is to break or renegotiate past commitments, on pensions, social-security benefits and welfare. Programmes become defended by clientele and constituencies, which means they can continue to have a life long beyond their usefulness. One reason why the welfare state is under such pressure is that the public sector finds it difficult to adapt at the speed of the society around it. A new system of social finance must be quicker to adapt to new sources of revenue and new needs for investment. That may well mean devolving power to put more tax and investment decisions into the hands of individuals, towns and regions.

Second, the social-investment system must be capable of matching the diversity of the needs it serves, with finance from different sources. The financing must be matched to the activity that is being financed. In the case of pensions, that should mean moving towards a system in which pensions are funded from income from investment, rather than by transferring resources from one group of the population to another. The kinds of taxes we will pay in the future will be quite different. For example, taxes for education might be organized quite differently from taxes for general government expenditure. One could imagine the introduction of a variety of tax covenants or temporary and local taxes, with a limited life, designed to fund a specific set of projects – for example, improvements to school or transport. And as the Shorebank example showed, it is possible to leverage private investment into social welfare, with the state playing a background role. As society becomes more diverse and differentiated in its needs, so will the system for funding social welfare and insuring people against risks.

Third, the scale of the challenge posed by the ageing population, the rising demand for education, and growing inequality, means we require a society-wide response. A modernized system for raising finance needs to mobilize very large resources.

Fourth, for that reason, any new system cannot be entirely privatized or entirely dependent upon self-help. It will require public and political leadership to be legitimate and to include everyone. Private-sector solutions – for example, in pensions – run the risk that people will choose to under-fund their pensions in the expectation that the state will eventually help them out anyway. To avoid this and to deliver the degree of organization necessary for an insurance scheme to work properly, the state will have to be involved. While the private sector could play a much more significant role in the welfare systems of the future, the regulation and oversight of markets for welfare will always have a political ingredient.

Fifth, developed countries are not just facing a tax revolt but a service revolt as well. People are more willing to fund public services if they can see a tangible, lasting return from their investment.

What would a system formed around those guiding principles look like, in the conditions set by the new economy?

Mobile, intangible assets, products and people will be harder to tax than immobile, physical ones. As a result, taxes on corporations, capital and savings are likely to yield less and less. This is the extension of a long-run trend. Before the Second World War, federal corporation tax in the US provided a third of tax revenues. These days it is down to about 12 per cent. It is almost certain that corporation taxes in Europe will be collected by the EU and allocated on a quota system to individual member states in an effort to overcome tax competition between different countries. This is how states levy corporate taxes in the US. Mervyn King, deputy governor of the Bank of England, in a 1996 speech on the future of tax, warned policy-makers that the effective tax on income from capital was heading towards zero. If taxes on company profits, dividends and savings are going to yield less, the slack will have to be taken up by taxes on income from labour, consumption, or entirely new taxes.

As far as income tax is concerned, the most mobile, skilled workers will be attracted by low taxes and high rewards. One option would be to swim with this tide, by cutting top tax rates in the hope of attracting footloose brainpower to the UK. The burden of income tax would fall on those who are easiest to tax: immobile people, in regular employment, which means the moderately skilled people who make up the reasonably educated middle classes. They would find themselves paying proportionately more of their income in taxes than more mobile, skilled people but with no guarantee that they would get better public services in return. A different approach would be to make Britain's income-tax system more progressive, but to offer internationally mobile workers other attractions, like vastly enhanced, zero-tax equity-option schemes, higher investment in research to attract scientists, safer streets and an improved environment.

To prevent tax systems being held to ransom by highly mobile factors of production and people, it is likely that governments will turn, on economic and environmental grounds, to consumption taxes. The trouble is that, in future, more consumption will be organized over the Internet in ways that may escape sales taxes such as VAT. One response, suggested by Luc Soete of the University of Maastricht, and chair of an EU commission of experts on the social impact of information technology, would be to impose a 'bit-tax' on the transmission of digital data. Such a tax would raise a lot of money. Elio di Rupo, the Belgian telecommunications minister, estimates 10 sextillion bits are transmitted in and out of Belgium a year. A tax of 1 cent per bit would yield $10 billion, about 4 per cent of Belgian GDP. The cost would be that such a tax would depress and distort Internet commerce. Consumption and energy taxes will become more important in the twenty-first century and companies such as AT&T and Microsoft will be essential to the collection of these taxes. Of course, technology will be only part of the tax regimes of the twenty-first century. Politics will be at least as important.

Tax-raising will require greater political ingenuity. Hypothecation – taxes specially designated for a particular purpose, such as pre-school education – will become much more common. Non-tax ways of raising and spending public revenues – such as the Lottery – will become more common. Another might be the growing use of 'tax convenants' which link a specific tax on specific people or companies to specific projects. For example a regional government might persuade a group of local companies to pay a higher corporate-tax rate for a specific period, in exchange for specified improvements to the local schools and transport system. It is possible to take this idea of 'tax covenants' even further by applying it to individuals. It should be possible to devise a tax-and-benefits system in which people could sign up to different options over and above their basic taxes. Local councils already adopt a similar approach to housing estates whereby tenants are offered different levels of service, depending on the amount of rent they are willing to pay. It should be possible to offer pensioners and parents for example, different levels of service depending on how much they are prepared to put into the system. Consumers are used to being provided with greater choice and individualization. To remain legitimate in such a society, the tax system will also have to become more open to individualization. What might this mean at a national level?

Imagine a society in which all welfare was organized by five to ten mutually owned, consumer-controlled, welfare providers. These welfare providers would be independent of the state, but awarded a contract by the government to run the whole gamut of welfare services, from unemployment benefits to pensions. At the age of 18, one would sign up to join one of these large mutual organizations. The competition to run one of these franchises would create a spur to innovation. Good performance would be rewarded: customers would drift towards the more efficient and effective services. The public comparisons between the performance of the different welfare providers would help highlight good and bad practice, creating pressure on poor performers to improve. Welfare consumers would have a choice. Some of the welfare organizations would provide perhaps low benefits for low contributions. Others would provide a different mix, with more education and less health. Others could provide you with German levels of taxes and benefit. The entire system would be overseen by government, which would regulate the welfare market to make sure that no one slipped through the net and the poorest contributors were properly provided for. The great welfare bureaucracy of the state would be broken up. The case for greater diversity and choice in welfare provision will grow.

Put the argument a different way. We are able to buy German cars, with German engineering, at German prices, if we want. Why shouldn't we be able to opt into German levels of tax and benefit if we want to? Within the European single market, twelve governments provide a range of different packages of taxes and benefit. Why shouldn't there be a similar degree of choice and differentiation within a single state such as the UK?

That is not, in any sense, a plea for more privatization. These welfare bodies would be mutually owned by their members and consumers. They would be new national organizations of self-help. It is an argument for a new constitution for the welfare state, in which the state plays a strong, strategic and regulatory role, with a large role for modernized mutual organizations and collective self-help. The success of Shorebank, remember, came from a mixture of local self-help, a strong commercial institution and a background of federal guarantees for loans which helped Shorebank to minimize the risk of its small-business lending, for example. This is the kind of mixed economy of welfare – state, mutual and commercial – which we need to encourage, to tap into different sources of finance and to earn a higher return from our social investment. Modernized forms of mutual organizations, in which people provide one another with mutual help and aid, already play an important and growing role in housing, crime prevention, education and savings. What we need in welfare are more hybrid organizations, in strong, structured national bodies which can account for finance and regulation, combined with local bodies which are capable of acting entrepreneurially to use local knowledge to create lasting social capital.

A central ingredient in this new mixed economy of welfare should be a new kind of financial institution, known as a Social Capital

Bank. A Social Capital Bank would operate a venture-capital fund for social improvement by investing in social projects with the aim of making a commercial rate of return. Its aim would be to set in motion the virtuous circle of social and financial capital that Shorebank created in Chicago. A Social Capital Bank would be run as a bank, to make money. It could take in deposits and lend money. It would raise money from shareholders and investors – in particular, mainstream commercial banks – to lend in distressed areas. The Social Capital Bank would invest in specific localities, with the aim of making a commercial return from social ventures aimed at property renewal, retail development, small businesses or public-facilities management. The borrowers would be like the borrowers in Shorebank: poor people, with few conventional assets but a lot of sweat equity and determination. The government would be a regulator and help to minimize the risk to the lenders. It could do this by offering to provide public funds to match the bank's investments and by providing loan guarantees to make lending less risky. In addition the government would play a critical role in encouraging the commercial banks to back and create this new breed of Social Capital Bank. This policy should proceed with the offer of a carrot followed by a stick. Banks should be offered a very modest tax inducement, for perhaps three to five years, to invest in a Social Capital Bank. Thereafter, commercial banks operating in the UK should be required to make a minimum investment, perhaps 1 per cent of their turnover per year, in Social Capital Banks. An initial aim might be to license fifteen Social Capital Banks in cities across the UK, with the aim of allowing the best to develop and spread to other cities.

It is not enough for a modern welfare state simply to be more efficient, leaner and meaner. Efficiency does not create lasting social capital. That task – creating social capital from thin air – is the one to which we now turn.

CHAPTER SIXTEEN CREATING SOCIAL CAPITAL

West Walker primary school was almost on its knees when Norma Redfearn arrived as headmistress in June 1986. West Walker is on the outskirts of Newcastle upon Tyne, in an area badly hit by unemployment, poverty and dereliction. The shipyards that once sustained the community are long gone. When Norma Redfearn arrived she found a demoralized community, heavily dependent upon the state, with low expectations and few ambitions. Many of the parents with children at the school were unemployed, lone mothers. Few had fond memories of school; most had left with no qualifications. The school was in dire straits. It had been designed to take 250 children, but due to falling school rolls it had just 143 pupils. Only six of its eighteen classrooms were occupied. Had the number of pupils fallen any further the school might have closed. About three-quarters of the pupils were on free school meals. As Norma Redfearn recalled: 'There were no churches, no factories and no work. The school was about the only place for people to come to get together. If it had closed there would have been nothing.'

Soon after she arrived Norma Redfearn set in train a process which has transformed the school. The educational achievements have been impressive: attendance has improved as have scores in national tests. The school is over-subscribed. Norma Redfearn quickly realized that to educate the children she had to engage the dispirited parents, and to engage the parents she had to reinvent the role of the school. West Walker has become a better school only because Norma Redfearn and her team have turned it into much more than a school: it has become a focal point for communal renewal at the heart of initiatives to improve health, housing, the environment and employment in the area. Norma Redfearn is a new model head-teacher. She has generated additional social value by managing the public assets under her control far more effectively. She is a civic entrepreneur.

Norma Redfearn began by talking to parents over a cup of coffee in the morning. It was the first time anyone had asked them what they wanted from the school. Their first priority was to do something about the barren windswept playground, which was so unpleasant that many children spent most winter playtimes huddled in doorways. Redfearn contacted a group of community architects, who worked intensively with parents and children to turn a muddy field into an award-winning play-park. This was tangible evidence for parents that by working together, with allies, they could make their school better. Staff from the architectural workshop facilitated an away-day at which teachers and parents talked about what they wanted to change at the school. That initial meeting created a consensus and sense of commitment. One priority was to make better use of the empty classrooms, which left the school prey to vandalism and budget cuts. Redfearn, the parents and staff drew up a plan to turn the classrooms into a 'community wing', to provide parents with classes while their children were at school. The plans were blocked for almost eighteen months by the local-authority education department. Eventually, with the help of local councillors who sat on the school's board of governors, the school used money from the council leisure department to develop the community wing. This has drawn parents into the educational life of the school alongside their children. The traditional educational activities of the school are enveloped by a wide array of community activities, which have in turn mobilized local support for the school.

A café, funded by local companies, runs a breakfast club, attended by thirty to forty children, which provides a free breakfast between 8.20a.m. and 8.55a.m. with fresh orange juice, cereal, toast, tea and hot chocolate for any child at the school. Before the breakfast club was created, many children were arriving at school without having had anything to eat. The club has improved the school's attendance record. Norma Redfearn says: 'You cannot hope to teach children if they are hungry. To give them a chance to learn you have to make sure they are properly fed.' About fifty children attend a homework club after school. The community wing comprises a library for the parents, a computer room for children and parents and a training room for classes such as assertiveness-training, sewing and keep-fit; it also conducts empathy and counselling courses, where parents learn about parenting skills. The community wing has become a home to other services, which are becoming more closely integrated with education. The school hosts the warden who looks after the urban park which runs along the Tyne, and a social worker who works with lone mothers, many of whom suffered abuse and severe deprivation as children. By being in the school, she is that much closer to the women she is working with. Mothers at the school have created a small business, running a crèche, which employs about fourteen mothers. A group of parents who met while creating an environmental garden at the school, went on to set up a housing association which has built an estate of new homes opposite the school. According to Norma Redfearn:

> There is nothing in this that does not come from the parents. Unemployment had created an area in which they were used to other people doing things for them: the government, the council, the social services. It had bred a passivity that was undermining. There was a culture of blaming it on other people, waiting for other people to come up with the money or the answers. It wasn't just economically and socially deprived, it was inward-looking. The community did not have wide horizons; the poorer it got, the more it turned in on itself. That is what we have to change. Not just how children are educated but how the community sees itself.

West Walker has done more than become more efficient at delivering a service. It has created a new kind of organization, a new kind of school. Norma Redfearn is a knowledge entrepreneur, working in the public sector. And she is not alone. Throughout the public sector a new breed of managers are emerging who understand that their job is to generate more value from the public assets they are stewards of. The public sector does not need more restructuring or rationalization; it needs reviving and renewing. That means more than running the public-sector machine faster to deliver more output from fewer resources. The problem is not just that the public sector is inefficient. The problem is that it does not produce enough value; it seems to consume resources, not replenish them. The public sector will only start to generate more value on the public's behalf when it becomes better able to learn, adapt and innovate.

The public sector is a vital part of the new economy. The public sector produces some of the intangible goods that we value most highly: public health, safe streets, a clean environment, educated children. The public sector owns substantial physical assets – roads, hospitals and schools – but many of its most valuable assets are intangible. We trust the public sector to store great repositories of information about ourselves, the raw materials of the information economy. The Inland Revenue, the National Health Service and car-insurance agencies are the richest databases in the economy. Much of the public sector's work is processing information. The public sector is a significant investor in the knowledge economy, particularly through its investments in education. Even though many people disdain public services, it has created some of the most valuable brands: the Bank of England, the National Health Service, the BBC.

The intangibility of the public services used to be seen as one of their great weaknesses. Public services were seen as occasionally adding to, sometimes serving, but most often feeding upon, a real, wealth-creating economy based around manufacturing. That demarcation line between the real, private-sector economy and the ephemeral, parasitic public sector is being erased. The real, wealth-creating economy is dematerializing. The private and public sectors are increasingly using the same sorts of intangible inputs – people, knowledge, ideas, information – to generate intangible outputs – services and know-how. The private and public sectors face many similar problems.

Large organizations in both the public and private sectors have found it difficult to learn about and respond to change. The NHS is full of wasteful bureaucracy, but so too are Philips and IBM. Not only does the public sector find it difficult to learn from the outside; it finds it difficult to learn from itself its own best practice. The popular criticism of the public sector is that it is hidebound by rules that enforce uniformity. The reality is that the public sector is bedevilled by wide disparities in performance – often wider than within the private sector – between the best and the worst schools, hospitals and police forces. The real problem with the public sector is not that every service is the same, but that there is no discipline to make sure the worst learns from the best. The regulations which wrap themselves like bindweed around the public sector do not impose uniformity or ensure equitable treatment; nor do they create incentives for innovation and experimentation.

The most admired private-sector companies – British Airways, Intel, Hewlett Packard – innovate to create new products, markets and industries. Traditionally public-sector organizations have done the opposite: they have held on to old ways of doing things until they were so clearly obsolete that they were doing harm, and only then – often in the face of a crisis – have they begun the painful process of developing alternatives. The pharmaceuticals industry is driven forward in part by heavy spending on research and development to create new products; the public sector has no R&D budget to speak of, it does not consciously invest to create the organizations of the future. The biotechnology and software industries have been driven forward by dynamic entrepreneurial companies working at the fringe of the industry. In contrast the public sector is largely made up of large organizations, with no entrepreneurial, creative wing to develop innovative new products. In short, the public sector finds adapting to change so hard because so little is invested in creating new ideas, organizational models and services. Most public-sector organizations were designed to deliver public services on a large scale, honestly, fairly, and with a modicum of efficiency. But that is not good enough in a world which is changing as fast as ours.

Public organizations were designed as bureaucracies to process large numbers of cases in identical ways. Their audit trails were designed to prevent fraud but in the process they suppressed experimentation and risk-taking. These organizations are divided into professionally dominated departments with activity concentrated into narrow specialisms, with little cross-fertilization of ideas or practices. Public organizations generally have heavy-handed management systems which provide limited autonomy or personal responsibility for front-line staff. These constraints make it difficult for the public sector to learn.

The public sector has undergone dramatic change in the past two decades. The Conservatives shook up public provision through compulsory competitive tendering, privatization, restructuring and the introduction of business-like management methods. Challenged to become more efficient, to produce more 'output' from finite resources, most public-sector organizations have responded. Management systems and training programmes have been introduced. Public organizations now go in for strategic business planning, re-engineering, downsizing, unit-cost analysis, performance measurement and quality assurance. In many public agencies, customer service has improved. Many organizations are more open to partnerships, at least in name. Yet, despite these improvements, the public sector still often falls well short of its potential.

The starting point for renewing the public sector must be a renewal of its relationship with the society it serves. That in turn means focusing the public sector more on the outcomes that society wants, rather than the outputs that public-sector organizations produce or the physical assets they have at their disposal. We need to focus more on providing a better-educated society, community safety, well-being and health, rather than just on examinations, arrests made, sentences issued or hospital beds occupied. The pursuit of greater efficiency within the public sector needs to be set within a larger goal of creating a public sector which is more effective in helping to prevent and solve complex social problems. What we need is a knowledge-creating public sector.

Britain needs a public sector better able to create public value from public assets instead of consuming, spending or merely transferring resources. We still spend a lot on public services, about 43 per cent of GDP, but too much is spent processing problems rather than solving or preventing them. The public sector needs to be refounded upon a new mandate: to generate new services to create lasting public value, by helping people prevent or solve complex social problems. Alongside honest, efficient delivery of services, the public sector needs more innovation, creativity and entrepreneurship. We need a model of excellence in public services which promotes creative, ingenious problem-solving as well as the traditional virtues of honesty, fairness, efficiency and accountability. Government will only become more effective and adaptive in an era of rapid social and economic change if public employees at all levels become engaged in a continual process of renewal and innovation, driven by a mission to deliver better value to the public. The problem is that innovators in the public sector face particularly large obstacles.

Innovation requires autonomy, decentralization and risk-taking, financed by risk capital. Traditional methods of holding civil servants to account for how they spend public money stress the virtues of predictability and standardization. The neutrality of the civil service is meant to ensure that it can serve democracy, by acting faithfully for whichever government is elected. Civil servants are meant to be empty vessels, waiting for a political leader to fill them with purpose. A fair and honest civil service depends upon people following, not bending, rules. We do not want tax officials to make discretionary judgements about how much tax people should pay, or prison officers to decide when to let out criminals, or benefit officers to calculate who deserves what level of benefit. Innovation involves taking risks: trying out a new idea that might fail. That creates particular difficulties in the public sector. Even the smallest mistakes in the public sector can be magnified into an embarrassment or even a scandal. Political leaders have a much lower tolerance for failure than their counterparts in business. This aversion to risk is compounded by how long it takes for a success to deliver. The returns from innovation are long-term and may accrue to the next administration. Public servants enjoy few of the incentives of innovators in the private sector. Successful private-sector innovators make more profit or win promotion within their company. Successful innovators in the public sector, who, for instance, find a cheaper way to deliver a service, may find themselves rewarded with a lower budget or more work for the same pay. It is little wonder there is so little innovation within the public sector: the space for innovation is minimal, the costs of failure are alarming, the incentives are feeble, the personal rewards uncertain and the pay-off from success only comes in the long term.

Capping this long list of obstacles to innovation in the public sector is the lack of funding. Left-wing critics are fond of complaining that the City of London and British companies are short-termist. The worst examples of short-termism are in the public sector, where investment decisions are driven by political cycles and the power of the Treasury. Innovation in the public sector depends upon bringing together professions and agencies to jointly devise more integrated, holistic solutions to complex problems. Youth crime, for instance, can only be tackled effectively by bringing together teams from the police, probation services, schools, social services and housing. Yet there are no public-sector budgets to fund collaborative innovation. There are only departmental budgets, for departmental schemes, which encourage narrow, departmental thinking.

We can no longer afford this under-investment in public-sector innovation and renewal. We are inclined to view imagination and initiative among public-sector managers as dangerous, while we regard the same qualities among private-sector executives as essential to economic growth. By discouraging civil servants from acting entrepreneurially we deny the public sector access to the ingredient which the private sector relies upon to remain dynamic and responsive: the imagination of its managers to sense new demands, reconfigure resources to meet them and thereby create new sources of value. We need more entrepreneurs, social and civic, working within the public and voluntary sectors, whose goal is to create lasting social capital.

The Social Entrepreneur

The idea that there could be entrepreneurs in the public or voluntary sector will strike people as odd. Entrepreneurs are supposed to be buccaneering, profit-seeking businessmen, out to get filthy rich. Yet there are growing signs that an entrepreneurial generation of managers is emerging both at the grass roots of the public sector and in the third sector of voluntary and social organizations. Take, for example, the work of Andrew Mawson and his team at the Bromley by Bow Centre in London's East End.

Andrew Mawson arrived in Bromley by Bow, one of Britain's most depressed districts, in 1984, as the newly appointed minister at a United Reformed Church which was on its last legs. The church hall had a leaking roof, a central heating system that barely worked, a piano so old that the keys were stuck together and a congregation of ten elderly parishioners. Tower Hamlets is one of Britain's poorest boroughs and Bromley by Bow is one of its poorest wards. The area has been subject to repeated state-led initiatives and spending programmes. None has left much of a lasting mark. Mawson persuaded his ageing congregation that the only way the church could respond to the mounting social crisis of unemployment, illiteracy and ill-health in the neighbourhood was by putting the church's facilities at the disposal of local people. This strategy has produced a remarkable transformation. The once-cold and leaking church has been refurbished and opened out to serve as a nursery and crèche during the week and a sacramental centre at the weekend. The adjacent hall is thriving with activity, ranging from a large community-care programme to a set of artists' workshops for local people. The centre is the base for a literacy outreach programme for 300 local Bengali families. The staff, volunteers and centre members usually eat lunch in a self-financing café attached to the building. A health centre, which the centre says is the first in Britain to be owned by its patients, is about to be opened, after an investment of more than £1 million in a building designed to the highest standards. The Royal Sun Alliance insurance group is financing a £300,000, three-year project to create new ways of diverting young people away from crime. NatWest awarded the centre £220,000 for a three-year scheme to promote young local entrepreneurs. The adjacent park, which houses the centre, is being redesigned with a series of sculptures. Housing is being created for single homeless people and an enterprise centre for local businesses.

Out of nothing has emerged a thriving social centre which combines health and welfare with work and enterprise, serving young and old, black and white, pulling together resources from the local and central state, the private sector and the church. Everything has been done to the highest possible standards. The centre is driven by a powerful ethic of creativity, excellence and achievement. The Bromley by Bow Centre is an inspiring example of social entrepreneurship at its best. The centre works through people rather than structures or systems. The centre has released creative energy from people who have been written off by the state, the education system and employers. At the centre's core is the vision and commitment of a small team of driven, determined people, led by Mawson, and including his deputy, Allison Trimble, and the finance director, Donald Finlay. This full-time team had the flexibility and drive to create the sense of mission and momentum which has driven the centre's growth. However, as the centre has grown, more power has been devolved to managers of specific projects, who decide the content of the project and its day-to-day operation. Allison Trimble, the centre's chief executive, describes the approach this way:

> It's a loose-tight framework of management. Loose enough to allow
> people the freedom either to be proactive or to respond quickly to ideas
> but tight enough to offer a framework of values which contribute to
> a sense of direction. The key staff are charged with being socially
> entrepreneurial. They are employed not so much to manage projects
> but to create environments which will encourage a sense of vision and
> motivation. We spend a lot of time with project managers when they
> first start, talking and talking about the values of the centre, telling and
> re-telling the stories of how it started and grew, until the project
> managers start creating their own stories themselves.

The centre starts from its clients and their needs, rather than an
imposed idea of what they want or what it should do. As Allison
Trimble puts it:

> The reality of people's lives on these estates is too complex to legislate
> around ideology or rigid policies, and so, for instance, we do not
> exclude people from the project for racism or sexism. There is instead
> a recognition that the language of the street does not always have the
> abusive meaning interpreted by the politically correct and even when
> it is abusive the context is generally too complicated to be resolved
> simply by a policy of exclusion. We have found that excluding people
> or views simply denies the complexities of the issues.

The centre excels at setting ambitious challenges for itself and its
members, which can transform people's sense of self-confidence.
Mawson insists the centre should match the best standards in the
private sector in everything it does. The buildings are designed
and furnished to the very highest standards. The work of artists
associated with the project is used to create a cultural and imaginative atmosphere. People are encouraged to think big and aim high.
The centre's youth project does not provide a draughty hall, with
the occasional disco and game of table-tennis. It sends young people
on trips across the Sinai desert or for tea at the Ritz.

The centre's most important resources are the ideas and knowledge of its staff, helpers and users. Art plays a vital role; its influence
runs throughout the centre. Allison Trimble explained: 'We have
used the arts to set up environments which encourage contradic-
tions, allow the unexpected to flourish and force people to look again
at situations with fresh eyes.' The Centre embraces the complexity of

the community it serves. More than eighty dialects and languages are spoken within fifteen minutes' walk of the centre. A sense of belonging and cohesion can only be created from such complex ingredients through similarly complicated, overlapping negotiations between users and groups. If the centre chose to engage with the community in a sentimental, ideological, bureaucratic or compartmentalized way it would not be entrepreneurial and creative, regardless of the drive and imagination of the staff. Bromley by Bow's social entrepreneurs are relationship brokers: bringing together people to address an issue they are all concerned with but have failed to resolve. This pursuit of holistic, integrated solutions underpins the design of the centre's buildings. Spaces are kept open, to be used by different groups at the same time, so encouraging people to share and rub shoulders. Allison Trimble explains: 'We have to find ways for the tensions which arise from our diversity to become an opportunity for dialogue and understanding rather than becoming a block to communication. This encourages people to have a sense of ownership about the space and the centre, without that entailing privatization.' The management of the centre is open and informal. Trimble spends a lot of time simply wandering around the centre, talking. The high level of trust and integration means that information is readily shared and spread. That means it is easier for the senior managers to keep track of what is going on.

Bromley by Bow is an inspiring model of social-capital creation. But it also highlights the obstacles social entrepreneurs face. Can small organizations manage growth? To whom are these social entrepreneurs accountable and how? Can an organization heavily dependent on the vision and drive of a few individuals organize an orderly succession once the founders are ready to move on? Can the value of these schemes be measured in concrete terms? Can the lessons of a small scheme be spread and taken up within the public sector as a whole?

Social and Civic Entrepreneurs

To promote social entrepreneurship, within and beyond the public sector, it's first essential to work out what social entrepreneurs do and how they do it. Social entrepreneurs mobilize under-utilized resources, people and buildings written off by business or the formal education system, to meet unmet social needs. Social entrepreneurs' assets are mainly the relationships they build with their clients, staff, partners and funders. Their output is entirely intangible: goodwill, trust, self-confidence and security. Yet these are not do-gooders. They are entrepreneurs: driven, determined, ambitious and creative. Successful social entrepreneurs are good leaders. They are very good at setting a mission for an organization and mobilizing people around it. Social entrepreneurs have to be good at communicating the mission to users, staff, funders and partners. That is why they are good storytellers. Social entrepreneurs are visionary opportunists. They communicate their aims in moral terms. But they do not get hung up on plans and strategies. They are pragmatic. If an opportunity to do something useful comes along they will try to take it up, even if it does not fit their original plan.

Social entrepreneurs are great alliance builders. Their organizations are usually too poor and too frail to survive on their own resources. They can only survive by depending upon a wider network of support. Social entrepreneurs, driven by the need to address real problems, have already gone beyond the traditional divisions of left and right, market and state. Their language is caring, compassionate and moral. Yet they are highly critical of the statism of the politically correct, old left and sentimentalized versions of working-class communities. They reject the libertarian right's radical individualism. Yet they accept much of the right's critique of the way the welfare state has helped to create a dependency culture among many benefit recipients. They believe in individuals taking responsibility for shaping their lives, that welfare should be active. Entrepreneurial social organizations tend to have flat management structures. They rely on a small band of full-time staff and employ informal management styles. Social organizations are more likely to be entrepreneurial and innovative if they operate in a relatively complex and fluid environment, in which new demands and opportunities open up, and if they develop an evolving relationship with their clients. The best entrepreneurial social organizations are porous at the edges; the boundary between the organization and its users is not fixed.

Entrepreneurs in the public sector – people like Norma Redfearn – have many of these qualities but they also have distinctive skills because public-sector organizations pose particular challenges. Public organizations are usually larger than most voluntary organizations or community projects such as Bromley by Bow. Public organizations usually have statutory responsibilities and use public money, for which they are held to account. They often have a more formal governance structure than voluntary organizations, in which managers have to answer to elected members. For these reasons, entrepreneurship in the public sector must be different from entrepreneurship in business or the voluntary sector. Crucially, civic entrepreneurship in the public sector is necessarily as much about political renewal as it is about managerial change. Public organizations cannot be revitalized unless they renew their sense of purpose and that is a largely political process. Entrepreneurship requires risk-taking. In the public sector, managing those risks requires political skill and leadership. Entrepreneurship in the public sector means bringing together people and resources in new, more effective ways. Often these new collaborations can only be brokered politically. It is not a purely 'managerial' task. That is why, in the case of West Walker school, Norma Redfearn went to such lengths to win the support of parents and local political leaders.

We need a much healthier balance in the public sector, so that a far stronger, more widely spread capacity for entrepreneurship goes hand in hand with sound administration and good operational management. The best way for the public sector to become more entrepreneurial is to learn from its own best practices in entrepreneurship. There is far more entrepreneurship within the public sector than most people realize. There is a lot of latent entrepreneurship waiting to be tapped. The debate about the public sector in Britain has been befuddled by crude questions such as how large it should be. The fundamental question is not how large the state should be, but what the public sector is capable of doing. Britain needs a public sector that is much more creative and innovative, inquisitive and intelligent. That means developing an approach to the governance, funding, management and evaluation of the public sector, which promotes innovation.

National policy can spur innovation by forcing public organizations to reassess their purpose and effectiveness. Central government can lead by example, by developing a more integrated, holistic approach to policy-making, by pulling together departments into cross-functional teams to address common problems. The Downing Street Social Exclusion Unit is one example of such an integrated policy-making unit, which could be applied to other areas. These experiments could lead to an even more radical overhaul of central policy-making. If national government followed the best models available in local government, such as the councils of Kirklees, West Yorkshire and South Somerset, the role of the cabinet and government departments would be dramatically changed. One approach would be for cabinet members to be given responsibility for strategic issues and social problems which cut across departments, such as community safety, youth crime or the elderly. The minister's job would be to address a clear social need. They would call upon the resources of various 'back office' departments to bring them together to solve the problems. Ministers should be held accountable for solving problems which electors want solved, not running government departments.

The government should create a central Innovation Fund, to fund projects which cut across departmental budgets and which are difficult to finance. Every other large business in the country has a budget for innovation or research and development, why not the government itself? Such a fund could be linked to the creation of innovation zones, akin to business enterprise zones. Local authorities and partners could bid to host such zones, where the normal rules of funding and so of public accounting would be suspended to allow public bodies to find new ways of working together. This approach would be strengthened by providing more funding by bidding, along the lines of the City Challenge initiative. Central government could specify the range of issues and outcomes it wanted tackled – for instance, innovative approaches to youth crime, early release from prison, or joint initiatives between social services and health services – and seek bids from partnerships created to experiment with new solutions.

Public-sector innovation and excellence need greater explicit recognition. One option would be to create a Queen's Award for Public Excellence, to stand alongside the awards for industry and export, to recognize the achievements of the best public organizations and managers. Each government department should have a Lessons Learned unit whose only job is to find and disseminate best practice, in the UK and internationally. The US Army's system of 'after-action-reviews', and its small but highly effective central Lessons Learned unit, is one model of how a public organization can learn systematically from itself. The machinery of auditing and accounting within the public sector needs overhaul. The National Audit Office, the Audit Commission, the Office of Public Service, the Cabinet Office and the Public Accounts Committee all have important roles to play. But much of their time is take up with administration. Their aim is to prevent fraud. We need to complement that with an audit system designed to promote value-for-money by spreading best practice and good ideas.

At a local and regional level we need a range of institutions to act as public-sector venture capitalists, with the job of picking up good ideas from one school or hospital, for example, and showing how they could be applied elsewhere locally. Dorset Health Authority's role in brokering joint approaches between its general practitioners, hospitals and drugs companies is a good example of the creative role that intermediate, regional bodies can play in promoting innovation. We need a more entrepreneurial, creative middle layer in the public sector: a new breed of public-sector venture capitalists. Creating a local political system more open to innovation is vital. At the heart of this must be reforms, possibly quite radical, for example: the direct election of mayors; greater use of local hypothecated taxes and direct election of boards to oversee their use; the extension of the idea of jury service to a form of democratic service, in which citizens would sit on advisory panels. And we need to develop a new cadre of public-sector managers capable of acting entrepreneurially.

To revive the public sector by giving it entrepreneurial capabilities, the government must promote innovation, through new funding mechanisms; disseminate good innovations, and reward and recognize innovators.

Social-Capital Creation

During the heyday of the welfare state in the post-war era, the voluntary sector became the state's junior partner, complementing services provided by the public sector. There was good reason for this. Voluntary, charitable, welfare provision had not been up to the scale of the social problems created by industrialization and urbanization. State provision offered more professional, sounder management. Many on the left believed charities and voluntary organizations were antiquated organizations, remnants of an old social order which provided help motivated by pity. Yet the state has only played a central role in welfare provision in the latter two-thirds of the twentieth century. Before then, most of the most important developments in welfare provision came from the voluntary sector. One of the greatest periods of social innovation in Britain was in the twelfth and thirteenth centuries, when more than 500 voluntary hospitals were founded. In the sixteenth and seventeenth centuries, charities and voluntary organizations were one of the few stabilizing forces in a society racked by forces of instability far more powerful than in our own time: epidemics, wars, the enclosures, the growth of a landless poor. It was in this period of unprecedented social instability that charities came into their own. The end of the nineteenth century was probably the heyday of British charity and philanthropy. Many of its social organizations were formed by women excluded from business or politics. The labour movement helped to spawn friendly societies, co-operatives, and mutual-assurance schemes. By the latter years of the century, according to some surveys, donations to charity were the second-largest single expense in the average middle-class household after food. In the twentieth century, inquiries into the charitable failures of voluntary universities and hospitals high-lighted some of the financial and managerial weaknesses of the voluntary sector. The economic dislocation of mass unemployment in the 1930s, followed by the sense of solidarity and the scale of state economic organization during the Second World War, paved the way of the welfare state of Keynes and Beveridge that followed.

The future of our education, welfare, unemployment and health systems may be to recuperate in modern form this voluntary, local, mutual tradition of welfare. Social and civic entrepreneurs who create social capital are helping us to find answers to the most pressing questions our society faces: can a secular society, exposed to the rigours of the global market, based on individual choice, lacking the settled ballast of religion or traditional social hierarchy, in the midst of a global communications explosion, also foster a sense of belonging, trust, respect and cohesion?

Answer: no, not of its own accord, nor by imposition from the state. It will take a new generation of innovators, social-capital creators. As people search for ways to bring greater stability to a society that seems rootless, social and civic entrepreneurs are among a small band of people who are coming up with practical ways to build social capital. They do not retreat from the modern world into cosy nostalgia. They do not want to take us back to a supposed golden age of community. They recognize we need to start from social reality as it is now, by addressing real, messy needs. Above all, they create a sense of confidence and optimism that a modern, mobile society does not have to seem rootless and indifferent.

CHAPTER SEVENTEEN **THE POWER OF FANTASY**

The new economy seems to offer most people rather little. Society is becoming more unequal. Experience of failure is becoming widespread. More of the economy resembles Hollywood: only a handful of the hundreds of projects under development become films, only one in six films released makes money and fewer still become hits. The same odds are at work in science-based industries. Only one in 4,000 synthesized compounds ever becomes a marketable drug and only 30 per cent of those that make it to market recover their costs. The more we create new ideas and new knowledge, the more likely we are to experience failure. This rising failure rate plunges occupations and organizations into a state of constant upheaval. Nothing can be relied upon for too long. Work that can be all-consuming one minute can be gone the next, swept away by the markets, technology, downsizing and enforced downshifting. The average professional worker, equipped with a laptop, a mobile, pager and modem, can work at home and at the office, in the early morning, while on an aeroplane, in a hotel lobby, even while dropping the kids off at school. Work goes everywhere and, for those who have it, there seems to be no escape. For all the promise that we will be working for less hierarchical, more open organizations, the global economy seems to be ruled by ever larger corporations.

The combination of the scale and speed of our own ability to innovate unsettles us. Our own capacity to accelerate, our foot permanently on the pedal, seeking to do more and more with less and less time, leaves us feeling mildly hysterical. Acceleration has caused anxieties at least since the late nineteenth century, when men with flags walked in front of motor cars. It was only under pressure from the railways that the federal government took charge of time. Soon the great acceleration began. In the 1890s, critics warned that bicycle-riding would lead to an epidemic of bicycle face, a permanent disfigurement caused by pedalling into the wind at high speed. In 1899 the leisurely 3/4 time of the waltz was on its way out after Scott Joplin published the bouncy ragtime classic 'Maple Leaf Rag'. Ragtime marked the start of the acceleration of music to match the acceleration of industry: jazz was followed by boogie-woogie, rock-and-roll, disco, punk and techno (which races along at 200 beats a minute). Now we often feel tyrannized by our ability to do so much, so quickly. There is a frenzied search for time-saving devices, short cuts and, most importantly, 'quality time' with children or partners.

The impact of all this, as Richard Sennett argues in *The Corrosion of Character*, is to put more people under more pressure. Of course, it can be liberating for the small minority who can be sure of being well paid and continuously employed because of their special talents or skills. But, for most people, just getting by in a more competitive culture has become increasingly demanding and uncertain. Success in the new economy requires inner resources of confidence and resilience, that most of us lack. The solution cannot be to re-engineer ourselves to become entrepreneurs, internalizing these pressures. The most humane, democratic and in the long run efficient solution is to create more supportive yet flexible institutions which will pick us up when we fall down.

Knowledge about communications and computing, our genes and brains, the forces of nature and the origins of the universe, is erupting all around us, and yet the gleaming, new economy born by virtue of all this knowledge seems empty, lacking a soul or animating values. We have pragmatism, realism and cynicism in abundance. We need a more uplifting, utopian vision of what our society could become. Not the utopia of technology painted by the true believers that the brave new world will be created by interconnected computers and digital communications, or genetics and neurosciences. The new economy needs a mobilizing vision which must be primarily, social, cultural and political, not scientific and technological.

This is one area where the old economy still triumphs over the new: it had a more potent mass-fantasy life. Fantasies are meant to be private, something we engage in during idle moments in the bath or staring out of a train window: daydreams about winning the Lottery or getting out of the rat race, of winning awards and being fêted by colleagues. Fantasies are willed and chosen; they tell us what we yearn for, in private and public. American society is devoted to fulfilling a fantasy: the American Dream. Most nationalist movements are animated by the fantasy of a pure, untouched homeland. Thatcherism gave us a powerful mobilizing fantasy of a society that could rekindle its Victorian glory.

The old economy, for all its limitations, delivered a potent mass fantasy: if you worked hard and saved, you would be rewarded with security, a steadily rising income and a stable and settled retirement. Your living standards would improve throughout your life. This aspiration is lovingly played out in *Ethel and Ernest*, Raymond Briggs's account of his parents' marriage from the 1930s to the 1970s, which begins with his mother working as a domestic servant and ends with them as owners of a car, hi-fi, television and the trappings of modern life. Post-war societies had confidence their institutions could make this mass aspiration a reality. Judged by those standards, the new economy looks feeble. The old economy offered mass affluence, the new economy rewards an entrepreneurial élite. The old economy made everyday life better by providing the mass of people with tangible benefits: housing and transport, health and education, better kitchens and indoor bathrooms. The benefits of the new economy – an e-mail address – are more esoteric. The old economy created durable institutions, through which people combined to better themselves. The institutions of the new economy seem feeble and fragile. The new economy needs a mobilizing vision and institutions fashioned to make it real. Bit by bit, our institutions are changing through reform, reorganization and restructuring – but the process is much too slow, haphazard, and piecemeal – it must become more conscious, imaginative and radical.

A Narrative for the New Economy

Narratives provide meaning and order, two features conspicuously absent from life in the new economy. Democratic societies need an engaging and compelling account of their future that captures the popular imagination, and which people can buy into, endorsing and enacting it in their everyday lives. Powerful narratives have to be at once credible and yet novel, encouraging people to see a familiar world in a new way. Unfortunately, credibility and novelty are often at odds. The most powerful narratives for the new economy will focus simply on: the promise of science and technology (too impersonal, double-edged); the imperative of flexibility to respond to the market (too impersonal, hand-to-mouth); the salvation of community (too cloying, backward-looking); or the merits of regulation to bring markets under control (too defensive, implausible). A narrative that is going to grip the public imagination will not be about how we cut costs, make profits or compete more ferociously but about how we create value, realize potential and unlock talent, in financial, social and human terms. We need to show how societies can combine innovation and inclusion, knowledge capital and social capital, to generate lasting value.

A modern society's goal should be to maximize the production and distribution of knowledge, to combine in a single ideal democratic and economic imperatives. Societies become more democratic as people become more literate, numerate and knowledgeable, capable of making informed choices and challenging authority, so allowing them to take charge of their lives. We make ourselves better-off, as a society, by our ability to generate, store, distribute and use knowledge more effectively. Political empowerment and economic opportunity stem from the same root: the spread of knowledge. This is the core of the utopian vision of the new economy.

This is a vision we can all buy into and take action to make real, through our individual efforts in education and lifelong learning. Yet the implications extend well beyond the individual. A society organized to maximize the production and distribution of knowledge would have radically redesigned institutions and organizations, both private and public. Companies would be owned and organized very differently. The government would have to engage in more direct democracy, to involve citizens more and to innovate new services. We would have to find new ways to invest in social capital and welfare. Education would migrate throughout our culture, well beyond the Victorian-inspired classroom, and we would need quite different ways to measure economic value and understand its sources. The conventions, laws, codes and organizations we have inherited from industrial society would become redundant, irrelevant, largely washed up.

The new economy is compatible with many varieties of cultures and communities, which value different kinds of knowledge. The ideal would be a hybrid culture that mixed these two approaches: an inclusive society in which the mass of people were well educated which was also capable of radical and incremental innovation. Such a society would need effective public institutions to invest in the knowledge foundations of society, to provide the infrastructure of education, telecommunications and culture, which a dynamic learning society needs. That would have to be combined with a culture that encouraged entrepreneurship, experimentation, risk-taking and diversity. Knowledge societies must be cosmopolitan, liberal communities.

The most effective way to empower ourselves, make ourselves better-off and enrich our cultures is by organizing our lives and our societies around self-improvement and learning. That goes with the grain of change: democratization, the rise of the intangible economy and growing cultural diversity. Yet it also exposes how many of our old institutions, laws and codes need demolishing. A society built on knowledge must differ from one built on industry, labour and capital. That is why we need a new constitution for the new economy.

A New Constitution for the New Economy

A constitution embodies lasting values which help describe how a society should be organized, with a division of powers, rights and responsibilities, which explains how a social vision pays out in individual rights – for example, to a vote or a fair trial. Most importantly, it provides people with a sense of their rights and responsibilities within a wider society, with a sense of belonging, security and stability in a fluid and shifting world. Any new constitution should cover politics, welfare and economics. What follows is no more than a sketch of what would be involved.

The political constitution of the knowledge economy should have two central features. First, it must be inclusive, by extending political equality and democracy. Prejudice, snobbery and social stereotypes cut people off from their ability to make the most of their own resources. The knowledge economy carries a powerful, democratic impulse. Rewards must flow to talent, creativity and intelligence; not to birthright. Second, the political constitution must promote a knowledge-rich culture. California is home to innovators because its laws and politics are friendly to creative people with diverse lifestyles. To promote economic well-being a political constitution must foster a culture of dissent, diversity and experimentation that would directly feed knowledge-intensive industries. Narrow, nationalistic, inward-looking, conservative and moralizing cultures are a recipe for slower growth in an economy which needs a flow of new ideas. A knowledge-creating society needs a liberal, permissive political constitution which encourages experimentation, diversity and dissent.

In a knowledge society decisions should be made where the knowledge is, not where the hierarchy decides power lies. In an increasingly educated and informed society, more power should flow directly to and from the people. The knowledge society's political aspiration is to use information and communications technologies to realize the utopian goal of self-governance. Politics is an exercise in collective problem-solving. The more that a political constitution allows us to engage in that process, intelligently and effectively, the better-off we will be: this will accelerate the shift towards more direct forms of democracy, including electronic referenda, direct election of mayors, the use of citizens' juries to advise on policies, and more direct election of public officials running semi-autonomous parts of the public sector.

Nations as much as companies will need be networked and integrated. A centralized nation state which does not empower cities and regions will be at a disadvantage. A state that dissolves into a war of competing regions will lack a capacity for concerted action. The nation state will still have a role in setting standards – for instance, educational standards. Regions and cities will have to have more freedom to meet and exceed these goals, using different means. Cast your mind forward, twenty or thirty years. The citizens of that society will have the technology to allow them to vote directly on European legislation as it passes, in effect bypassing the moribund European parliament. There could be global or continent-wide votes on environmental taxes, for example. In addition it is likely that, in the UK, Scotland, Wales and the English regions will have far more developed indigenous political systems, as will large cities such as London. The constitution will be more like a constantly shifting mosaic than a set of principles written in tablets of stone.

A new welfare settlement is needed, to show how we can come together to protect one another against the risk and turbulence inherent in the new economy. The task is not simply to reform the welfare state but to create a welfare society in which the state is one player, alongside new mutual organizations, the family and the voluntary sector. The welfare constitution must be inclusive and innovative, shifting more resources from social spending to social capital creation by promoting an active form of welfare in which people are not passive recipients of benefits but active in improving their well-being. This must be founded upon a new contract with individuals, in which rights and responsibilities, entitlements and contributions go hand in hand. Delivering that will require new mutual, co-operative institutions of welfare, in which people can help one another to make contributions of time and effort to receive benefits in services and money. The future of welfare will depend on a reinvention of old traditions of mutual self-help, to re-humanize and reconnect a welfare system which has become routine and bureaucratic. The state will play a critical role in this system but as a regulator, standard setter and commissioner of services, as much as a direct provider of welfare. Above all, we need a welfare system which is focused on delivering outcomes – better health, better-educated children – rather than more outputs (more lessons) or more efficient institutions (more, better-run schools).

When the three motive forces in the new economy – financial capital, knowledge capital and social capital – are in harmony, the economy grows and society is relatively secure and stable. When they are at odds, as they have been for much of the past two decades, growth falters, as does social confidence. The most impressive societies combine innovation, economic growth and social solidarity. To deliver that combination we need an economic constitution.

The first pillar of such a constitution would be a new approach to ownership, to maximize the social and individual returns to the creators of knowledge. Within companies that would mean giving a much greater stake to employees. One possibility would be for every employee to have a right to own equity in their company and to be paid in part through equity. Another would be to require companies to put a far higher proportion of their stock, perhaps 30 per cent, into employee ownership and equity programmes. In some areas – genetics, neurosciences and genomics, for example – new forms of social ownership are needed. Fundamental knowledge and research created in universities or other publicly funded research institutes could be banked with 'knowledge capital banks', which would be charged with earning the maximum return compatible with the maximum dissemination of the knowledge. The knowledge economy should develop through a hybrid mixture of private and social ownership rights which reflect the different sources of knowledge.

In the 1980s, the new right taught a powerful but ultimately misleading lesson that price and value were one and the same. The best way to determine the value of something was to find out how much consumers would pay for it in an open market. In the knowledge economy, the role of markets as the ultimate arbiter of value will be put more into question. We are likely to see a proliferation of new measures of the value of human, environmental and social capital, which challenge traditional financial and market measures. In a knowledge-creating society, which is devoted to allowing people to make better choices about their lives, value will come in many different shapes and sizes; it will depend on our perceptions and imagination; in an intangible economy, providing information, entertainment, culture and media, growth and value are increasingly what we decide them to be.

An open innovative economy needs flexible, dynamic labour markets that create jobs and respond to change. That has to be matched by minimum standards, for wages, employment conditions, education and lifelong learning opportunities, which provide people with greater security. If an employer uses the know-how of an employee to create a product, they should have a duty to replenish that knowledge capital, through training, learning and sabbatical programmes. The employment contract needs to become akin to an investment agreement, in which the employer agrees to invest in the marketability and employability of their employee. Employees should not be paid a wage but more like a licence fee for use of an asset.

The new economy requires a new mixed economy of competition and collaboration. Competitive, open markets are the sharpest spur to innovation and productivity and the best way to reward talent and creativity. But collaboration is essential to creativity and knowledge creation. To compete more effectively, people need to collaborate more intelligently. An economy that promotes individualism will not generate the collaboration needed for sustained creativity. Public policy has to play a new role to bring the new economy to life. The job cannot be left to markets alone. The government, as a regulator, must open up markets to reward innovation and allow incumbents to be challenged. As an investor, the government must help build the generic capabilities business needs to compete but which private investment will not fully finance, including investments in education, science and research. Strong economies need deep reservoirs of know-how. Finally, the government, particularly at a regional and city level, can act as a catalyst, helping people and businesses, universities and schools, to collaborate to compete.

The critical differences between societies, in terms of growth, welfare and democratic empowerment, will be explained by their differing abilities to expand and apply their combined know-how. Future generations will not be as constrained by access to raw materials and energy but only by their inability to capitalize on their talents. Fewer and fewer men and women will have to work in hazardous conditions, mining, forging, welding, loading and shipping products. The economy will become less environmentally destructive. Yet predicting when the new economy will flower is difficult. In the late nineteenth century, inventions emerged from all over the place: the typewriter in 1874, the telephone in 1876, the internal-combustion engine and the phonograph in 1877, the electric light in 1880, the zip in 1891 and the radio in 1895. These products mesmerized people and created vast fortunes for their inventors and producers. Yet it took perhaps sixty years before the combined potential of these revolutionary inventions started to be realized thanks to the giant corporations and public-investment policies of the mid-twentieth century. It could be 2020 or 2030 before we start to reap the full benefits of the Internet and 2050 before the fruits of the current biotechnology revolution are accepted parts of daily life.

Culture – not science, technology or even economics – will determine how deeply embedded these changes become in our daily lives. The same was true of mass-produced products of the industrial economy. Economic and cultural innovation went hand in hand. Henry Ford's River Rouge plant in Detroit was in full swing as James Joyce was writing *Ulysses*, the first challenge to the orthodox novel. The first films were shown commercially in 1903, as Ezra Pound was writing his first formalist poems, marking the start of modern poetry. And in 1907 Picasso put on view perhaps the most shocking painting of the century: a portrait of three prostitutes which marked the start of cubism and modern art. Economic and scientific modernization succeeds when it is accompanied by a cultural creativity that revolutionizes the way we see the world. The future will belong to people who make scientific and technological innovations serve human needs for pleasure, entertainment and fantasy.

The Future: Tense

Societies are shaped by their distinctive tensions and conflicts: that was one of Karl Marx's lasting insights. Feudal society, according to Marx, was feudal because the tensions between master and serf were played out through a closed, hierarchical social order, not an open market. Capitalist society was capitalist because everyone was either capitalist or worker, their position determined by their role in the production of commodities for the market. We are not entering a frictionless world of abundance as the optimists of the new economy claim. The knowledge society will be shaped by the conflicts that will be distinctive to it. These will not be the class tensions of industrial society. We are moving into a post-capitalist society. But that does not mean it will be free from inequality and conflict.

One of the most powerful social groups created by the knowledge economy are so-called 'knowledge workers': mobile, skilled, affluent, independent, hard-working, ambitious, environmentally conscious, people who can trade on their skill, expertise and intellectual capital. These knowledge workers will be highly mobile. For the élite there will be a transfer market, akin to the market for sports stars. Many will be able to ply their trade across the Internet. The tension between the knowledge-rich and mobile and the knowledge-poor and immobile could become a central feature of life. The richer, more mobile parts of society will be less willing to pay tax; the more immobile will be easier to tax but relatively poorer. This tension between the mobile and immobile groups will translate into different attitudes towards nationalism and the global markets. The historic national ties between the mobile elite and the immobile are being broken. As the mobile identify more with an international class of competitors and collaborators, so their loyalty to those they leave behind may weaken. The immobile may react with a more intense identification with nationhood.

The knowledge economy, particularly as it is conveyed through the Internet, may promote a universal culture, values and sense of democratic rights. As the globalizing knowledge economy erodes cultural differences, it should undermine the basis for nationalism. It is just as likely, however, that people will seek to bolster their endangered sense of identity even more strongly in an economy in which everything, including national currencies, could disappear into thin air. Nationhood, industrialization and knowledge have long been tangled together. As Ernest Gellner argues in his *Nationalism*, industrialization created a mobile society in which old industries and occupations based on cities and regions had to give way to innovation in search of profit. Such a society had to have a common, codified national culture that would allow people to move around within a larger national market and yet still fit in. Nationalism provided the glue for industrialized societies in the nineteenth century. The knowledge economy is so wedded to change it will need strong glue to hold together. These days nationalism is dormant, flaring into life only occasionally. Yet it never goes away. The central task for most national leaders will be to negotiate their countries into a productive nationalism, one that recognizes dependency on the world market for goods and talent as well as protecting distinctive national cultures.

Attitudes towards nationalism will be shaped by another divide that will take on growing significance, between knowledge radicals and knowledge conservatives. Knowledge radicals stand for open societies prepared to engage in the diversity and experimentation that goes with radical knowledge creation. Politicians who embrace innovation and change will stand squarely in the Enlightenment tradition which puts reason and ideas at the heart of politics. Knowledge conservatives will take a much more cautious, risk-laden view of progress. Conservatives value tried and tested old knowledge and prefer a slower rate of innovation. The knowledge conservatives will come in different stripes: communitarians, new environmental romantics, authoritarian populists or, simply, traditional conservatives. Conservatives will argue that knowledge should be controlled, restrained or suppressed for the sake of some greater good, like tradition or the environment or a sense of community.

And, finally, there will be repeated disputes between knowledge producers and consumers. Knowledge producers will want to earn as much as possible from their expertise by restricting its supply through arcane procedures for training and licensing: doctors, lawyers, accountants and other traditional professions fall into this camp. Knowledge consumers will want to break up these old-fashioned monopolies, using new technology, their own know-how and the skills of para-professionals. I am very aware that the acute and chronic insecurity and inequality generated by this stage of globalization is the biggest issue for most people and that the measures proposed in this book to tackle rising inequality do not go far enough. We need to expand and improve our basic educational infrastructure to ensure equal access to a wider diversity of education and learning throughout life. We need radical measures to spread ownership of productive resources, via employee ownership and entrepreneurship, so that people have more of a chance to enjoy the wealth their talent and know-how can create. We need new forms of social ownership of knowledge, public–private partnerships, to ensure we get the best mix of incentives for people to share and exploit their knowledge. We need a welfare state that is increasingly focused on investment in social capital, to create public value and to develop people's capabilities to look after themselves. That means an accelerating shift from social spending to social investment, passive to active welfare. Above all, this book has been an attempt to argue that a revived sense of civic purpose and an ethic of collaboration will be as central as markets and competition in the knowledge era.

When financial, social and knowledge capital work in harmony, through institutions designed to reconcile their competing demands, society will be strong. When these forces are at war, society will malfunction. A society devoted to financial capitalism will be unbalanced and soulless. A society devoted to social solidarity will stagnate, lacking the dynamism of radical new ideas and the discipline of the competitive market. A society devoted solely to knowledge creation would be intelligent but poor, if it did realize the value of its know-how to the full. When these three forces of the new economy work together, they can be hugely dynamic. Too often they seem in danger either of spinning out of control or of being trapped by a society unable to stomach the institutional reforms needed to move forward. That is where we are, trapped between the gridlock of the old and the chaos of the new. As *Going on a Bear Hunt* reminds us: 'We can't go over it. We can't go under it. We'll have to go through it.'

CHAPTER EIGHTEEN A MANIFESTO FOR THE NEW ECONOMY

Let me describe a country to you. About 40 per cent of families live in homes with no running water or sanitation. People's health is so poor that 4 of every 10 volunteers for the army are rejected on grounds of ill-health. There is no national secondary education system, so it should be no surprise that most children spend less than 7 years in full-time education, only 3 in 100 children make it into secondary schools and only 1 in 100 go to university. This country spends less than 1 per cent of its gross domestic product on education, less than the average state in modern Africa.

Inequality is extreme. Four per cent of the population own 90 per cent of the wealth. More than 80 per cent of the population are property-less: they have no savings, do not own their homes, nor any consumer goods. Ten per cent of people earn so little that they cannot feed themselves. Many of those in work are domestic servants. There is no system to sustain people through unemployment, nor one to help them find jobs again. In rural towns each year, farm labourers gather in groups in the market-place wearing signs of their calling – a shepherd with a crook, a dairymaid with a milk pail – to offer themselves to employers in a ritual which goes back to the Middle Ages. Although there are railways, transport is still rudimentary. Horse-drawn carts carry almost 90 per cent of goods traffic. There are only 23,000 registered cars in a country with a population of more than 40 million. Most people do not have holidays: only a handful can afford to go abroad. Many of those that do leave are fleeing for a better life: about 300,000 people a year emigrate. Political leaders worry about a crisis of depopulation.

This country is socially backward and regressive. There is no system for compensating workers for accidents they suffer at work;

neither are there systems for providing social security and pensions. Until recently children as young as twelve worked in mines. Politically life is no better. Women do not have the vote. A clique of hereditary landowners exerts such control over politics that they can block the national budget. One of the country's leading playwrights was recently sentenced to two years' hard labour as punishment for his homosexuality.

That was Britain in the year 1900.

Just to paint that picture shows how far we have travelled in the last hundred years. After a century beset by recession and war, it is easy to underestimate the progress that has been made. In many ways our century has seen a remarkable expansion of human population, productivity, inventiveness and achievement. The most obvious measure of that progress is economic. In two years the modern world economy adds the equivalent of total world output in the year 1900. In the nineteenth century world industrial output trebled. In the twentieth century it rose thirty-five-fold. Such was the pace of change that world industrial output in the twenty years to 1973 was equivalent to total output in the previous 150 years. A much more telling measure of progress is the way we have transformed the range and richness of our experience. Our horizons and aspirations have expanded more in this century than perhaps any other. We live longer and are able to make far more of our lives, largely thanks to our ability through medicine and public health to eliminate diseases such as tuberculosis, bronchitis and pneumonia. A British male in 1900 could expect to live for forty-five years. A British boy born this week can expect to be alive close to the end of the next century. We take for granted the car and the aeroplane. But this is the first century in which we have been able to relinquish our reliance on horse-drawn transport. We can walk down our high street and arrange to travel further than the most intrepid explorer a century ago. We can pipe more entertainment at higher quality into our living rooms than the average emperor could call up at the turn of the century.

The twentieth century has transformed society, not just in Britain but increasingly globally. Agrarian-based, hierarchically governed and largely self-sufficient communities whose social structures have been legitimized by tradition and reinforced by religion are being transformed into mobile, globally interconnected, innovative, urbanized societies in which political authority rests on popular consent. It is a shift we are still coming to terms with. Our growing and systematic capacity to produce change drives our societies forward. But it also creates our most troubling dilemmas. Change and innovation bring with them upheaval. New ideas and technologies drive out the old. But people, institutions and cultures change far more slowly than ideas, technologies and products. That is why we find it so difficult to cope. Coming to terms with the disruptive consequences of our own capacity for change is perhaps the central question facing modern politics.

Why has change accelerated to such an unsettling extent? First, we invest more and more systematically to generate change. In the nineteenth century inventions were often made by chance; now we search incessantly for innovation and improvement. In the early years of the century there were perhaps 20,000 scientists and researchers in US industry; now there are more than 1.5 million. In 1900 about 80 per cent of US patents were granted to lone inventors; these days corporations, universities and charities account for the lion's share. Second, discoveries get turned into products far more quickly. The electron was discovered in Cambridge in 1897. But the electronics industry did not come into being until after the Second World War. These days it takes a few years for fundamental innovations to get translated into products people use in everyday life. Third, new products get spread more widely. It took decades for the car to become a mass consumer product. In the knowledge and service economy products are weightless. They replicate like viruses at the speed of modern computers and communications systems. That is why Internet usage is multiplying at five times the rate that television spread in the 1950s. Fourth, we encourage an appetite for novelty and change especially among young educated consumers, who want to be the authors of their lives. Fifth, change is not simply a faster version of the past. The trajectory of change has become more uncertain and unpredictable. Communications, software and genetics are being driven forward by radical and disruptive inventions which few predicted a decade ago.

Our capacity for change is as alarming as it is inspiring. Innovation and knowledge creation have allowed people more choice over lives that are richer and longer than those of our grandparents. Yet we find it hard to come to terms with the globally interdependent, mobile, fluid and inventive society we inhabit, in part because our public institutions and collective behaviour are so slow to respond. As consumers we can easily grow accustomed to e-mailing people around the world or interacting with our television. Yet many people, especially older generations, worry that young people live in an impatient and permanently depthless present, in which there is no sense of perspective and little sense of obligation. We live in a world that seems creative but anonymous, inventive but fleeting, innovative but alarming.

Looking Forward: Five Principles

The central question we face is how to unleash our potential for innovation and change while maximizing benefits and minimizing wasteful disruption. In a moment I will set out some practical proposals which the British government could enact in the next few years. But as important are the five core principles which should guide these detailed policies.

First, we must invest heavily in the creation and spread of knowledge. Knowledge has become the dynamo of economic growth through a powerful combination of complementary factors, which have come together only in the closing decades of the century: the spread of information and communications technologies; the growing productivity of scientific research; the still recent and incomplete development of mass education systems; and the emergence of more open, global markets. In an economy organized around the creation and use of knowledge everyone has a chance if they can learn, learn and learn again, from their early years to old age. In 1900 countries were held back by their lack of coal and iron ore. These days the only thing that holds us back is our own inability to make the most of our combined brainpower. The future is in our hands and heads, it does not lie buried beneath the ground. The ability to generate, apply and exploit our combined know-how is central to competitiveness in the modern economy, for teams, firms and societies.

Second, we must innovate *and* include. The ingredients of the

Silicon Valley model – fuelled by venture capital, rapid innovation, global ambitions and huge rewards – are increasingly well known, even if the recipe is difficult to follow, especially in Europe. An economy will be dynamic only if it orchestrates talent, money and ideas to rapidly open and exploit opportunities in large and growing markets. Yet Silicon Valley's downside is growing inequality and the political system's incapacity to address the most basic issues: housing, the environment, education and transport. We need a more balanced approach: a knowledge economy in which everyone has a chance to make it. The more we invest, at an earlier stage, in the talent, skills and imagination of everyone, the bigger the returns will be. That is why, in a knowledge-driven economy, economic growth and social inclusion must go hand in hand. That is why we need to: invest more in places and people left out of the new economy, create new forms of welfare to help people cope with volatility and ensure that all children, from all backgrounds, have the basic skills to make their livings. That commitment, by giving everyone a chance, has far-reaching implications for how we organize public services.

An innovative, open and entrepreneurial society is always in motion as it seeks better ways to organize itself. The trouble is that civic life and public institutions – councils and schools, health and welfare services, the civil service and parliament – upon which we rely to adjust to change are often slow to adapt. This shortcoming matters because it most affects those least able to cope. Those who are rich in know-how, contacts and finance find it relatively easy to take advantage of the opportunities of the new economy. Those who lack these assets risk being left behind. Thus, a society that seeks to innovate *and* include must be committed to profound change in its public and social institutions, in the way people learn, save, vote, pay taxes, claim welfare benefits and look after their health. We must renew and reshape old and established organizations, both public and private, with their long histories, embedded cultures and traditions resistant to change. That will require great determination to overcome the vested interests preserving these institutions as they are. Creating a sleek but fleeting Silicon Valley start-up is exciting. Transforming an old, slow-moving organization, upon which many thousands of people may rely – a social security system, a health service, a large company – is much harder grind.

Third, our goal cannot be purely economic. We will create a successful knowledge economy only if we create a society that takes a democratic approach to the spread of knowledge. We must breed an open, inquisitive, challenging, ambitious society. The spread of knowledge underpins democratic self-governance. People are better able to take command of their lives when they feel confident they can make and then act upon well-informed judgements. That is true whether you are a citizen or a consumer, a parent or a patient. Electorates and consumers are better informed and educated, largely because technology is migrating towards them, putting them in a better position to compare and contrast offers made to them, whether those offers are made by politicians or retailers. In a world of digital television and instant communications it will become increasingly difficult for a political élite to govern thanks to the ignorance of its citizenry. That is why the knowledge economy and democratic, open politics will grow together. Only democratic political systems breed the independence of spirit needed in the knowledge economy.

Our aim should be a society in which knowledge, and the power to act on it, are widely spread: distributed intelligence rather than centralized intelligence. Societies create, diffuse and use knowledge in quite different ways. In general we in the West are still wedded to a hierarchical model, in which knowledge is first created, usually by scientists and professionals, academics and other specialists, then diffused, through products, services, education or books, and finally used by passive consumers. In the twentieth century production lines for specialist knowledge have become vastly more productive. As a result, ironically, we are increasingly relatively ignorant because we depend so much on the specialist knowledge of other people, who make the products and services we use. Our house, for example, is stuffed with equipment: computers, digital television, mobile phones, freezers, microwaves. Neither I nor my wife has the slightest idea how any of this equipment works. We are made richer by our ability to remain ignorant, by trusting in the knowledge of other people. This pipeline model invites policy-makers to focus on the creation of specialist knowledge, for example by investing in universities, encouraging the growth of specialist qualifications and providing tax breaks for research and development. Specialist knowledge will remain critical to progress, for example in the creation of new genetic treatments for disease. However, this model of society driven by specialist knowledge is increasingly at odds with a more democratic model of the knowledge society.

Scientists and other specialists cannot simply lay down the law to trusting consumers. Ideas have to be explained and justified. It will become increasingly difficult to separate the creation of knowledge from how it is diffused and used. The specialist knowledge invested in genetically modified foods will be wasted unless these new products command popular assent. Specialist knowledge creation will increasingly have to work in tandem with a more democratic and open approach to spreading, verifying and developing knowledge.

Fourth, the knowledge economy creates a global agenda. If we retreated into narrow nationalism, it would be like our ancestors a century ago seeking to retreat from the cities to their country communities. The stage of global integration we have reached at the turn of the century will seem primitive to people standing in our shoes in a few decades, let alone at the end of the next century. Our task, in this generation, is not to retreat from globalization, but to create the political and regulatory institutions for a more stable, interconnected global economy. The knowledge economy goes to the heart of issues of global inequality and development. It is not a frivolous add-on. Modest improvements in our ability to diffuse tried and tested knowledge can generate huge gains in health and life chances. A study of 45 developing countries found that the average mortality rate for children under 5 was 144 per 1,000 live births when their mothers had no education, 106 per 1,000 when they had primary education only and 68 per 1,000 when they had some secondary education. A country with an income per head of $8,000 in 1950 would have had, on average, an infant mortality rate of 45 per 1,000 live births. By 1995, a country with the same real income per head would have had an infant mortality rate of 15 deaths per 1,000 live births. The drop in the mortality rate was largely due to the spread of education, which put people in a position to make better-informed choices about how to care for their children. Food production, the most basic of industries, is increasingly knowledge-driven. Between 1970 and 1994 world rice farming was made 55 per cent more productive, maize 70 per cent and wheat 95 per cent. In Asia and South America cereal yields have risen from about 1 tonne per hectare in 1950 to more than 3 tonnes in 1997. These gains have been made possible by the creation, spread and use of agricultural know-how, in the form of more disease-resistant seeds and improved farming techniques.

For many people globalization is a dirty word. The worst response would be a retreat into nationalism and protectionism. The way forward is to create a global economy which is both more inter-dependent and more stable. That will require reform to many established institutions: the IMF, the World Bank, the WTO. We also need inter-global institutions for a global knowledge economy: a World Knowledge Bank to fund young entrepreneurs in developing countries, a global education fund for poorer nations.

Fifth, there is no one best route into the knowledge economy. The old economy was dominated by the search for the 'one best way' to do things. That was the ideology of Frederick Winslow Taylor, the apostle of efficiency. His goal was optimization: to find the one best way to process steel or make a car. In a society of mass standardized products, mainly made with heavy equipment and physical processes, this fascination with finding the one best way to make a product may have made sense. Yet in a knowledge economy, driven by creativity and imagination, there is no one best way. The production of new ideas, within schools, colleges, companies and teams, can be organized in a vast array of different ways. Firms, governments and societies have a widening range of choices over how to organize themselves. This is why European societies, such as France and Germany, with strong education systems, weak entrepreneurial cultures and powerful state machines, will find a route into the new economy quite different from the silicon valley model.

However, there will be common ingredients, or at least societies will face common dilemmas. All societies will need to strike a balance between diversity and integration. Creativity stems from the interaction of a diversity of viewpoints, disciplines and outlooks, in which ideas are abducted from one area and transplanted to another. One argument for bio-diversity, for example, is that it is a unique stock of genetic knowledge. We need to value the diverse, marginal and apparently redundant who are written off by the mainstream – older workers, middle managers, ethnic minorities – because they may be the source of the most imaginative ideas. Creative societies have to be open and cosmopolitan. The fact that so much knowledge creation comes from diversity is an argument in defence of pluralism. But creative organizations – whether firms or societies – also excel at integrating knowledge. That means that convening people to collaborate and share ideas is essential. A knowledge society thus needs to be diverse and integrated at the same time. A fragmented, atomised society without the capacity for collaboration will be creative only spasmodically. The balance between trust and competition is also delicate. Sharing ideas is often impossible without high degrees of trust. However, new ideas will emerge only if old ideas can be challenged. That requires open competition. A higher rate of innovation implies a higher rate of rejection and turnover, as old ideas are thrown out or once promising ideas are rejected. But that also implies a higher rate of failure and upheaval, not just for ideas and products, but for people. Societies will differ in how they combine diversity with integration, competition with collaboration.

The Next Decade

Finally, let's get down to some specifics. What should we do in the next few years, in Britain, to create a knowledge-driven economy which is both inclusive and innovative?

Let's start with education. We have only just begun to scratch the surface of what is possible and needed in revolutionizing education. We should invest heavily in early years education. Every child up to the age of three could be assigned a Learning Visitor, a bit like a health visitor, whose job it is to help parents give young children access to opportunities to play and learn. An army of Learning Visitors on our poorer housing estates would particularly help single parents get access to shared facilities for learning. Beyond that we should create not just more nursery places but new family learning centres in which parents and young children can learn and develop together. Often the children who find it most difficult to learn are the offspring of parents who had a disastrous time at school. We need to invest in encouraging entire families to learn together. How would this be funded? By establishing a new golden rule of public investment: that investment in education should be doubled from about 4.5 per cent of gross domestic product as it stands now to about 9 per cent by 2010. Much of this extra spending could be raised by a hypothecated and time-limited education taxes, linked to structural reform in how we deliver education. What would that structural reform consist of? The agenda is virtually endless.

First, we need to make it easier for people to create and open new schools. There is massive pent-up demand for new forms of schooling, but the supply does not meet this demand because the state exerts such control over the creation of new educational institutions. Imagine a world in which every budding Internet entre-preneur had to queue at the Department of Education to win the right to launch their business. We need to make it far easier for groups of parents or teachers to start schools, which might teach a variety of curriculums and be funded through a wide variety of mechanisms. Of course that will be possible only if the national curriculum sets minimum standards. As long as a school meets those standards, we should encourage as much diversity as possible in additional teaching. Teaching of core subjects needs to be com-bined with teaching creativity and problem solving. By the year 2010, at least a third of what our children do while in education should be about creativity, problem solving, working in teams and running enterprises and projects of one kind or another. None of that will be possible unless we address whether Local Education Authorities dominated by committees, bureaucracy and party poli-tics are the right bodies to control local education. We should encourage the creation of new kinds of democratically accountable intermediaries to take over from underperforming LEAs – associ-ations created by schools, services run by charities and private companies – to provide this role. Only then will we also get the diversity of approaches to pay and reward needed to make teaching really attractive. If a junior or secondary school head teacher can create lasting social and economic value by turning around a school, they should be rewarded by being paid £80,000–£100,000 a year. We should find ways of giving public sector workers the public sector equivalent of stock options, through sabbaticals and leaves of absence, in which they could study and retrain. If a teacher in the bottom half of the league table manages to improve the performance of a class by 10 per cent in a core subject, like maths, then they and *every* other teacher in the school should get a bonus of £15,000. If the school improves its performance by more than 5 per cent across the board, it should get an extra £100 per child in funding in the following year. Teachers might be able to choose which performance-related rewards to aim for: some might choose time off, others a cash bonus, or to reinvest in school facilities. In education we have to put our money where our mouth is and challenge teachers: if you really want decent rewards you can have them if you deliver a first class education.

In further and higher education we have only just begun to realize what may be possible. Universities will be at the heart of the knowledge economy but only if they become capable of far greater dynamism and innovation. Universities are stifled by government regulation and closed academic cultures. The way forward is to largely free them from this by creating a much more open market in further education, with degree courses largely funded by income-contingent loans. That should be combined with the growth of a range of new universities, some funded by companies, others organised entirely through digital television and the Internet. Courses should become increasingly modularized, so that students can pick and mix their own courses and dip in and out of education throughout their twenties and thirties. A combination of new funding mechanisms, technologies, organizational structures and approaches to academic pay should lead to an explosion in adult learning. Why shouldn't great academic brands, like the London School of Economics, extend their scope by allowing people to study an LSE course whether they are in Scotland or South Africa? Universities as they are currently organized will not deliver the expansion of opportunity that we require.

Higher education will be an expanding global industry in the next fifty years as countries and companies set up universities to help their people upgrade their skills. The UK already has a strong position in this industry and should exploit it to the full. UK universities should be brought together with the BBC to create the largest virtual university and library in the world. The BBC is already a world leader in online education. One of the main barriers to creating a new university is the cost of setting up a library. The books alone in a decent university library probably cost close to £750,000. Our universities already have them. If we simply put all those books online we could make the UK's virtual university library available to all sorts of new universities around the world. Once we have invested the fixed cost in creating a virtual university library the marginal, additional cost of making it available to other users would be quite small. This would dramatically lower the cost of creating a university and encourage all sorts of new entrants into the industry. New universities in richer developing countries might have to pay, say, $50,000 for access to the virtual university. But the UK government could choose to give the virtual university free to the twenty poorest countries in the world. It would be the largest global give-away of knowledge the world has ever seen. It would establish Britain's reputation as a worldwide centre for learning and education. It would dramatically symbolize the UK's commitment to equality of opportunity on a global scale. By 2005 the UK should have created the largest virtual university and library in the world.

The current agenda for education – to extend nursery provision, drive up standards and widen the intake of higher education – is just a very modest beginning of what must become a much larger, more radical and imaginative revolution in what education delivers, how it is delivered, to whom and how it is paid for. At the moment we are still correcting mistakes and failings of the past; we have not begun to really create an education system for the future.

Education is the first priority; a policy for mass entrepreneurship is the second. We need to encourage everyone to feel as if they can make something of their own talent and ideas in the knowledge economy, especially the young. What might this entail? First, cut capital gains tax to 20 per cent to encourage entrepreneurs to create wealth by starting growth businesses. Second, the creation of a new kind of Knowledge Bank, which would be a public–private partnership, focused on providing seed capital for young entrepreneurs who can present a credible business plan. We need to create ways to funnel micro-credit to entrepreneurs in our poorest neighbourhoods. Third, we should reward companies which provide stock options for all employees and include measures of employee ownership, and we should make it easier for companies to issue up to 25 per cent of their stock in the form of options. Fourth, we should change pension fund legislation to make it far more attractive for pension funds to invest in venture capital.

Next, we need a far more radical reform of the public sector, to make it more able to engage in the entrepreneurship and innovation which drives the private sector. What would that mean? We should create a venture capital or innovation fund – perhaps worth £150 million to begin with – within the public sector to invest systematically in the creation of new services and the dissemination of new ideas, especially those which combine different departments. Venture capital-style investment in the public sector should match that of the private sector, as a proportion of GDP. We need to create a much more active market for money to flow to people with talent and ideas in the public sector, regardless of their rank and standing. So, for example, it should be a requirement that people going into the senior civil service should have been involved in at least one public sector start-up, that is an attempt to create a new form of organization. The public sector needs to learn from large private sector organizations which have innovated by creating 'skunk works' to come up with new ideas, internal venture capital markets, ideas fairs and smaller sub-brands and spin-offs, with a more innovative culture. And finally we need to create new rewards to recognize the role of civic entrepreneurs, not necessarily in money, but through time off for study, for example. The entire welfare system should be broken up and operated by a group of competing mutuals and social enterprises. They would be mandated to meet minimum national standards of service, but they would compete in terms of their effectiveness in getting people back to work or providing quality of service. Only through creating more competition within the public sector will taxpayers be in a position to compare the relative cost and effectiveness of different ways of delivering welfare. That in turn will drive up performance. And within the next few years we should start to make more of the public sector's vast intangible assets.

The privatization programme of the 1980s focused on the industrial economy: steel, cars, oil, gas, electricity, water. In the next ten years we could raise hundreds of millions of pounds to be ploughed back into education by seeking to extract more value from the public sector's vast stock of largely dormant intangible assets.

This New Economy privatization programme would in turn depend on the creation of public–private partnerships to exploit these assets. As a simple example take the BBC's *Top Gear* website. *Top Gear* is an outstanding brand name. Its website gets thousands of hits from fans both of cars and of the programme's former presenter, Jeremy Clarkson. At the moment the TopGear site just sells merchandise related to the programme. However, it could become Europe's leading motoring website, allowing people to trade cars, buy accessories, search for insurance deals, upgrade their in-car navigation software and the like. That would take TopGear beyond the realm of the BBC and into the much larger marketplace for e-commerce. But to do that the BBC would have to sell say 49 per cent of the TopGear Web-business to a private partner with e-commerce expertise. As a purely BBC website TopGear will be marginal to the emerging e-commerce marketplace for cars. In a public–private partnership it could be a huge commercial success. This recipe could be followed with a string of BBC websites covering food, travel, home decoration and the like. The BBC has done a brilliant job in creating some of the best websites in Europe. Even at today's depressed stock-market valuations for Internet companies, the BBC's online assets are probably worth about £8bn. If the BBC realized half of that by selling minority stakes in its online businesses to private partners, it could fund a massive expansion of its education activities.

The political process and the character of the state could, in theory, change dramatically. Over the next few years an electronic and online political world will develop alongside the physical one we inherited from the Victorians. How long will it be before we have our first online election? The technology to make online voting possible is readily available. We should set ourselves the target to make the election after next – 2007 – the first one in which people can vote electronically. And if we can vote electronically once, then we could do so over and over again, not once every five years but on legislation as it passes through the House of Commons. The House of Commons, rather like other intermediary bodies, is designed to represent large groups of people. But when technology allows people to plug into the political process directly, then Members of Parliament, like other intermediaries, such as insurance brokers and travel agents, may find themselves looking for a new role in life. When people can buy, sell, trade and invest directly using the Internet and its successors, as they will in the next five years, they will want to know why they cannot interact with the political system in the same direct way.

The Commons itself would continue to exist, perhaps mainly as a tourist attraction and symbolic font of parliamentary democracy, but much of the business of government, the largest paper-processing business in the country, could be conducted electronically. Just to give you one example of what that might mean, think about what happens when you get your next prescription from your doctor. First your doctor types into her computer and prints out a piece of paper. Then you take the paper to the chemist, who writes into her computer and prints out a label for your bottle of pills and another piece of paper which goes off to a central paper-processing unit in Newcastle. When that paper arrives in Newcastle an operator opens the envelope, takes it out and inputs the details into her computer before printing out another piece of paper which goes to the Department of Health to pay the chemist. The whole paper trail costs £40 million a year. No extra value is created and the entire procedure could be largely automated. The money saved on processing could be reinvested in services which really help consumers. Gains of that scale are available throughout the public sector.

Or take another example. The government partly funds itself by borrowing, by issuing gilts or bonds. To arrange the sale of bonds it pays middle-men in the City who find buyers. But quite soon all this could be done across the Internet. In late 1999 Pittsburgh made history by conducting the first sale of municipal bonds across the Internet. It sold $55m worth of bonds, simply by posting them on the Internet and asking investors to make bids electronically. The middle-men were cut out and the cost of public borrowing dramatically reduced. The UK Treasury should create Europe's leading e-bond market in the UK. The aim should be that most government bonds should be issued to investors over the Internet by the year 2007.

The prospects for the e-state extend well beyond simply processing information more efficiently.

The NHS Direct telephone service is moving on to the Internet. This will allow anyone, at any time of day or night, to consult a doctor, look up information and chat to other patients across the web. You will never be more than a mouse-click away from an NHS doctor. Even when you are abroad on holiday you could consult an NHS doctor via the Internet. Of course that also means that you could consult a US doctor just as easily through one of the US health advice websites that are already up and running. If you do that, why not order your pills through Drugstore.com, a US online pharmacy? If we buy books from Amazon.com why not pills from Drugstore.com?

The implications are far reaching. We need to think of health services becoming international, if not global. And as a result we will start to pay for health in a range of different ways. If we start using US-based Internet health services for advice and consultation, we will get used to paying for health advice with our American Express card. The National Health Service will no longer be purely national. Just as we can access web-based services in the US, people in Texas could log on to NHSDirect. We should aim to make NHSDirect the world's leading Internet-based health service within the next five years. The largest, most responsive and cheapest web-service for providing people with help regarding their health in the world. Rich people and rich countries that wanted to dial into NHSDirect would have to pay. But we could give free access to NHSDirect to twenty of the poorest nations in the world. It would be the biggest ever gift of health know-how. The NHS was created in 1948 as a purely national institution in a largely industrial economy. Our aim in the next decade should be to take the NHS into the knowledge economy, and that would mean taking the NHS global.

E-commerce should change the character of public services in other more prosaic ways. Take public procurement as an example. In late 1998 Ford announced it was planning to move most of its worldwide procurement, worth about $80bn, from 30,000 suppliers, on to an e-commerce platform called AutoExchange. The idea is that Ford will put out tenders for parts on to a vast electronic market place and take the lowest bids from around the world. Massive amounts of paperwork will be cut out. By shaving a little off millions of transactions, Ford hopes it will eventually save about 20 per cent from its procurement budget. The same savings in principle should be available within the public sector. The UK public sector should lead the way in creating the largest e-commerce public purchasing market in Europe.

Finally, we need a competition policy which will attack the role of vested interests and knowledge monopolists who seek to control access to know-how and skills to protect their position. Chief amongst these are the professions. In many professions – law, accounting, some aspects of medicine – it is increasingly possible for consumers, armed with computers, to work with para-professionals to help themselves. Much legal work, for example, could be done by people working with standard forms provided on the Internet. By late 1998, 6 per cent of all uncontested divorces in the UK were being completed over the Internet, only ten weeks after the service was set up. That is an indication of the potential to cut out middle-men like lawyers and make it far easier and cheaper for people to use the legal system. The online service provided by Desktop Lawyer costs just £59 compared with about £400 in a high street solicitor's office. The same goes for accounting. We should not protect the knowledge monopolies of the professions from this new competition. The Internet is ushering in a new age of self-service professionals, where people armed with computers will be able to do much of what they turned to lawyers and accountants for in the past.

There is a large potential for us to harvest the power of the knowledge economy to extend equality of opportunity, reinvigorate public services and open up politics. The implications extend well beyond the scope of this conclusion to embrace the family, tax and welfare, the environment and Europe.

Out of Thin Air . . .

As we stand at the turn of the century it is worth looking back. Many of the scientific breakthroughs that allowed huge improvements in the quality of life in the twentieth century were made in a short time either side of the turn of the last century. The X-ray was discovered in 1895, the electron in 1897, radioactivity in 1898, relativity and quantum theory came a few years later. Charles Parsons, an English entrepreneur, invented his steam turbine for electricity generation in 1897, and Rolls and Royce formed their partnership to exploit the recently developed combustion engine in 1904. The first flight from English soil took place four years later and the first rudimentary jet engine was tested in 1910.

By the end of the first decade of the twentieth century many of the basic inventions which so opened up people's lives had already been created. We are the beneficiaries of this extraordinary period of inventiveness. Had our ancestors put a man with a red flag in front of inventors to slow knowledge creation, our lives would have been impoverished. We should take note before we rush to rein in scientific curiosity. In 1899 Marconi proved to a sceptical public that a radio message could be transmitted across the English Channel. Every day millions of people still rely on his invention for news, entertainment and education. This year a young person, perhaps like Marconi an immigrant, will be working on an idea which he hopes could shape the century ahead, expanding the horizons and life chances of millions around the globe. We must not stand in his way. This book has been an imperfect attempt to sketch the forces driving the knowledge economy and some of what we would need to do to create a society that was open, entrepreneurial and inclusive. This has been no more than an incomplete sketch. A more rounded and considered picture will have to wait, but not too long for another book.

SELECT BIBLIOGRAPHY

This is not an academic book, so I have not used formal footnotes and references, in part because I think these can put off readers. Instead I have compiled a bibliography of some of the most useful and interesting books and papers which I read to research the book.

General

BOOKS

Beck, Ulrich, *The Risk Society* (Sage, London, 1992)

Buchan, James, *Frozen Desire* (Picador, London, 1997)

Coyle, Diane, *The Weightless World* (Capstone, Oxford, 1997)

Crouch, Colin, and Streeck, Wolfgang, *Political Economy of Modern Capitalism* (Sage, London, 1997)

Drucker, Peter F., *Post-Capitalist Society* (Butterworth Heinemann, Oxford, 1993)

Dyson, Esther, *Release 2.0* (Viking, London, 1997)

Frank, Robert H., and Cook, Philip J., *The Winner Take All Society* (The Free Press, New York, 1995)

Gellner, Ernest, *Nationalism* (Weidenfeld and Nicolson, London, 1997)

—*Plough, Sword and Book* (Paladin, London, 1991)

Gray, John, *False Dawn* (Granta, London, 1998)

Haack, Susan, *Evidence and Inquiry* (Blackwell, Oxford, 1995)

Haas School of Business, *Knowledge and the Firm* (*California Management Review*, Special Issue, Spring 1998, University of California, Berkeley, 1998)

Hagel, John III, and Armstrong, Arthur G., *Net Gain* (Harvard Business School Press, Boston, 1997)

Hamel, Gary, and Prahalad, C. K., *Competing for the Future* (Harvard Business School Press, Boston, 1994)

Kaku, Michio, *Visions* (Oxford University Press, 1998)

Kauffman, Stuart, *At Home in the Universe* (Penguin Books, London, 1995)

Kelly, Kevin, *New Rules for the New Economy* (Fourth Estate, London, 1998)

Landes, David, *The Wealth and Poverty of Nations* (Little, Brown, London, 1998)

Lester, Richard K., *The Productive Edge* (W. W. Norton, London, 1998)

Luttwak, Edward, *Turbo Capitalism* (Weidenfeld and Nicolson, London, 1998)

Popper, Karl R., *Conjecture and Refutations* (Routledge, London, 1963)

Rose, Jacqueline, *States of Fantasy* (Clarendon Press, Oxford, 1996)

Stewart, Thomas A., *Intellectual Capital* (Nicholas Brealey, London, 1997)

Tapscott, Don, *The Digital Economy* (McGraw Hill, New York, 1995)

ARTICLES

Cassidy, John, 'How to stop the global crash' (*New Yorker*, November 1998)

Centre for European Policy Studies Working Paper, 'Valuing Intellectual Capital' (Brussels, 1997)

Goldfinger, Charles, 'The Intangible Economy and Its Challenges' (paper presented to Business Intelligence, Knowledge Management Annual Conference, London, 25 November 1996)

Intangibles Research Project, 'Intangibles and Capital Markets: Conference Papers' (Stern School of Business, New York University, 15–16 May 1998)

Lev, Baruch, and Zarowin, Paul, 'The Boundaries of Financial Reporting and How to Extend Them' (Working Paper, Accounting and Finance Dept, Stern School of Business, New York University, 1998)

Quah, Danny, 'Increasingly Weightless Economies' (*Bank of England Quarterly Journal*, February 1997)

—'The weightless economy: Nintendo and heavy metal' (*CentrePiece*, London School of Economics, Vol. 2, Issue 1, February 1997)

—'The weightless economy: the weight of evidence' (*CentrePiece*, Vol. 2, Issue 2, Summer 1997)

Romer, Paul M., 'Beyond the Knowledge Worker' (*Worldlink*, January–February 1995)

—'Evaluating the federal role in financing health related research' (Collo-quium Paper, *Proceedings of the National Academy of Science*, Vol. 93, November 1996)

—'Implementing a National Technology Strategy with Self-Organizing Industry Investment Boards' (in Brookings Paper on Economics Activity, *Macroeconomics 2*, Brookings Institution, Washington DC, 1993)

—'In the Beginning was the Transistor' (*ASAP Forbes Magazine*, 1996)

Teece, David J., 'Innovation and Business Organisation' (Second Claren-don Lecture, 6 May 1998)

—'The Knowledge Economy and Intellectual Capital Management' (First Clarendon Lecture, 5 May 1998)

—'Technology Strategy and Public Policy: The Meaning of "Monopoly" in High Technology Industries' (Third Clarendon Lecture, 7 May 1998)

The Knowledge-Creating Company and Organizations like Brains

BOOKS

Albert, Steven, and Bradley, Keith, *Managing Knowledge* (Cambridge University Press, 1997)

Barton, Dorothy Leonard, *Wellsprings of Knowledge* (Harvard Business School Press, Boston, 1995)

Boisot, Max H., *Information Space* (Routledge, London, 1995)

Chalmers, David J., *The Conscious Mind* (Oxford University Press, 1996)

Choo, Chun Wei, *The Knowing Organisation* (Oxford University Press, 1998)

Davenport, Thomas H., and Prusak, Laurence, *Working Knowledge* (Har-vard Business School Press, Boston, 1998)

Davis, Stan, and Meyer, Christopher, *Blur* (Addison Wesley, Reading, Massachusetts, 1998)

Edvinsson, Leif, and Malone, Michael S., *Intellectual Capital* (Harper-Collins, New York, 1997)

Fruin, W. Mark, *Knowledge Works* (Oxford University Press, 1998)

Gates, Jeff, *The Ownership Solution* (Allen Lane, London, 1998)

Greenfield, Susan, *The Human Brain* (Phoenix, London, 1997)

Kao, John, *Jamming* (HarperCollins, London, 1998)

Kay, John, *Foundations of Corporate Success* (Oxford University Press, 1995)

Law, Andy, *Open Minds* (Orion Business Books, London, 1998)

Morgan, Gareth, *Images of Organisations* (Sage, London, 1996)

Nonaka, Ikujro, and Takeuchi, Hirotaka, *The Knowledge Creating Company* (Oxford University Press, 1995)

Pinker, Steven, *How the Mind Works* (Allen Lane, London, 1998)

Senge, Peter M., *The Fifth Discipline* (Century, London, 1990)

ARTICLES

Chesbrough, Henry W., and Teece, David J., 'When is Virtual Virtuous?' (*Harvard Business Review*, January–February 1996)

Hill, Charles W. L., 'Establishing a Standard: Competitive Strategy and technological standards in winner-take-all industries' (*Academy of Management Executive*, Vol. 11, No. 2, 1997)

Iansiti, Marco, and West, Jonathan, 'Technology Integration: Turning Great Research into Great Products' (*Harvard Business Review*, May–June 1997)

Liebeskin, Julia Porter, 'Knowledge, Strategy and the Theory of the Firm' (*Strategic Management Journal*, Vol. 17 (Winter Special Issue), 1996)

Miles, Raymond E. et al., 'Organising in the knowledge age: Anticipating the cellular form' (*Academy of Management Executive*, Vol. 11, No. 4, 1997)

Teece, David J., Pisano, Gary, and Shuen, Amy, 'Dynamic Capabilities and Strategic Management' (*Strategic Management Journal*, Vol. 18, No. 7, 1997)

Public Policy and the Knowledge Economy

'Collecting Tax in Cyberspace' (*Information Strategy*, June 1997)

Kay, John, 'The Economics of Intellectual Property Rights' (*International Review of Law and Economics*, 13, 1993)

King, Mervyn, 'Tax Systems in the 21st Century' (Bank of England, 1996)

'Property Rights and Entrepreneurship in Science' (*Small Business Economics* 8, 1996)

Sagoff, Mark, 'Patented Genes: An Ethical Appraisal' (*Issues in Science and Technology*, Spring 1998)

'The Tap Runs Dry: Disappearing Taxes' (*Economist*, 31 May 1997)

'What Chance for the Virtual Taxman?' (*OECD Observer*, No. 208, October/November 1997)

Wilkie, Tom, 'Lords of Creation' (*Prospect*, July 1998)

Wolfe, Tom, 'Sorry But Your Soul Just Died' (*Independent on Sunday* Review, 2 February 1997)

Intelligent Regions and Silicon Valley

Cooke, Philip, and Morgan, Kevin, *The Associational Economy* (Oxford University Press, 1998)

Henton, Douglas, Melville, John, and Walesh, Kimberly, *Grassroots Leaders for a New Economy* (Jossey-Bass, San Francisco, 1997)

Leadbeater, Charles, *Britain: The California of Europe* (Demos, London, 1997)

Saxenian, Annalee, *Regional Advantage* (Harvard University Press, Cambridge, Massachusetts, 1996)

Scott, Allen J., *Regions and the World Economy* (Oxford University Press, 1998)

The Rise of the Knowledge Entrepreneur

BOOKS

Audretsch, David B., *Innovation and Industry Evolution* (MIT Press, Cambridge, Massachusetts, 1995)

Leadbeater, Charles, and Oakley, Kate, *The Rise of the Knowledge Entrepreneur* (Demos, London, 1999)

ARTICLES

Acs, Zoltan J., and Gifford, Sharon, 'Innovation of Entrepreneurial Firms' (*Small Business Economics* 8, 1996)

Autio, Erkko, '"Atomistic" and "Systemic" Approaches to Research on New, Technology Based Firms' (*Small Business Economics* 9, 1997)

Baumol, William J., 'Entrepreneurship: Productive, Unproductive and Destructive' (*Journal of Business Venturing* 11, 1990)

Jones-Evans, Dylan, 'Technical Entrepreneurship, Strategy and Experience' (*International Small Business Journal*, 14 March 1995)

Ripsas, Sven, 'Towards an Interdisciplinary Theory of Entrepreneurship' (*Small Business Economics* 10, 1998)

'Small Firms in High Tech – A European Analysis' (*Small Business Economics* 10, 1998)

Symeonidis, George, 'Innovation, Firm Size and Market Structure' (*OECD Economic Studies*, No. 27, 1996)

Trust

Fukuyama, Francis, *Trust: The Social Virtues* (Hamish Hamilton, London, 1995)

Hollis, Martin, *Trust Within Reason* (Cambridge University Press, 1998)

Kramer, Roberick, and Tyler, Tom R., eds., *Trust in Organisations* (Sage, London, 1996)

Lane, Christel, and Bachmann, Reinhard, *Trust Within and Between Organisations* (Oxford University Press, 1998)

Misztal, Barbara A., *Trust in Modern Societies* (Polity Press, Cambridge, 1996)

Rechheld, Frederick F., *The Loyalty Effect* (Harvard Business School Press, Boston, 1996)

Ridley, Matt, *The Origins of Virtue* (Viking, London, 1996)

Seligman, Adam B., *The Problem of Trust* (Princeton University Press, Princeton, New Jersey, 1997)

The Knowledge-Creating Public Sector

Altshuler, Alan A., and Benn, Robert D., eds., *Innovation in American Government* (Brookings Institution Press, Washington DC, 1997)

Leadbeater, Charles, *The Rise of the Social Entrepreneur* (Demos, London, 1997)

—and Goss, Sue, *Civic Entrepreneurship* (Demos, London, 1998)

Moore, Mark H., *Creating Public Value* (Harvard University Press, Cambridge, Massachusetts, 1995)

Networks and Social Capital

Burt, Ronald S., *Structural Holes: The Social Structure of Competition* (Harvard University Press, Cambridge, Massachusetts, 1992)

Castells, Manuel, *The Rise of the Network Society* (Blackwell, Oxford, 1998)

Ebers, Mark, ed., *The Formation of Inter-Organisational Networks* (Oxford University Press, 1997)

Nohria, Nitin, and Eccles, Robert G., *Networks and Organisations* (Harvard Business School Press, Boston, 1992)

INDEX

Abraham, David, 65–6, 67
Adobe, 83–4, 105
Advanced Rendering Technologies, 97
Amaze, 101–2
American Airlines, 73
Apple computer company, 105
ARM semi-conductors, 97, 136
Arrow, Kenneth, 151
Arthur, Brian, 62–3
assets see intangible assets; tangible assets
Audi, 146
Audretsch, David, *Innovation and Industry Evolution*, 104, 106
authority, respect for, 74–5, 107

background trust, 161, 165–6
Baldrige, Malcolm, 102
Balfour Act (1902), 110
bank lending, 116
  for social capital, 183–8, 200–1
banks
  branch networks, 22–3
  and Internet, 194
Barton, Dorothy Leonard, *Wellsprings of Knowledge*, 53, 77
BBC, brand name, 51
  and online education, 243
  websites, 245
Bellhouse, Brian, 94–7
Bellhouse, Elspeth, 94, 96
Bentley, Tom, *Learning Beyond the Classroom*, 110
Beveridge, William, 188
biotechnology industry, 47, 50, 172
  collaboration in, 14, 132–3
  knowledge base, 50
Blair, Tony, 16, 149–50
BMW, 44, 161
Boisjoly, Roger, 71–2
Bosch, 146, 147
brain, human, as network, 88–9
branding, 20, 22, 34, 43, 71

and market value, 78, 118
  in public sector, 51
  and trust, 152, 161
  for universities, 113–14
Bretton Woods system, 3, 7
Bringley, Jim, Shorebank, 185–6
Britain, in 1900, 232–3
British Airways, 130
British Biotech, 116
Broers, Sir Alec, 14
Bromley by Bow Centre, 209–12
BSE crisis, 122, 155
Bush, George, Jr., 16
business skills, need for, 101
Butler Education Act (1944), 110

California
  culture and politics of, 107, 224
  economic strength, 140, 143
  education system, 41, 109, 144, 195–6
  taxation levels, 143–4, 195–6
  see also Silicon Valley
Cambridge Display Technologies, 97, 136
Carlsson, Chester, 104–5
celebrity, cult of, 12–13, 19–21
cellular self-management, 80–1, 82
Challenger space shuttle disaster (1986), 71–2
Chapchall, Danny, 97
chemical industry, 34–5
Chiat Day, 65–6
Chiat, Jay, 66
Chicago, community banking, 183–8
China, 44–5, 60, 120, 161
China, Ancient, 108
Cisco Systems, 76
cities, power of, 13, 145
Clarkson, Jeremy, 245
Clinton, Bill, 16
closed trust, 165–6
CMG, self-organization in, 81–2

collaboration, 10, 11, 226, 227
  in science, 13–14
  and trust, 167
collaborative leadership, 85–6
collaborative networks, 130–1, 132–3
communications, 20
  and co-ordination, 134–5
communitarianism, 15–16, 107
  and trust, 150–1, 155–6
community
  and schools, 203–4
  and social entrepreneurship, 209–12
community banking, 184–7
companies, 102–5
  collaborative networks, 131–2, 135
  confluence of flows, 70–1
  global consolidation, 60–1
  joint-ventures and alliances, 128–9
  market-to-book ratios, 46–7
  nature of new, 62–4, 134–6, 178–9
  networked, 61–2, 124–9
  and outsourcing, 129–30
  ownership of, 66–8, 176–9
  and tax collection, 191–2, 197–8
  traditional, 4, 58–9, 64, 69, 87–8
  and trust, 157, 165–6
  value of unlearning, 79–80
  see also institutions; knowledge-creating
    companies; organizations
competition, 45, 48, 227, 240
  and risk, 123
competition policy, 115–21, 248
complementary products, 132
complementary skills, 106
computer industry, 76
computers
  personal, 105
  spread of, 41–2, 131–2
  vulnerability of, 119–20
consciousness, nature of, 89–90
consensus, and innovation, 146
consumers, 46, 230
  direct sales to, 22–3
  as joint-producers, 25–6, 32–3
consumption, nature of, 24–5
consumption taxes (VAT), 193, 198
contracts, 227
  as basis of trust, 162–3
cookery knowledge, 30–2
corporate networks, 128–9
corporations see companies
cottage industries, pre-industrial, 55
creative failure, 77–8
creativity, 72
  rewards for, 224
  and trust, 152–3

Crick, Francis, 171
cultural entrepreneurs, 49
culture
  challenges to, 52, 228, 229
  trust across boundaries of, 157

Daimler-Benz, 146, 147, 192–3
Darwin, Charles, 90
Davies, Philip, 97
DEC, rejection of Intel, 105
Dell Computer Corporation, 100
Dell, Michael, 100
democracy, xi, 222, 223
  radical, 167–8, 216
Dennett, Daniel, 89
Denso, 137
Department of Health, 246
dependent trust, 158
development banks, 183
development costs, 31–2
Diana, Princess of Wales, 18–22, 25–7
directness, power of, 22
dissent, for radical innovation, 107, 146
distributed intelligence, 88, 90, 91–2
diversity, for radical innovation, 107,
    239–40
DNA analysis, 39, 41, 169, 171–2
double-entry book-keeping, 117–18
Drayson, Paul, 93–7
dualism, of mind and body, 90

economic growth, 7
  organization of, 180–2
economy
  constitution for new, 225–8
  networked, 114, 124–6
  see also knowledge economy
education, 108–14, 230, 232, 238–9
  community integration in, 203–4
  financing, 188, 196–7
  investment in, 40–1, 49, 52, 240–4
  structural reform, 241–4
efficiency, 69
  of knowledge transmission, 30–1, 33
egalitarianism, in companies, 82
elections, online, 245–6
electronic bond market, 246–7
electronic commerce, 247–8
  and taxes, 193–5
Ellison, Larry, 143
EMI, and CT scanner, 131
employee ownership, 65, 66–8, 81–2, 178
employment policies, 115, 188, 189
  see also labour
Enlightenment, tradition of, 230
entrepreneurs, 93–8

defined, 98–101
and risk, 99–100
see also knowledge entrepreneurs; social
  entrepreneurs; Internet entrepreneurs
entrepreneurship
  encouraging, 243–4
  in Britain, 106
  in organizations, 82–3, 105
equity pay, 68, 83–4
ethical dilemmas, 52
  genetic engineering, 121–3
Etzioni, Amitai, 15, 107, 150
Europe, company valuation, 47
European Union, 7, 197, 224, 248
explicit knowledge, 28–9, 72–3
  see also tacit knowledge
explicit trust, 158–9

failure, 106, 219
  creative, 77–8
Fairchild Semiconductor, 142
families, and learning policy, 109–14
family model, 188
fantasy, 220–1
Federal Express, 100
Ferguson, Sarah, 21
finance capital *see* community banking;
  venture capital
finance capitalism, 5–8, 225, 226
  and globalization, 192–3
financial accounting, 117–18
financial flow, 70
financial markets, 3, 5–8, 24
  in intellectual capital, 118–19
financial services, 22–3, 49
  see also banks
flexibility, 61–2
Ford Motor Company, 37–8
Fukuyama, Francis, Trust, 150
Fung, Victor, 124, 125, 126

Gates, Bill, 32, 98, 105
genetic research, 39–40, 50
  ethical dilemmas, 121–3
  and ownership rights over knowledge,
    171–5
  see also biotechnology industry
Gennen, Harold, of ITT, 58
Germany, 11, 35, 109, 148
  Baden-Württemberg region, 146–8
  nature of trust in, 161, 165–6
  social costs, 147, 189–90
Geschke, Dr Charles, 83
globalization, xi, 7, 60, 144–5, 192,
  233–4
  effect on tax system, 192–3

and intangible assets, 44–5
and nationalism, 229
Goldman Sachs, 179
goods, rival and non-rival, 29–30, 180–1
Gray, John, 15, 107, 150
Great Britain, 77, 106, 187
  collapse of corporate model, 59–60
  education and training, 40, 51–2
Grzywinski, Ron, Shorebank, 184–6

Hamel, Gary and C.K. Prahalad,
    Competing for the Future, 123
health services, 216
  financing, 189
Hewlett Packard, 49, 76, 77, 80, 161
hierarchies, 57–8, 61
  and big corporations, 58–9, 178
  limitations of, 59, 153
Hobsbawm, Eric, 39
Hoff, Ted, 105
Hong Kong, 125
House of Commons, 246
Human Genome Project, 169
Hutton, Will, 15, 150
hypothecated taxes, 199, 216

IBM, 41–2, 79
  and Microsoft, 59, 105
ideas, 70–1, 77, 238
identity, 52, 156
Illich, Ivan, 112
increasing returns, 26–7
  and trust, 159
incremental innovation, 50, 54, 71–5
  combined with radical, 78–9
  consensus and, 109, 146
India, 60, 183
individualism, and trust, 167
Industrial Revolution, x, 134
  Second, 35
industry
  knowledge content of, 38–9
  mass-production, 55–7
  traditional, 47–8
inequality, x, 11–13, 167, 219, 230, 236
information, 29, 51, 126
  efficient use of, 42–3
  shared, 164
  see also knowledge
information technology, 39, 41
  tax on, 198
information warfare, 119–20
Inland Revenue, 191–2, 205
innovation, 10, 47, 114–21, 227–8,
    234–5, 249
  in large companies, 102–4

innovation – *cont.*
  in public sector, 206–9
  rewards for, 173
  as threatening, 79–80, 235
  and trust, 166
  units of, 141–2
  see also incremental innovation; radical
    innovation
Innovation Fund, proposed central, 215,
  244
insecurity, ix, 157, 230
  in new organizations, 63–4
  social, 217, 221
insider trading, 116
institutions
  need to reconstitute, 4, 147, 221
  outmoded, 3, 27, 52
  Victorian innovation in, x, 4–5, 54
  see also organizations
insurance companies, 22, 48, 122
intangible assets, 14, 18, 101, 117, 181
  importance of, 44, 45–6
  market price of, 78–9, 118
  and public sector provision, 205–6, 244–5
  see also branding
integration, 85, 135–6
Intel, 49, 79, 105, 142, 159, 161
intelligence
  and distribution, 88, 90, 91–2
  nature of, 88–90
internalization, of knowledge, 29, 73
International Monetary fund, 7
international trade, liberalization, 44–5
Internet, 23, 39, 140, 234
  and tax collection, 191, 193–4, 198–9
  and trusted third parties, 163
  entrepreneurs, 241
investment
  inward, 114–15
  state, 40, 196–7, 227
Italy, 11
ITT, management principles, 58

Japan, 11, 37, 75, 109, 114
  computer industry, 76, 77
  and corporate organization, 58–9,
    72–3, 77
  nature of trust in, 159, 160, 161, 162–3,
    165, 167
  reliance on tacit knowledge, 74–5
Jobs, Steve, 105
John Moores University (Liverpool),
  101–2
John Paul II, Pope, 174
Joint Venture Silicon Valley initiative, 144
joint-stock companies, 4

joint-ventures, 13, 60, 128, 160–1
Jospin, Lionel, 16
J.P. Morgan investment bank, 129

Kaku, Michio, 39
Kay, John, 176
Keynes, John Maynard, 7–8, 99
Kirzner, Israel, *Discovery and the
  Capitalist Process*, 100
Knight, Frank, *Risk, Uncertainty and
  Profit*, 99–100
know-how
  as competitive advantage, 101
  importance to companies, 47, 69–70
  protection from imitation, 70–1, 181
  variations in application of, 49–50
knowledge
  company reservoirs of, 70, 84
  creation and spread of, 16–17, 29, 230,
    237–8
  and economic growth, ix, xi
  incremental creation of, 71–5
  in manufacturing networks, 126
  ownership of, 169–70, 180–1
  radical creation of, 76–9
  and risk, 123
  see also explicit knowledge; innovation;
    tacit knowledge
Knowledge Bank, 243
knowledge capitalism, 9–10, 225, 226
knowledge economy
  arrival of, 227–8
  constitution for, 223–8
  entrepreneurs for, 97
  global agenda, 238
  investment in, 235–6
  narrative for, 221–3
  ownership of, 180–2
  risk in, 63–4
  tensions and conflicts in, 228–6
knowledge entrepreneurs, 93–8
  characteristics of, 100–2
  in education, 204
  importance of, 102–5
  networks of, 106–7
knowledge push, 39–43
knowledge-creating companies
  ownership of, 177–8
  principles of, 80–6
Korea, 76

labour, 18, 226–7
  cheap, 44–5
  mobility of, 192–3
Landes, David, *The Wealth and Poverty of
  Nations*, 11–12

Lane, Christel, 165
Latin America, 5, 154, 183
Laubacher, Robert, 134–5
Law, Andy, Chiat Day, 65–6
leadership *see* management
learning, 29, 92
    families and, 109–14
    and unlearning, 79–80
Lev, Professor Baruch, 47, 103
Li Fung, Hong Kong, 124–6
Linux club, 134
local government, 215
Local Education Authorities, 241
London School of Economics, 242

McDonald's, 50, 56
Malone, Thomas W., 134–5
management, 58, 68, 85–6
    in entrepreneurial social organizations, 213–14
    of networked companies, 135–6
    of new organizations, 61–2, 65–6
    in public sector organizations, 206–7
    self-management, 80–3
    Taylor's scientific principles, 56–7
manufacturing networks, 124–6, 127–9, 130–1
Marconi, Guglielmo, 249
market economy, 14–16
    and efficiency, 180
    limitations of, 116, 126, 226
    see also knowledge economy
market pull, 43–6
marketing, 34
Marshall, Alfred, 70, 99
Marx, Karl, 99, 228
materialism, 90
Mawson, Andrew, 209–10, 211
membership, sense of, 83–4, 177
Micro Compact Car joint venture, 130
Microsoft, 26, 98, 105
Miescher, Johann, 171
Mill, John Stuart, 99, 151
Millar, Andrew, 116
MIT, 141
modification, and re-invention, 90
money, electronic, 194–5
monopoly policies, 115–21
Monsanto, 153
mortality, child, 238–9
motor industry, 37–8, 130, 131, 154–5
multi-media companies, 143
Murdoch, Rupert, 113

narrative, for new economy, 221–3
NASA, and Challenger disaster, 71–2

nation state, 145, 224–5
nationalism, 220, 229–30
NCR, 79
neo-classical economics, 99
    see also market economy
networks, 11, 114, 148
    collaborative, 131–2
    in education, 111–12
    of knowledge entrepreneurs, 106–7
    manufacturing, 124–6, 127–9, 130–1
    in new organizations, 61–2
    and relationships, 126, 137–8
    stages and transitions, 136
neuroscience, developments in, 89
New Labour, 149–50, 163, 170
NHS, 247
    as brand name, 51, 205
    see also health services
Nike, 21, 127–9
Nokia, 50–1
Nonaka, Ikijuro, and Hirotaka Takeuchi, The Knowledge Creating Company, 72–5, 92

oil prices, 6
Open University, 111
openness, 82
    and trust, 161–2, 164
Oracle, 49, 76, 143
organizations, 53, 54, 80
    bureaucracy in, 205, 206–7
    and distributed intelligence, 88–92
    and Taylorism, 55–7
outsourcing, 129–30, 157
ownership, 170, 178, 225–6, 230
    of companies, 65, 66–8, 81–2, 176–9
    of knowledge, 169–70
    of knowledge economy, 180–2
    moral rights of, 173–4
    social, 179–82, 230

Paccioli, Luca, 117–18
participatory management, 68
partnerships, 13, 101, 136, 160, 178, 230
patents, 71, 95, 132, 174–5, 181
pay, equity/stock, 68, 82
pay structure, 67–8
Penrose, Edith, 70
pensions, 188, 197
performance, improvement of, 73–4
Perkin, Will Henry, 34–5
personal contact, in networks, 144
Platt, Lewis, of Hewlett Packard, 80
political constitution, for new economy, 223–5

politics, public trust lost, 150
Popper, Karl, 77
Porsche, 146, 147
Potter, David, 97
Powell, Walter, 132, 133
PowerJect painless injection, 93, 94–7,
    136
Prahalad, C.K. see Hamel, Gary
private sector
    and scientific research, 39, 40, 174–5
    and social ownership, 179–82
profit-sharing, 83–4
property rights, 178, 179–82
Psion, 97
public policy
    and economic management, 145
    and innovation, 143
    integration in, 215
    and social investment, 196–7
public sector
    bureaucracy in, 205, 206–7
    civic entrepreneurs in, 213–14
    disparities in performance, 205–6
    and exploitation of knowledge, 170, 175
    innovation deficits, 51
    innovation in, 207–9, 215–16
    need for renewal, 204, 207, 236, 244
    and social ownership, 179–82
public trust, 85, 123, 153–5
    and transparency, 162, 163

Qualified Employee Share Ownership
    Trust (Quest), 67
Quinn, James Brian, 129

radical innovation, 48, 50, 76–9
    culture of dispute and diversity for, 146,
        166
Real Holidays, 97
recipes
    and economic theory, 34
    as knowledge transfer, 30–2
Redfearn, Norma, 202–4, 213–14
regions, and networked economies, 145–6
regulatory barriers, 128
relationships
    in entrepreneurship, 213
    in networks, 126, 137–8, 144
    and trust, 159–60
religion, and genetic patents, 173
reproduction costs, 31–2
research and development, 40, 48–9, 76,
    78, 118
responsibility, in companies, 59, 67
rewards, 21, 173, 224
Ridley, Matt, 151, 156

rights, 169–70, 223
    moral, 173–4
    see also ownership
risk, 2–3, 10–11, 99–100, 123
    aversion, 208
    globalization of, 121–2
    in new economy, 63–4, 100
    in trust, 158
Rock, Arthur, 142
Rolls-Royce brand, 44
Roman Empire, 108
Romer, Paul, 34
routine, value of, 70, 87–8
Royal Family, 18–19, 23–4, 25, 27
Russell, Bertrand, 18
Russia, 5, 161

Safeway, 42
St Luke's, 65–9
Sako, Mari, 154
Sanger, Fred, 171
Sara Lee, 129–30
Sarphie, David, 94, 95, 96
Saxby, Robin, 97
Say, Jean-Baptiste, 99
Scandinavia, trust in, 154
Schroeder, Gerhard, 16
Schumpeter, Joseph, 100, 102
science, 9–10
    collaboration in, 13–14
    and technology, 35
scientific knowledge, explosion in, 39–40,
    234
self-employment, 2–3, 192
self-governance, 224
self-help, co-operative, 134, 137, 167–8,
    225
self-interest, 15
    and trust, 167
self-management, 81–2
Seligman, Adam, The Problem of Trust,
    156
semi-conductor industry (US), 48, 142
    radical innovation in, 76–9
Sennett, Richard, 220
Seven-Eleven (Japan), 42
share options, 82
shareholder ownership, 176–9
Shockley, William, 142
Shorebank, community bank (Chicago),
    183–8, 200
short-termism, 208–9
Silicon Valley, 76, 115, 143, 144, 236
    and computer assembly, 45–6
    economic recovery, 139–40, 142–3
    knowledge base, 49–50

networked economy, 141–2, 145–6
  origins, 142–3
  social networks, 11, 146, 167
  venture capital in, 106–7, 139–40, 142–3
Smith, Adam, 99, 151
Smith, Delia, 27, 30, 31, 32, 34, 97
Smith, Fred, Federal Express, 100
Smith, Hamilton, 171
social capital
  creation, 217–18, 230
  financing, 183–8, 190, 200–1
  in networks, 126, 138
Social Capital Banks, 200–1
social capitalism, 10–14, 225, 226
social contract, for companies, 85
social entrepreneurs, 209–14
  and voluntary sector, 217–18
Social Exclusion Unit, 215
social ownership, 179–82, 230
social welfare, 188, 225
  funding for, 196–7
  state role in, 200–1
  welfare providers, 199–200, 217, 225
  see also taxation; welfare state
socialization, to share tacit knowledge, 72
society
  post-capitalist utopia, 167–8, 220–1, 223
  and spread of knowledge, 222–3
  tensions and conflicts, 228–6
Southeast Asia, 5–6
specialization, 57
sports and entertainment, 118–19
standardization, 57
Stanford University, 76, 83, 142–3
state
  as investor, 40, 196–7, 227
  role in setting standards, 224–5, 226–7
  role in welfare provision, 200–1
  see also public policy
stress, 220
Stutterheim, Cornelius, 81
Sun Microsystems, 49, 76
supermarkets, 22
Sybase, 76
symbolism, use of, 149–50
Symeonidis, George, 103

tacit knowledge
  compared with explicit, 28–9
  conversion to explicit form, 72–3, 74
  and fixed assumptions, 74–5
  as inefficient transfer, 30–1, 33
  as intangible asset, 45
tacit trust, 158–9

Takeuchi, Hirotaka see Nonaka, Ikijuro
tangible assets, value of, 46–7, 116
tax covenants, 197, 199
taxation
  hypothecation, 199, 216
  ideas for, 197–201
  individual, 198, 199
  and public spending, 195–6
  system outmoded, 190–6
  to fund welfare state, 188–90
Taylor, Frederick Winslow, 239
  Principles of Scientific Management, 54–7
Taylorism, influence of, 56–7
technology, 35
  advances in, 9, 48
Teece, David J., 45
telephone call centres, 130
telephone companies, and Internet, 23
tensions, in new economy, 228–6
Texas Instruments, 41
Third Way, 16
3Com, 49, 105
3M, 80
time-and-motion studies, 56
tools, as store of intelligence, 91
Torvalds, Linus, 134
Toyota, 136–7
training, 49, 52, 166
Trimble, Allison, 210–12
trust, 137, 148
  complexity of, 155–6
  and creativity, 152–3
  critical role of, 150–1
  deficit, 156–7
  economic value of, 151–2
  and exchange, 151, 162
  and hierarchy, 153–4
  loss of, 149–50
  nature of, 158–62
  new sources of, 162–4
  public, 153, 162–3
  surfeits, 164–6
trusted third parties, role for, 162, 163–4

unemployment see employment
United States, 5, 40, 47, 76, 119–20, 187
  biotechnology industry, 172–3
  collapse of corporate model, 59–60
  companies, 47, 103–4
  patents for genetic products, 132, 172–3
universities, 41
  branding for, 113–14
  British, 112–14
  and growth of science, 35–6
  role in companies, 50, 101–2, 114

unlearning, value of, 79–80
utopian vision of society, new, 167–8,
    220–1

value, 15, 24
    of knowledge, 116–19
    and price, 78–9, 226
venture capital, 106
    in Silicon Valley, 106, 107, 139–40,
    142–3
Visa, 128
Volkswagen, 44
voluntary sector, 217, 225

Wal-Mart, 159, 161
Walras, Leon, 99

warfare, intangible, 119–20
Warnock, Dr John, 83
Waterford Wedgwood, 43–4
Watson, James, 171, 172
welfare state
    obsolete, 11, 188–90
    see also social welfare
West Walker primary school (Newcastle),
    202–4
working from home, 1–2

Xerox, 79, 105

Youlton, David, 97

Zarowin, Professor Paul, 103